T0147009

A WEEK
ON A WARD

VINCENT BLADE DOUGLAS

BALBOA.
PRESS
A DIVISION OF HAY HOUSE

Balboa Press books may be ordered through booksellers or by contacting:

Balboa Press
A Division of Hay House
1663 Liberty Drive
Bloomington, IN 47403
www.balboapress.com
1 (877) 407-4847

Because of the dynamic nature of the Internet, any web addresses or links contained in this book may have changed since publication and may no longer be valid. The views expressed in this work are solely those of the author and do not necessarily reflect the views of the publisher, and the publisher hereby disclaims any responsibility for them.

The author of this book does not dispense medical advice or prescribe the use of any technique as a form of treatment for physical, emotional, or medical problems without the advice of a physician, either directly or indirectly. The intent of the author is only to offer information of a general nature to help you in your quest for emotional and spiritual well-being. In the event you use any of the information in this book for yourself, which is your constitutional right, the author and the publisher assume no responsibility for your actions.

Any people depicted in stock imagery provided by Getty Images are models, and such images are being used for illustrative purposes only.
Certain stock imagery © Getty Images.

Print information available on the last page.

ISBN: 978-1-9822-1469-2 (sc)
ISBN: 978-1-9822-1468-5 (hc)
ISBN: 978-1-9822-1484-5 (e)

Library of Congress Control Number: 2018912609

Balboa Press rev. date: 10/24/2018

PREFACE

I am a diminished person. This is the story of my diminution.

Some 50 years ago, I was introduced to the worlds of psychedelics and psychic phenomenon. It did not end well. Although I only spent a week in a closed psychiatric ward, that one week would drastically affect the rest of my life. It took me at least six months to get the full use of my hands back. I'm not so sure I have ever gotten the full use of my mind back.

This is my story. This is my song. I would have thought that after a lifetime of learning and experience that I would understand what happened to me and that I would learn from it and help others. This has not been the case.

The bulk of this book was written many decades ago, I have chosen to share it at this time in my life.

DISCLAIMER

This is a first person account of a week spent on a psychiatric ward. Much of it was written while I was delusional and still hallucinating. It is as true and as real as I can make it. Names have been changed and identifying items omitted. Also, considerable time has passed. Please note, however, that all thoughts and words are mine and note that I was hospitalized on a closed ward. Some of what I observed and have reported probably never happened.

THEN

This book was started while I was still mad (Paranoid schizophrenic? Bipolar? Nervous breakdown? Drug flip out?). Sheer will power, together with the all-pervading conviction that I had something very important to say drove me to its writing. I persevered, despite impaired use of my hands, memory lapses, hallucinations, little energy and ohmigod, the fear.

The first draft of my story was completed in some six months following my release from a psychiatric ward. Much of it was rewritten in the next couple of years. I was then forced to put it aside. Now, so many years later, an inner need has forced me to finish it. The memories are true. The pain was real. Any philosophy, explanations or rationalizations that have crept in are simply words used to describe something that I still don't understand. I was crazy. This is my story.

AND NOW

AND NOW

The bulk of this ego trip to myself was written immediately after being released. It took some six months to do a first draft. After revisions, it was not touched for years, and resurrected briefly in the year 2001. It was finished only now. About a year after my ward experience, I was lying in the dead man's yoga position (flat on my back, arms at my side), meditating. Suddenly, it was as though I had been shot in the heart by a long distance rifle. I knew my own mortality and knew with complete knowing that I would die someday. Yes, we all know we will die, but I **_knew_** (or grokked it as used in Heinlein's *The Stranger in a Strange Land*). I broke out of my reverie and begged God to let me live to the year 2000, fully knowing that I had a limited time on this planet and that all kinds of magical things were going to happen at the turn of the century. And now here I am, still going on. Trying to clean up unfinished business and get on with my life. Sharing this experience has become a driving force in my life.

CONTENTS

INTRODUCTION

INTRODUCTION

This is a first person account of a week spent on a psychiatric ward. Its writing was triggered by the visit of one of my professors while I was hospitalized. I had begun to become rational and attempted to tell him about my experiences. He suggested that it would be meaningful for me to write about them, especially due to my background in psychology.

I began attempting to detail my ward experiences shortly after my release from the hospital. My writing, however, became much more than an attempt to detail a one-week experience. It became my reason to be. It gave purpose and meaning to my struggle to survive and regain my sanity. Writing the first draft of my experiences, done during the six months or so following my release was one of the most difficult and courageous things that I have ever done.

First of all, there was the lack of physical dexterity. For example, a week or two after my release, I had written a one-page letter of thanks to the two professors that had visited me on the ward. I had used a portable typewriter, for goodness sake (the common use of computers and the internet were not yet here). It had taken me an entire afternoon of concentrated effort with many pages thrown away (a word processor would have been helpful). Simply, my hands didn't work. Although it was difficult for me to hold rational thoughts for any length of time, my greatest frustration was the inability of my fingers to hit the right keys on the typewriter. Tears formed in my eyes and dripped down my face as I inserted blank page after blank page into the typewriter. I was finally able to type a short letter that was readable. My physical difficulties slowly abated over a period of several months.

Then there was the fear. As I got into my story, I was telling secrets, chronicling the voyage of an inner space traveler through nightmare country. As such, they came out of the walls, from beyond the veils of my rational mind. Misshapen, vulture-like monsters perched on my shoulder, monitoring my thoughts, ready to control my writing. I ignored them. My story must be told. The hallucinations changed. As I continued to tell my story, typing away, a golden chain formed around my ankle, with one end holding me to the typewriter. I was obviously on to something; the truth must be told and in its telling I would be set free.

There were the impaired memory processes. I had gone quickly from waking up on the ward with no memory at all to a recall of only my long term memory to a jagged memory filled with quite vivid, complete histories as well as blanks and blurs. In attempting to detail my experiences, I would occasionally blank, not only forgetting what I was trying to say, but also what I was doing. Sometimes I would be back in minutes; other times it would take me hours to resume what I had been doing.

Finally, I was not rational in the truest sense of the word. That is, I was unable to hold on to a single train of thought, any consistent system of logic or sense of purpose. Hindu's have compared the mind to a drunken monkey needing to be disciplined. The mind has also been compared to a vast switching unit, with us attending very quickly to now one subject, then another and then another, with an illusion of continuity. As this drunken monkey switched from one thought to another, I would slide into the side pockets of my mind, forgetting where I had started and where I was going. Most of us are able to concentrate on one thing, ignoring or dismissing irrelevant thoughts. Not me. Not then.

In my weakened, post-ward condition, trying to hold or keep my concentration was very difficult, if not impossible for me to do. I would skip from thought to thought and from subject to subject with each new entry into my consciousness becoming the main idea. My reasons for writing continually expanded. I was beset by a whole series of existential questions: Who am I? Why am I? What am I? Why did this happen to me? What did I do to deserve all of this grief and suffering? In addition to trying to answer these questions, I was determined to expose the apparent absurdities of our hospitals and mental health professionals as well as the pain involved in the healing process. There was also the need to understand the madness and hallucinations that beset me as well as my love affair with Linda, which had taken me beyond the limits of my experiential capability. Was she a goddess, Siva's mistress Kali coming to bedevil me? A saint? Or was she just a decent, nice young woman who happened to fall in love with a jerk? Okay, I really believe that it's the latter one.

Anger and determination enabled me to finish that first draft. Rereading it, I was surprised that I had used "fuck" about every other word. Fuck me. Fuck the ward. Fuck them. Later, rewriting it, I would attempt let go of my anger and to limit it to a more objective account of my experience.

On one level, my story is a simple one. I was a bright, idealistic, religious youth that grew up in the Midwest. I was an egghead, geek, nerd, or whatever the current term is for a shy academic. At the age of 17, I sat across from the Dean of Men at a large, Midwestern State university. He told me that based on my high school record and test scores, I could be anything that I wanted to be. I could succeed at any academic course of study the university had to offer. All I needed was interest and motivation.

I was only moderately successful in college, however, having discovered booze, broads, and agnosticism. By my mid-twenties, I had obtained a bachelor's degree in psychology; a master's degree in education, had taught Russian, math and psychology at the high school level, switched to industry and was working as a senior systems analyst. A series of personal crises led me to introspection and a questioning of who I was. Still in my 20s, after all of my gold stars, I found myself to be balding, growing fat, and smoking and drinking too much. Where had all my promise and idealism gone?

My answer was to return to school and become the teacher and psychologist that I had always dreamed of becoming. I was able to obtain a four-year fellowship to a major university in School Psychology with an emphasis in Computer Assisted Instruction. For me, it was a dream come true. I would be able to combine my interest and expertise in the fields of education, psychology and computer systems.

As it turned out, I would only spend a year in graduate school, returning to my previous job in Chicago with a raise and promotion. Some 15 months later, I would attempt to return to graduate school. Although I had given myself a month to re-acclimate myself to school before winter enrollment, I would meet Linda, with my plans exploding in ecstasy. Two months after meeting Linda, I would find myself weak and broken on a psychiatric ward.

Whether my insanity was the accumulation of bad habits, a magnification of personal faults, a situational psychosis due to pressures pushing and pulling me here and there, the result of emotional overkill with Linda, or simply, the result of drugs as I told the doctors, I do not know.

Although it was probably the result of battling myself, I like to think of my madness as a fall from grace, necessitated by my attaining knowledge of techniques and power far beyond my wisdom and understanding. Whatever the case, in order to understand my story, it is necessary to understand **_Magic_**. Magic, or rather, altered states of awareness permeated my existence for some 2 ½ years prior to my breakdown.

The three major techniques, interwoven, that I participated in were tripping (psychedelics), yoga and mind control. The psychedelics taught me that the experiential possibilities of any single human being are virtually without limit and for all practical purposes, infinite. Yoga, and at best I was a novice, gave me control, allowing me to pass through mountains, so to speak, and return to my normal state. Mind control opened doorways to the void, allowing me to move through time and space.

Following is an overview of some of my experiences with these techniques, emphasizing the psychic and mystical aspects of my adventure that ended so badly. Although I still meditate, I no longer actively participate in any of these things. I am reminded of Hesse's _Journey to the East_, in which the main character begins telling of an exotic spiritual journey that he experienced in his youth that is no longer taking place. He is then led to realize that it is he who has changed and not the voyage. I feel like that. Although my ward experience can be understood in isolation and, indeed, has a number of elements of a classical breakdown, I feel a need to mention these search vehicles as background in order to give set and setting to my ward experience.

Tripping

The world has certainly changed. Drug usage and drug experiences are so very different today as opposed to then. So many books have been written regarding the psychedelic experience that it would be foolish for me to try to supplement them, except, perhaps, to relate some of my personal experiences.

My life has always been cyclical with the highs and lows, bad and good coming in bunches. As I prepared to return to graduate school, I was on the strongest natural high of my life. My mind had opened with me becoming incredibly productive at work as well as free of the gloomy depression and bothersome illnesses that had dogged me for much of my early life. Perhaps my major problem is that I have never been satisfied; when the good happens in my life, I always look for better.

In this totally open frame of mind, riding the tide of good, even outstanding events, a friend visited me from the west coast. He was doing his guru trip. He had been totally caught up in the west coast shtick, had turned on, and returned to the Midwest to tell all of his old friends about his new world. He spent a week or two with me in Chicago, talking continually about his new life style. We decided to travel together. We drove down to Florida with me lining up courses and an apartment for the coming semester. We then drove up the east coast to Cape Cod. He would remain there while I flew back to Chicago and then move to Florida.

Ah, what an experience. To that point, I had smoked some marijuana. Although enjoyable, I had done it for purely recreational reasons. He turned me on to Acapulco gold, which at that time was already legendary marijuana in head circles. More importantly, he talked to me about a way of life that promised insights into the wonder of it all. As he said, "I've taken mescaline three times and after the last trip I never came down." To him, psychoactive drugs were a gateway into a newly found spirituality and wholeness. He spoke of a way of life and philosophical insights that were reminiscent of Alan Watts and Timothy Leary. As we talked, he would constantly ask me questions, then wait for answers and listen intently to my responses. Always a latent seeker and a heavy reader, bits and pieces of Lao-tze's *Tao-Te-Ching*, Greek mythology, Zen Buddhist writings and more, spiraled upward from forgotten memory vats into my consciousness. It was as though I gave historical precedent, cognitive background and verbalization to the life style that he had discovered.

As we drove, talked and smoked grass, he turned me on to his version of head philosophy, which was, in effect, a "know thyself" colored by the drug experience. Now, it seems almost blasphemous. Then, it was so very new and different. As one guru out of the East, referring to LSD, had commented, it was so typical of us materialistic westerners to find spirituality through a physical substance like acid.

After constant driving, rapping and smoking, we became so in tune with each other that it became eerie. While we've all experienced the "I was just going to say that" phenomenon while talking to a friend, our rapport became continual. I would have a taste for ice cream and he would be turning off the road, driving into the parking lot of an ice cream stand. My mouth would be dry and he would be handing me a breath mint, as I was about to ask for one. He would start to ask me for directions and I would be telling him which way to turn before he could complete his question. This interpersonal sensitivity became so constant that I began babbling about it. He simply shook his head, "Don't you understand? When you talk about it, it isn't happening." Ah, yes. There is knowing (experiencing) something and then there is knowing about something. If you're there and start talking about being there, you're no longer there, but rather, in a state of being of talking about being there.

My major lesson of that two-week interaction as well as the key to understanding trip philosophy was simply, to live directly as opposed to the "aboutism" of straight society. With mass communication and the information explosion, each of us is aware of so many things with so much of our schooling predicated on learning about things. We have the illusion of knowing quite a bit. I learned, however, that with regard to certain modes of existence and experience that we know less than a simple savage. Although drugs are a magnifier of certain aspects of experience as well as a source of change, they are not necessary for tripping. Indeed, per head philosophy, each of us, whether we know it or not, is in on the trip. We are all tripping. Always. Each of us is a traveler. "The only thing constant in nature is change." "Changing is." It is impossible to stand still. Whether our trip be viewed as a journey through life, the life-death process, itself, or as a cyclical sleeping and awakening, it is not possible to stop it, for even death, as Shakespeare noted, may be just another phase.

My interactions with this friend left me both curious and confused. What, exactly, did all of this mean? Live in the present. Live directly. Experience. I spent the fall adjusting to academic life, caught up in new friends and study. Although I had some ego problems (going from a senior analyst playing a small but important role in a multi-million dollar merger to a first year graduate student was a little like asking me to sweep the floor when I had been designing buildings), I adjusted well to graduate school, thoroughly enjoying it and loving Florida.

Although I took a modicum of grass with me to graduate school, I stayed straight and had some success. I was still curious and confused about both drugs and the philosophy to which I had been exposed. Over Christmas break, I returned to Chicago and together with another friend drove to the west coast in order to visit my mentor and learn more about this new way of life. There, I met hippies, got involved in endless discussions with THC, strong grass and a mescaline trip changing my perceptual world. As I prepared to fly home to Chicago, I was still light tripping on the mescaline; I asked my old friend and current guide for some marijuana, as I was not one of the "in" crowd at school. I needed to more fully explore this world.

As a goodbye present, he threw me a quarter pound or so of decent marijuana. When I asked the price, he replied, "The first bag is free." It would take me a full week before I came completely down from the mescaline. I had a physical release in about three days. The psychological release came at a marathon encounter group a few days later, when my fellow graduate students accused me of sitting in the corner like some kind of all-knowing Buddha. This, of course, was exactly what I had been doing, musing in my other world loftiness at their petty this-world concerns.

I spent winter quarter smoking grass and making new friends. I attempted to understand this alternative culture with its emphasis on living NOW as well as its lack of concern with materialism and the structures and standards of mainstream American society.

That spring, on my 28th birthday, I took my first acid trip. I no longer had to attempt to understand the NOW or IN society, the alternative culture of peace, love and happiness freaks. I became one. Tripping and the lifestyle associated with it became my way of life. That spring is perhaps the happiest time of my life. I went from an anxious, balding materialist to a person that I truly loved. Physically, I lost some 30 lb., including 4 inches off of my waist, began walking tall and straight, let my hair grow long (it stopped falling out) and both felt and looked years younger. I stopped smoking cigarettes, stopped drinking alcohol, ate less meat, and generally took good care of myself.

I was in love—with a young woman, with myself and with the northern Florida countryside. It was a time of rebirth and rejuvenation, with my life permeated with the discovery of self, others and nature. I was reborn both emotionally and spiritually. Although I smoked grass and tripped on weekends, it wasn't just the drugs. I also did yoga, became good friends with so many bright, young people and fell in love with nature.

As all things must change, however, so did my euphoric state of mind. We had a saying, "Some people have dreams; we live ours." The extended daydream of living simply and lovingly began changing to a world of paranoia and depression. Old concerns began plaguing me. Could I hold on and get that doctorate? What about money, status and the future? My life was nice, even beautiful, but what about tomorrow? I couldn't sit under a tree for the rest of my life. Could I?

First of all, I fell into depression. The entire world is a game; no game is worth playing. Why bother to do anything? Nothing really mattered. From a way of life that had freed up dreams and energy, I fell into lying around wasted and confused. Then, there was the paranoia. At the beginning of the summer, my friends and I had heard about drug busts. Then it was friends and acquaintances that were getting popped. Finally, the people that had been over last night were now in jail. Were we next? It was as though an ever-tightening web was closing in on us. I retreated from my fear and climbed out of my stupor by returning to Chicago. After a year of search and study, I was surprisingly able to return to my former company with both a raise and promotion.

Although I returned straight, I had been exposed to a world of wonder. Both tripping and yoga had blown me away, exposing me to a world that I had not even been able to dimly imagine.

Tripping. What is it? So many authors such as Huxley and Watts have written erudite descriptions of it; so many burnouts have told their stories. So many of us have seen friends and loved ones destroy themselves. The world, it is different now. I am no longer any kind of expert on any kind of drug; originally, however, it was very important to me to attempt to analyze and describe the experience.

Simply, you take a chemical. This causes chemical changes in the brain and central nervous system leading to a radically changed perceptual world. To me, taking a psychedelic was like having a very intense dream while awake. Basically anything could happen, including very little.

Initially, I could externalize anything that my imagination or fantasy life could come up with. Pictures on the wall would begin moving; melting wax on a candle could become an intricate mini-universe and so on. The major difference between the trip experience and certain types of psychosis is that when tripping, one normally knows that that dancing tiger is really just a wall hanging. In very intense trip experiences, there had been built-in warning signals to protect yourself as well as supportive friends ready to help.

To me, tripping was an intensification, magnification, narrowing and centering of experience. I viewed it as an overall narrowing as certain aspects are magnified while others are ignored. While tripping can key dreams of the future or memories of the past, one is usually centered in the present due to the intensity of the immediate. Tripping dramatically affected my attention, awareness, sensory perceptions, concept of time, and internal speed.

I originally viewed the psychedelics as a cleansing or toning of experience. As Huxley has pointed out, our bodies actually act as a reducing valve, limiting our experiences in order for us to survive as an organism. View any sensory input (through our eyes, ears, and so forth) as a tube. Put a screen in that tube. For many of us, that screen is covered with sludge. My mind always came up with the pun that LSD, indeed, acted as acid. At first, it seemed to dissolve the sludge, allowing clearer, sharper perceptions. Over time, however, as I introspectively watched the effects of the drug on me, the screen, itself, began to disintegrate, resulting in a reduced capability of rationalizing or delimiting my experience, as well as acid nightmares that I was being irrevocably changed and not for the better. Not only the screen, but also the channel or tube as well as the rate of input changed.

Although there are many ways to view tripping, the concept of easiness stands out. A strong willed person with a well-developed ego can trip, view it as a sensory experience and either forget about it or perhaps, as some have done, write a treatise or book about the experience. Others would be much more easy, tripping into increasingly exotic worlds, with some losing (or finding) it completely. Some were forced to leave the cities and the intense, scattered vibrations that one finds in them. Making love to a flower became more important than a raise or promotion to some, while others were tripped into ideas of how to make money.

No longer as easy, I no longer know anyone who trips today. Does anyone still do psychedelics? Or is it all opioids and other types of pain killers. All the heavy trippers that I had known have either gone on to other things or are otherwise lost to me. While some former trip heads may view it as an interesting experience, others have changed enough not to know or care or be able to function in any kind of a rational world that I can understand. Ambivalent toward the trip experience, I must admit that even now, I occasionally miss the heavens, hells and happenings of that time of search.

On the other hand as one of my professors cynically stated, "We use to have to rely on mothers for supplying us with mental patients. Now we have LSD."

Yoga

Although drugs were such a strong stimulus, yoga also played a role in my brief sojourn as a peace, love and happiness freak. While I had read about yoga in the 1960's and had attempted to do some exercises on my own, I actually discovered this discipline about a week before my first LSD trip.

A friend had turned me on to some very good smoke. I somehow arrived at my first yoga class still buzzed. Over the next several hours, doing exercises, chanting and meditating, I not only stayed stoned, I became even more peaceful and relaxed. I knew that I was on to something really good. After that first class, I stopped smoking cigarettes. I didn't quit or give them up, I simply spaced into a world where I could no longer smoke tobacco.

It was Kundalini yoga, one of the most powerful of the yoga's. At best, I was a beginning novice, never really possessing the discipline to fully explore this very powerful technique. Not meaning any disrespect, Kundalini yoga is sort of like a speed freak version of hatha yoga (physical yoga). It stresses certain breathing techniques, including the breath of fire, which, if done correctly while holding an asana or position, has the same power in minutes that would otherwise take the control of hours.

At one level, yoga means "discipline." At another level it can mean "union." Kundalini yoga is a method aimed at raising the Kundalini nerve that is coiled at the base of the spine. The goal is to move one's energy upward, sending it to each chakra (a chakra is roughly equivalent to a sensory-motor nerve center).

There are seven major chakras. These centers have physical, psychic, and psychological corollaries. Physically, they are roughly located at the anus, genitals, stomach, heart, throat, forehead and crown of the head. As one learns this discipline, tremendous power and energy is released with one's subjective world going through step-functions to higher awareness as the Kundalini is raised. This discipline is also referred to as serpent yoga due to the analogy of the sleeping, coiled serpent being raised.

While that spring is perhaps my happiest time, much of the credit must go to this discipline. Although I only did 30-45 minutes of exercise and meditation a day, my habits changed dramatically. I found that smoking cigarettes, drinking alcohol, eating heavy foods or keeping the company of coarse people were all hindrances to my wellbeing. On the other hand, I misused this discipline, combining it first with grass, and then psychedelics in order to get even higher, ever faster.

Perhaps even more important than the physical changes that I went through, was the exposure to a different world view. At the time, Yogi Bhajan was the Kundalini missionary to the United States. He was a tremendously powerful human being with a thick, black beard, broad shoulders and strong chest. He emanated strength and did not fit my stereotype of a thin, stoop shouldered, introspective yogi.

He held a lecture in which he demonstrated some breathing techniques. The seating for his lecture was an interesting study in life as it was then. The heads, the peace love and happiness freaks, sat cross legged at his feet, attentive and in awe. The straights sat further away in metal, folding chairs. As an indication of my ambivalence and/or schizophrenic tendencies, I sat at the dividing line between the two groups, albeit on the floor. I was not quite a "head," not quite a straight.

During his lecture, he strongly put down all drugs, including the psychedelics and alcohol. The trip heads (peaceful and in the presence of one, who was there) were stunned. One girl stammered, "B-but that's what g-got us here." The trippers sat amazed, mouths open, attempting to assimilate this new information. It was as though they had eaten enormous quantities of bread in order to see the Buddha, and after finally being able to obtain an audience, they were then told that bread was not good for them. There was little protest, only astonishment.

The middle class straights in attendance, sitting on their chairs, were not so easy. One person, in particular, refused to give up arguing and finally stated that even our Lord, Jesus Christ, drank wine. I loved Yogi Bhajhan's answer and will never forget it. "No, this I no believe. I do not believe that any being so powerful that he can raise the dead, could drink alcohol." I was entranced by the worldview that could easily accept that someone could raise the dead, even to the extent of putting restrictions on the habits of one who was able to do so. On the other hand, as I later tried to tell this story to an acidhead, he simply shrugged his head and said, "Hey man, we all have hang-ups."

At that same lecture, a friend had come over and whispered that he had scored what Liam and I had been looking for. I was on the verge of my first acid trip. As my friend left, a young woman I didn't know, gripped my arm, looked deeply into my eyes and emphatically stated, "Bad vibes." Perhaps.

While Kundalini yoga and the psychedelics were my twin entry into a brief interlude as a hippie, they also opened my perceptual world to a number of mystical-like experiences. While the practice of yoga and meditation can lead to psychic experiences and powers, these are basically put down as hindrances to enlightenment. While tripping, anything can happen. Although I had a number of mind-boggling trips, I remember the joy and wonder, rather than the disorientation and confusion.

Mind Control

My Eden had been short lived, however. Returning to Chicago was an escape to a safe environment. For the remaining year and a half prior to my breakdown, although I continued to smoke marijuana, I would trip only a couple of times and practice yoga only sporadically. I did, however, become a trained psychic.

I discovered Mind Control. It was through a series of coincidences. I would find out that "coincidences" would permeate the life of a Mind Control graduate as in, "Joe will call in about 20 minutes." As the phone rang some 20 minutes later, there would be a laugh and a wink, "My, what a coincidence."

The course I attended consisted of four, 12-hour days of training accomplished during two consecutive weekends. Techniques used in the class involved self-programming, visualization and the dropping to lower brain waves.

The brain emits a number of waves, classified according to their rate. Delta waves are the slowest, associated with very deep sleep and the unconscious mind. Theta waves are very slow, associated with the deep subconscious and creative imagery. Alpha waves are associated with the subconscious mind and the dream state. When we sleep and are dreaming, our eyelids flicker; this is REM or rapid eye movement. The predominant brain wave emitted during dreaming sleep is the alpha wave. Beta waves are associated with our awake, conscious self.

In mind control, you can view the mind as an upside down pyramid. We live on the surface, emitting beta waves. In a method similar to self-hypnosis, one goes to a deeper, more basic level of mind, the alpha level of slower brain waves and programs one's self. The theory is that what happens at these deeper levels of mind will subsequently affect our normal, awake self.

A simple exercise illustrates the potential of this self-programming technique. At night, in the reverie between being awake and falling asleep, visualize a clock and move the hands to the exact time that you want to wake up. Picture it clearly and let yourself know that this is the exact time that you want to wake up and that you will wake up feeling better than ever. While many of us have very good biological clocks, others of us don't. With a little practice, you will be surprised at how easily and accurately you can wake up at any given time. (I can no longer do this very well so don't feel badly if you can't do it either. At one time, however, I could consistently wake up to the minute that I had pictured in my mind.)

The first half of the course emphasized habit formation, control over the autonomic or involuntary nervous system, and positive reinforcement techniques. It became progressively esoteric, however, including the idea that one could project one's intelligence or awareness to any point in time or space. Think about that for a minute or two. **_Any_** point in time or space! It ended with one being able to build a mental laboratory at a deep level of mind where one could, among other things, work health cases. The end result of the course was that one could, given a person's name, age, sex and location, "work" that person, sending energy to aid that person's physical, mental and emotional health.

While the lecture portions of the course were somewhat simplistic, I absorbed them with the proverbial grain of salt. The training, however, was effective. Quite simply, it worked. Perhaps drugs and yoga had opened my mind to "anything can happen." Whatever the case, I very quickly became adept at this new technique. Although I have no evidence whatsoever as to any cures I caused or people I healed, the diagnostic capabilities were incredible.

For example, Joe, another student, went into an emotional tirade on the afternoon of the last day of the course. Angrily, he said that although the course had some good parts, it should be sold as an exercise in creative imagery as there was nothing psychic about it. Some four hours later, I would lead him through his first health case. I used my aunt. He went to his level (a semi trancelike state, the alpha state) and started describing what seemed to be a cross between my mother and my aunt. With some prompting by myself, he was able to sort out the images and described my aunt accurately, although given her age, sex and my guiding, this was not especially difficult. He then went into her maladies.

"Huh, gee, I don't know what the name of the disease is, but it's like the red and white blood corpuscles are fighting each other. There's a real heavy purplish color. There's too many red cells. I'll send some help."

My aunt had polycythemia, which is a blood disease where one has a preponderance of red blood cells, resulting in fatigue and dizziness, also diagnosed by Joe. I was hooked. It was amazing. Coincidence? How? He didn't even know what polycythemia was and I had to look it up.

A couple of days later, I was working cases at a graduate meeting with a somewhat flip cohort. His, "yeah, yeah, that's a hit", was not convincing. For example, I had seen a black woman as white. I felt that I had come down from a drug trip. It had been a nice dream but come on now, of course this couldn't work. Two weekends of training and I became psychic?

While working these cases, I heard my two instructors talking to a couple that had just come in. They had heard about the course and wanted a demonstration. "Sure, any of our graduates can work health cases. It's a money-back guarantee. Look, there's someone that graduated just two days ago. Let's have him work your sister."

I was called over. One of my instructors had been trying to work the sister, but kept on getting the wrong person. It happens. Mind Control isn't magic; it just seems that way. The two visitors, although earnest and hopeful, were doubtful, but not overly critical. They seemed nice enough. I was manic in my enthusiasm and told them that anyone could do it.

I dropped to my level and sat facing my mental screen in my mind's eye. My one instructor read me the sister's data, while my other instructor went to his level and sent me energy. The image was surprisingly clear and strong. "Ah, let's see, she has dark hair with some gray, appears to be about forty or so, wears glasses, appears to have a pleasant disposition." All hits.

"Ah, let's see, hmm, she has trouble around the mouth. Something's wrong with her teeth or gums; she may have false teeth or just had some pulled or something."

"Right. Go on."

"She gets headaches, tension ones at the sides of the forehead. I don't know why, though, as she seems very pleasant and easy going. There may be something wrong with the eyes; I can't tell. Maybe it's just her nerves. Ah, her fingers are very thin and long and very white, very pale. Her feet seem pale, too. She may have some kind of a circulation problem."

"Right, she does get headaches and you described the hands. No known heart or circulation problems, however. What else do you see?"

"I just keep on getting drawn to the mouth and the forehead. Let me send her some help... Okay, that's all I see. Should I come back?"

"Wait a minute, let's try some point-time correlation. Okay?"

"Sure." Now some mumbling; they were talking together in whispers. Although I had never done any point-time correlation, it was relatively simple in theory as there was no time or space at these levels of mind. Basically, one just kept the image secure on the screen and moved one's clock-calendar to the desired date. One of the problems in working cases was that at times one would get images of the person at different ages. For example, one may see a now thin person as being fat like they were two or three years ago. Being given a person's age was a good reference point; one had to check the calendar in one's head, however, in order to be sure that one was working things that existed now. The discerning reader may quickly jump to a, "Ohmigod, do you mean that the future can be known?" While this seems true in theory, it seems much trickier than seeing the past and I have refused to experiment with it.

"Okay. Adjust your calendar to January, 19xx."

"Uh, okay." It was a little tricky, keeping the image strong and clear while changing the calendar to the desired date. Arggggggh. Ow.

"Wow. I get some kind of cartoon witch screaming in pain. There is all kind of energy emanating from her. There's a golden glow around her hips."

"This is approximately the right area. Investigate further."

"Uh, can't really see anything. Very strong energy. Don't know what's happening. Look, I'm going to project myself into the image and see if I can find out what's going on." I guess it was kind of stupid, maybe even brave, projecting myself into all of that pain. I was so carried away by my successes that it didn't seem to matter. It's a relatively simple process. You're viewing a screen in your head with an image on it. You simply project yourself into that image. One can then get some idea of the pain, feelings, and so forth, that are bothering the person. In Mind Control, it's called "putting on someone's head." This is one way to "mind read." In retrospect, it also seems dangerously close to "possessions."

I projected myself into this image of a cartoon witch in my head, which seemed to be emanating all of this pain and energy. Oooops. Arggh. Ow. I began shaking and trembling much like a Holy Roller or someone speaking in tongues. I felt a strong rush of energy from my stomach and in my mind's eye, I saw a cartoon image of an infant in swaddling clothes. The picture was similar to the little kid in the Popeye comics, for those of you who remember Popeye.

"She either had or lost a baby in January of 19xx."

"A hit. Congratulations, you've just had your first baby."

Well, what to make of it? Although I was completely accurate and the couple were astounded, they left pale and shaken and never came back. Scary? To me, it was fantastically exciting. The import and possibilities were staggering. I was hooked. I had found a new source of wonder and promise.

Every day, going to and from work on a bus, I would go to my level and work health cases. I did relatives, friends, co-workers and referrals, sending golden, life giving energy to anyone that needed it. I realized that rather than a source, it was as though I were acting as a conduit or a relay station that channeled and directed a force that was beyond me. I became quite religious, going to the depths of my mind, saying a prayer of thanks and also, asking that I never be allowed to hurt anyone or to otherwise misuse such a marvelous skill.

Working cases had its humorous side. My boss and secretary had shown some interest, although to be perfectly honest, only my mother and one of her lady friends, who both were going to a Unitarian church at the time, were the only two people who would listen to me without total skepticism. One morning, early at work, as I passed my secretary I mentioned that her ulcers were in the lower portion of her stomach, just starting, and if she drank more milk and learned to relax, I didn't think that she would have any trouble. Returning from my coffee run, she was still frozen in the same position. She stared at me and asked me how I could have possibly known about her ulcers. She had just been to the doctor and discovered that she was developing ulcers. I just smiled and said, "After all, I am a trained psychic." We never talked about it again.

I had been working all of my relatives, just sending love at a deeper level of consciousness (it's really impolite to work someone without their request for a number of reasons, including knowing too much about them), when I came across my cousin's wife. Her mid-section was spilling forth a strong, whitish-gold light. From my "witch" case, I knew that this meant she was pregnant. On one of my infrequent visits home, I told my mother that someone in the family was pregnant. She guessed just about everyone and finally gave up. Smug, I told her about Barbara. "Oh gees. My son, the psychic. She's seven months pregnant and everyone in the family knows about it."

Working cases had its serious side. Cancer, which shows up as orange-red, proved the most difficult for me. One of my instructors asked me to work his aunt, who was dying from cancer. Although I tried several times, I wasn't so sure that I was getting through. After some time, I tried again.

She was virtually immersed in a sea of red. I tried to send some help and received a very strong image of her sailing away in a Spanish Galleon. She seemed very at peace and was waving goodbye to some distant shore. Weeks later, when I checked with my instructor, he verified what I had suspected. She had passed away.

Mind Control was not magic. It all seemed tied up in wider plan, karma, destiny, call it what you will. Also, not being "clear" (that is, still bothered my own perceptual inadequacies) or fully developed spiritually, my mind would give me cartoons and symbols instead of totally precise images. The next case illustrates some of this.

A very dear friend of the family was going into the hospital. I decided to work him. I received a very clear, strong image of him with a strong band of orange-red across his diaphragm. Since one is working cases in one's own mind, one can use any technique that seems suitable to send help. Nothing that I did seemed to work. For example, I tried using a giant eraser to erase the cancer off of my visual screen, but no, that didn't get rid of the red. Finally, in a burst of inspiration, I condensed the orange-red color into a little black pea, plucked it out of his body and threw it into a wastebasket in my laboratory. Several days later, I found out that he had been operated on and that the doctors thought that they had gotten all of it. They, however, had operated some 24 hours before I worked the case!

Trying to use psychedelics, Kundalini Yoga and Mind Control with no real teacher or guide, I was certainly playing Russian roulette with a very loaded gun.

But oh, did my mind fill in. I had always been considered bright with the praise of numerous teachers and high scores on standardized tests reinforcing this perception. Hah! My success in school consisted mostly of memorization and facile regurgitation of facts with some isolated stabs at original, creative thinking. I was a whiz at digesting textbooks written about the great thinkers, easily able to comprehend organizational schemes, critiques and analyses of their ideas. Studying original works of the masters left me bedazzled and confused, however.

Oh, how it turned around. As I became both an explorer and a knower of this huge brain with which most of us are gifted, I became quite arrogant. I found myself reading original works by the great masters, comparing their thoughts to my experiences, separating the chaff from the wheat. At the same time, however, the "aboutists," those numerous classifiers and arbitrators of knowledge became almost totally incomprehensible to me.

I think that either yoga or mind control with a good teacher would have been okay. I, however, had no guru and also, continued to try psychoactive substances. I began noting some strange things.

For example, about a year after my heyday as a peace, love and happiness freak, I had a week off and decided to try some LSD. I took two trips, hanging around Lincoln Park and Chicago's lakefront. Later, when I tried to go to my internal laboratory and work health cases, I found my laboratory totally wrecked with green a predominant color. It would take several sessions of me going to my level before I could reconstruct my laboratory. What did this mean?

I did a reverse guru trip, going out to the west coast to turn my former mentor on to mind control. He asked me to help him with his back. The problem is that he immediately got me stoned on stronger grass than I had been used to smoking. When I tried to work him, I got esoteric images. Instead of seeing his back problem as a regular picture (similar to colored x-rays), I saw a huge serpent coiled around his backbone.

What could this possibly mean? Was I just using drug-tinged imagery? Was my early Christian training coming to the fore?

And then, it all fell through. About six months before my hospitalization, I was doing yoga after smoking some very good grass. I accidentally did something that popped me through a (the?) Tibetan dorje into a world beyond my imagination. I was totally mad for several days. In the middle of this very strange experience, I picked up the *Tibetan Book of the Dead* and read a section describing a stage of experiences after a person is dead. It was similar to the world that I was living in. I would later find out that a man had died in the apartment above me and that his corpse had been rotting there for several days. I sincerely believe that I accidentally got caught up in his death vibrations. Whatever the case, my world went tilt and then some.

An understanding boss, a loving mother and a co-worker that did drugs were able to help me return from my walk through whatever had happened to me. I surfaced in a world of hedonism, losing myself in sex, ignoring the perceptual wonders that I had been able to experience. This too, turned to ashes. The various trips and psychic experiences had gotten to me. It was time to center; time to take care of my body.

Linda

Enough experimentation with my mind, it was time to become healthy and happy once again, time to return to being a person that I could love and cherish. My excesses had constantly exposed me to worlds that I didn't understand. No longer confident of finding enlightenment or of transcending my flaws and weaknesses, I decided to return to the beauty of northern Florida. I would be that teacher, that psychologist I had always wanted to be. I would work hard, pay my dues and live a normal, loving life.

Perhaps it would have worked. I don't know. On what was to be my last night in Chicago, a friend came over, bringing Linda with him. He and I did a goodbye trip to Chicago. It may as well have been a goodbye trip to me. It was the first acid that I had done in the some five or six months since my two trips in June. Something burst in my brain. I heavy tripped for some 30-45 days, not bad for a half a tab of acid.

For the most part, I was just manic and hyper with everything brighter than normal. One experience stands out, however, that shows some of the far side of what I was experiencing. Linda was working at a dress shop on State Street just south of Chicago's Loop (downtown Chicago is called the Loop because of the loop the elevated trains make around it). I had visited her, which was a little dicey because of the people and commotion where she worked. I was walking north along State Street toward downtown when I realized that I did not hear anything.

I was surprised as there were people and cars everywhere. I stopped and looked around. Across the street, standing in a doorway was this long hair who was selling underground newspapers. I had seen him in Old Town (where I lived, which was a couple of miles north of the Loop) several times. I was surprised that he came this far south. He seemed real. Substantial. He was okay. The rest of the world began turning gray as though I were standing in a cloud or a thick fog. Except for him, my world seemed to be disappearing. I started to freak out.

I put my head down, just watching my feet and the sidewalk as I continued to walk. I kept saying to myself, "I need a head. I have to find a head. I need a head." I knew what I was saying. I needed to talk to a trip head, someone who had done drugs and could tell me what was going on.

I continued to walk. At the corner, there were a couple of members of the Process. That summer, they had been around Old Town. They seemed to be color coded and wore different colored robes (I had seen, black, gray and blue). Today was a dark day and they were wearing black. They were sort of devil worshipers although the devil was viewed as a personage who executed God's will. I had been to one meeting of the Process. I had met a couple guys who were passing through town and I put them up in my Old Town apartment. None of us knew much about the Process. I knew very little and it would be gone shortly so I never did learn that much about what they really believed or practiced.

A woman dressed in her black robe stopped me and said, "Would you like to read about death?" She held up a glossy booklet with a skull taking up the entire front cover. I had found my "head."

"I find death kind of boring."

"What could be more interesting than death?"

"Why, the whole life and death _____." Hysterical laughter. Mine.

She smiled sweetly at me and said, "We're meeting down at the lake at 2:00. Be there."

Although I began meandering toward the lake, I realized that my world was substantial once again. Relieved, I made it back home. Coincidence? Searching for a "head" and having a picture of a skull thrust into my face? Sure. Why not? Of course. My whole life was a coincidence.

I have such regret. I fell so very in love with Linda. Linda and graduate work in psychology. My two loves. It was a dream that had come true. I had it all. However, my world kept changing. Eventually it went "pop." This, then, is my story of a week on a ward.

GETTING IN

GETTING IN

Sitting on the sofa, blind with rage, I waited for this too to pass. Then I was on my feet, shouting, "Okay, if that's the way that you want it, okay! If that's the way it has to be, okay. God damn it, okay!" I was shouting at my invisible demons. She hadn't done anything. Or maybe, it was a simple, "I don't care," to my, "What do you want to do tonight?" Throwing my jacket on, pulling on my shoes, gaining in anger, rage and maddening vibes, I knew that something had to be done. This had to be over. This must end. I hurried toward the door.

I was a wild pinwheel of discordant energy. On the other hand, Linda was a quietly pulsating, comparatively weak orb of life. She was miles away from me, with the two of us separated by a thick, tangible, heavy energy field. It was as if we were both underwater with her a self-contained, satisfied, shielded light source and with me an enraged, angry, drowning, not knowing which way to swim, not remembering how to float, not content to stay buried, thrashing, wild thing.

Flash. I knew what I had to do. I would drive north, driving until the VW bug gave out. With no money for gas or repairs, I would walk, just walk, walking north, toward home, toward Chicago, skulled out of my mind, putting one foot after the other until it was over. I would keep on going, like a blind insect ever climbing up a wall, zeroed into a single track, unable to stop no matter what obstacles are put in its way.

I could see, sense and feel a feverish me, buried deep in my fur parka, not making it, collapsing in the snow. A silly thought as a portion of me knew that the car wouldn't make it through Georgia. It would be a fitting end to a dull, dismal, unproductive existence. Let them write: He tried.

1

He really tried. Not making it, he did try. Shit, if they only knew how hard I had tried.

And then, I was outside of the apartment, running quickly. I knew what had to be done, knowing that it had to be done and done at once. It had to be done while the anger and rage were still there, done before reason had a chance to return and stop me. This must end.

Remembering: It hadn't been all that bad. Not really. A speeding, zipping, going out of focus me had made it out of the city and had been able to make it back to graduate school. The hassles had been met; getting an advisor, lining up books and classes, finding an apartment. After two weeks of classes, I had flown back to Chicago for my court date.

It had been an absurd bust. After all of the nights and days of paranoia in years past, I had been sitting innocently in Linda's apartment. She shared it with a roommate. Her roommate was going out with a friend of mine. I had met Linda through him. The rumor was that her roommate's ex had done light dealing.

Whether it was because of her former roommate/dealer or the vindictiveness of my friend's separated wife, the police had had a search warrant. There had been a buzz at the door, first a regular, quick buzz, and then an insistent one. As Linda got up to answer it, she said, "This may be something that's going to fuck up our whole evening." A kind of premonition and somewhat of a surprise to me as Linda just plain didn't swear. This was the only time I have ever heard her use the "f" word. Ever. Before, during or after my week on a ward.

When Linda opened the door, there they were, three narcs with drawn guns. They quickly moved to search the place. I stood up as they rushed into the room and was standing over a small bowl of marijuana. It was some weak grass that we had been smoking, pretending to get high. Although Linda's roomie had screamed out that anything that they found was hers, they had popped the four of us. My friend, Linda, and I had sat there like the three little monkeys, who neither saw, spoke nor heard any evil. Waiting for the search to be over, thinking our thoughts, we were quiet and had been told that we would be free to go. Her roomie had sort of flipped out, screaming at the cops, following them around as they searched, yelling that she had been through this before and that she knew that they would plant something. They found the bowl of mediocre marijuana that had been on the floor at my feet and two pills that looked suspicious. The roomie would later laugh that if she had known about the pills, she and my friend would have taken them.

Linda was an almost complete innocent, smoking only rarely. At the time, I smoked about a joint (a dozen or so puffs) a day and had never done any dealing. Except for the psychedelics (taken a couple of times now that I was back in Chicago and not lolling in the rain forests of northern Florida) and grass, I really hadn't gotten into drugs. Three big, old Chicago narcs, with speed and heroin everywhere, busting some kids and myself for some grass that was so bad that it could have been oregano sprayed with black flag. Busting us took over half their shift and would prove to be a costly mistake for us.

If the bust, itself, was absurd, the court date that I flew back for was an even greater joke. Our lawyer (obtained through connections) thought he was Clarence Darrow or some such ("Look, I know that I can get you off. Look, I can get you off, but this judge, see, it's an election year and he wants to ride this guy's coat tails, and he's taking a hard line and look, we got to lay off of this guy. Look, I never lose a case, just stick with me."). Linda was passive. Thinking of the plane fare and the charge (listening to other cases where pounds and garbage cans full of grass were found, it was hard for me to believe that anything bad could happen with the four of us popped for a total of less than an ounce), I wanted to go ahead with the court appearance. My friend and the roomie were adamant about "laying off of this judge." The case was continued. I had flown to Chicago for nothing. Linda and I had found out, however, that we needed to be together. We made plans for her to get to Florida the next weekend.

This was my second go-around at graduate study in northern Florida. The first time I had been searching for a Holy Grail, a reason to be. Corny, but true. That first time returning to college in my late 20's, a successful systems analyst, I had had my dream come true. I had received a four-year fellowship to a top graduate school. Aptitude, together with my work in systems and education had done it. While I did not have spectacular grades and had been out of school for some time, the work was to be in Computer Assisted Instruction. It was a perfect fit. I left work to cheers and best wishes. I had made good. To me, it was even more than that. I would get a chance to self-actualize and be all of the things that I had ever wanted to be.

Surprise. I was almost immediately shocked at the petty triteness (6 to 7 profs sitting around for hours trying to figure out how to revise a proposed grant in order to get a tape recorder included, while I had just left merger studies where the talk was in the millions), shortsightedness (okay, take all of those person hours spent by first year grad students learning the Core curriculum, an outmoded way of exposing each of us to the assorted facts of a dozen specialties that few of us will ever need or use, or how about all of that time spent in writing, individual, narrow theses—where do they tie in, what about the option of having everyone work on different aspects of the same thing, using an underlying theory or purpose in order to have some meaning, impact or relevance), the lack of idealism (with me searching for TRUTH and my department head continually saying that the Ph.D. is nothing but a union card, do meaningful work at the post-doctoral or career level), and the degree of specialization (holy cow, it takes three months of concentrated effort and study just to understand what these guys are talking about, just to use the same vocabulary). What a shock for this ex-teacher, then making it as a senior systems analyst on his way to solid, middle management.

That first quarter, I played the game well (A, A, B, and B), made ripples if not waves, tutored some people, learned my role of "student as low-life" and had more or less adjusted. Christmas break, with a visit to California, THC and mescaline, together with long head raps with an old friend, who was living high and thoroughly caught up in the west coast shtick of the late 1960's kind of changed my values. Winter quarter was spent rolling around in the grass with me receiving all B's and making new friends. School became a distant hassle.

Spring quarter (A, B, B, and C) became a time of search, peace, love and happiness. The psychedelics had been bridged. Rather than a hassle, school was a, "huh?" My grades were amazing. At mid-term, I actually had 2 A's, a B+ and a solid B going. It's funny, I can't remember ever cracking a book. Classes were something to go to if you weren't crashing at the pad or getting high. I held together and saw it through to the end. For finals, I gathered all of my books and papers together, literally thousands of pages, planning to read one line per page. Even this was too much. I took my Personality final crashing from my second psilocybin trip of finals week. With the pages blurring, I finished it in 45 minutes while the other graduate students sweated for two to three hours. It was a solid screw-up, with me receiving my only C in graduate school.

Summer quarter (B) was spent laying around wasted. I had one course and twelve hours of master's thesis, not even being able to come up with a topic for my thesis. I had fallen into depression--all the world's a game and no game's worth playing. I was strung out, almost catatonic and spent my time staring at walls, wondering how I had gone wrong. Where went the ecstasy, the glimpse (and what a glimpse) at infinity, the highs, and the dreams?

As I look back, it is difficult for me to believe that my great, hippie, trip head experience was only some 3-4 months long; it seemed like years. I crawled back to Chicago, retreating to a life style that I could handle. Surprisingly, I returned with a promotion and a major raise. A letter to my former secretary and company need had triggered my return. I had lost 30 pounds, straightened my back, and stopped smoking and drinking. I felt good, except for the cloud over my head. I had caught a glimpse. Yoga and the psychedelics had blown me away. The early 1970's evidenced paranoia and bipolarization of society. I became a double, living in two worlds. Mysticism and long raps with straights that at least smoked grass triggered memories of some of what I had found, while pressures of a 9 to 5 job kept me in the middle-class world.

I lived some 15 months divided against myself. Functioning at work, but always dreaming of what I was missing. The bad habits of cigarettes and alcohol began once again to color my existence. Imbedded in Chicago, not surrounded by rain forests, I found it increasingly difficult to cope, to be happy. Visions were no longer clearly seen, experiences were no longer mind-blowing ecstasy. I continued on. A delay in a raise at work due to Nixon's wage-price freeze, an aborted attempt to transfer to another department and management failing to act on a proposal that took months to prepare, provided the stimulus for me to try it once again. My only dream had been to be a college professor, to be an educated person. "One more time" was my driving force. I no longer did drugs, although I still smoked grass. This time, I would make it. I had learned discipline. I would cope.

I quit work on the last day of November. My boss begged me to stay. Once the freeze was over, he insisted that I had a fine future and that I would move right up the corporate ladder. I wouldn't listen, however. One more time at that merry-go-round, one more try at that elusive doctorate, that life-long dream. That was my dream and my motivation. Was the brass ring still there? Could I still make it?

I planned to leave for Florida immediately. I had horded my shekels (no fellowship now), planned to study a month and re-acclimate myself. This time, I would make it. Hah!

My friend came over to say goodbye. He was splitting from his wife and was going to bring over his new girlfriend. Sure. Instead, he brought over her roommate, a girl named Linda. As a goodbye trip to Chicago, he and I split some windowpane acid. Linda declined. After having seen her twice before, we had finally met. We fell in love. My plans exploded in ecstasy. The month of December was an orgy of sight, sound and sensuality. I had a reason to exist, a will to live. I was in LOVE. Something went "pop!" in my head and I never came down. I burst into trip consciousness and stayed there day after day after day.

Golden, vibrating energy was in me, through me, and about me. It wasn't just that she loved me, or I loved her or that we loved each other. We were IN LOVE. I used to say that yoga could prolong a high for several hours; Linda lasted more than a month. Somehow, I made it to Florida. After returning to Chicago for that absurd court date, we were finally together in Florida. The lack of time and urgency of finding a place had required us to move into a one-bedroom, plastic, efficiency-apartment, one in a cast of hundreds. We were together, however; that was all that mattered.

Linda had eased into the slow, golden pace of northern Florida like a fish so satisfied at finding its rightful element that it just sits there basking in the filtered sunlight, digging the stationary, non-moving, baby blue quiet. I, on the other hand, still a little scattered from a month plus of almost continual tripping and an orgy of the senses, continued to try and live a dual life. It didn't work.

Chicago had been firmer. The job was structured; the work was something that I was good at. A strong, ordinary environment had tempered even the head raps, meditation and mysticism that I had experienced. In Chicago, it was as if I were a messenger, bringing tales of the great beyond; here, I was the newbie. School represented my extremes. It was the far side of my experience.

I tried to make it with my head friends. I dropped some orange sunshine (once) and smoked copious quantities of grass. Even here, however, it was different. My friends had been structured by school with the trip experiences new and mind boggling. Now, they seemed adrift. Sharon, an ex-love had dropped out of school in her last quarter while student teaching ("It's a cage, these kids are kept in a cage!") and was living in a teepee on someone else's land. Bobby had made it through and was hanging around town while working a menial job. Tom had gotten his degree and was working as a garage mechanic. Liam, my true good buddy, after finishing his master's degree with a near "A" average, had voyaged across the country, then followed a guru to Houston, and had resurfaced in northern Florida. He was now hanging out at Bobby's, where he did the cooking and otherwise helped out.

On the one hand, I tried to get back in tune with these people with whom I had shared some of the most beautiful experiences of my life. On the other hand, I hit the books, trying to regain and remember the endless names and innumerable facts, attempting to interact with the Profs and the other grad students. There had to be some reason for my leaving a managerial position that was moving to good money and which promised a safe, solid, economic future. No longer searching for that Holy Grail of understanding, knowledge and awareness, there had to be some reason for re-exposing myself to the locked in world of profs and grad students with its endless preparation of monographs, theses, and dissertations that taken as a whole, seemingly had little impact on anything or anyone except those preparing them.

While having some difficulty in getting in tune with either my old, head friends or with graduate school, there was always the northern Florida countryside. I thought of town and the surrounding area as a woman. The first time around, seeking status, knowledge and power, while calling it truth, I had been seduced away from small-minded men to this open, sensuous woman. Sitting in her rain forests, basking in her bright but damp sun, soaking up her peace, I had been wooed by this beguiling, always beautiful, knowing yet capricious mistress. Coming down from the north, racing around, full of energy and ideas of mice and men, she had just smiled at me. She waited, knowing that I would come to her. And how I did.

Stoned, tripping, blitzed and just plain high, I had fallen in love with her. Lying in her fields, walking through her forests, swimming in her waters, I had meditated, merging with her. I would get off by myself, smoke a joint, and just lay around, listening to her, feeling her. To a city boy, it was so very good, so gentle and peaceful.

This time around, however, I wasn't ready to be seduced. December had been a mind-blowing explosion of essence, a climaxing of body and soul, a disintegration of the barriers of my mind. Rather than falling into the slow, lazy sensuality of northern Florida, I wanted to get it on, pull myself together, get another erection, hit those books, sharpen that intellect, and notch that degree. It hadn't worked before. It didn't work the second time around.

Things started going wrong, or perhaps a right so correct that I couldn't catch up with it all, quite quickly. Scattered, torn by these different aspects of my past and present, I began spiraling ever deeper within myself. I began losing touch with Linda, the marvelous creature with whom I had shared an almost eerie rapport. Liam was the only one that I could talk to and yet, even with him, I found it difficult to talk, to interact. Have you ever become a forest?

Things began happening in multiple dimensions with me getting increasingly frightened. To this day, I still don't know. I still have my regret. There I was, with a second chance at my dream, with the love of my life at my side. Everything that I had ever wanted was right there for me. Perhaps, if I had had the sense to give myself up to it, to just lay quietly in the surrounding fields for a few days, to just relax completely, perhaps it would have passed. I kept on fighting it, however, whatever IT was. Golden energy began creeping around my ankles. I could feel and sometimes, even see it. It was as if I were sinking deeper and deeper, slowly but surely. Finally, I was drowning, with only my head above water, and then I was fully submerged in some kind of thick, heavy, slow moving, palpable energy field. My strength and energy were being sapped with my reason freaking at what only I could see and feel.

Finally, whatever the trigger, although too disoriented to know what to do, strength, together with rage and anger came bubbling up. This must end.

As I ran toward my car, thoughts and images cascaded through my brain. As flashes of the last few weeks of horror entered my consciousness, my resolve tightened.

Outside of the apartment, running quickly in the cool, damp, February night, I could hear and feel Linda behind me. A glance behind me: she was running, tugging on her long, brown, suede coat, with her long, thick black hair all disheveled, blowing in the wind. She was yelling, "I'm coming with you." Oh Linda, how I love you. If only you could have stopped me. Or maybe, if left alone... Perhaps, I would have driven around town; disoriented and freaking, trying to find somewhere that would still the rage bubbling inside of me. Maybe, I would have returned to that hillock, where we (Liam, Sharon and all those others) had tripped some two years earlier. Perhaps I would have sat in the damp grass, huddled in my parka (a holdover from Chicago and not really needed in northern Florida) and been able to let it all go. Curled in the fetal position, rolling in the mud, perhaps I would have been able to cry and scream and beg forgiveness of a God that must show mercy as justice would destroy so many of us. A good cry, an honest repentance of all of my vain travels and imaginings and then, maybe then, just maybe, I would have had the sense to see Him in the lightening, in the rain, in those small pines twisting in the wind. But now, I had a witness, someone to hurt as much as I was hurting myself. Stubborn. I was so stubborn and stupid.

We were in the car. Linda and I were together, yet so many worlds apart. Starting the car, a familiar action, I calmed down, fell in an energy lull and was almost normal. Linda sat straight, rigid, all tight and apprehensive, like a small girl determined not to show fear as that big, old roller coaster crept up that first, huge hill. She had no idea what was happening, but she would stick by her man. Sure, I had been acting strange, sure she was frightened, but I was her love. She had never tripped or experienced an acid nightmare and she had no idea what to do or say. A bubbling, "Oh Vincent, you're so cute when you're flipped out," a screaming, "Stop the car, you mother fucker!" or a gentle, "Hey, let's go get stoned...," may have stopped me even then. She, however, in her own way, had entered my madness. I was determined to play this one out.

Gas pedal held down, I popped the clutch, attempting to gain an illusion of speed and power. We roared out of the parking lot. I used first and second gears and a sharply, turning steering wheel, in order to get the VW to match my rage. A sharp turn and then we were out on one of the main drags. Bright lights, traffic, motion and commotion surrounded me. Oh my, I was tripping my brains out with the VW a slow moving snail while my mind took off and soared.

Stopped in traffic, going south toward the center of the city, rather than north toward Chicago, I was totally disoriented, completely straight and fully mad. Everything was bright and strange. Out of the sparkling glitter of town by night, came only determination. This must end. The problem was simple. I hadn't taken anything. I could have understood it if only I had been on something. I hadn't even smoked any grass or had a beer. My metabolism was speeding out of control, but I had not taken anything. If tripping, I could have turned to Linda and forced a laugh, "Weird movies coming down. Sure do feel scattered tonight." No, this was something else. I hadn't taken anything. I held to my strength, to my madness.

Stopped at a light, waiting on one of many hills, clutch held at the friction plate with the engine vibrating due to too much gas, I had an urge to simply let go. Popping the clutch, crashing into that big, old Chevy in front of us, they could come and get me, scraping my essence off of the windshield. No, Linda was there, beside me. No sense in hurting both of us. Hang on.

I suddenly realized that, instinctively, I was driving toward Liam. He was both a friend and a head. He would know. He would be able to help. He could talk me down out of this. We could blow some weed, listen to some sound. It would be okay. Oh hell, Bobby would be there. I hated to have my friends see me so weak and jumbled. It would be okay, though. It had to be.

The car, as if on remote control, moved slowly but steadily toward Liam's and Bobby's apartment. I may have made it. I think that I would have, except for the sign. I was at the last stoplight before their apartment. I was moving on, about to make the light, when I saw the sign, a black "Hospital" on a rectangle of white with an arrow pointing to the left. A split second decision, a quick, skidding turn to the left, and I was lost. Perhaps forever, as even now, so many years later, I still feel diminished.

No longer on one of the main streets, I found myself driving down darkened side streets in a neighborhood which didn't look at all familiar.

No longer crawling, the VW raced down those desolate, darkened, foolish streets. Looking back, it was as though I had been climbing up a hill, following a golden path to a safe haven. Then, whoosh! I had taken a side trip to the hidden dark side of the road. It was as though I had been walking on the apex of one of those A-frame roofs and had suddenly fallen to the side. Making my way through a strange forest, I had fallen into a pit, cut off from the sun. Only a few blocks from safety and now...

I was a confused spectator, watching the VW race down a dark, silent, curved path to whatever?!? Remembering, feeling Linda next to me, I was able to ask her, "Where are we?" I had forgotten where I was, as well as my urgency and need. Anything could have happened. This was a totally new, but not really alien world. Linda was only able to mumble, "I don't know." I must have been terrifying her. Her response served as a cue. I was mad. This must end.

We rounded a curve and there it was. The hospital. Even now, so many years later, writing this, cold shivers start up my legs and down my back. Why did I have to do it? Why not? You count. I was just a fucked up druggie that needed a touch of hell. Sure, I had taken all kinds of things. But when was the last time I had taken anything? I was so screwed up that I even missed the turn into the parking lot. Oh dear Lord, please let me keep driving. Let it all be a joke. Let this be a happy story. Let me go on and finish graduate school and become a competent, well-functioning psychologist. Let me marry Linda and lead a normal life. Shit.

A quick turn-around and I made the parking lot.

WHY? Why was I doing this to myself? I had so much: comfort, success, an agile mind, a decent body, friends, health, love, hope and opportunity. So many of us are forced into worlds beyond our control, suffering pain and tragedy, with so many of us crippled and maimed by war and disease. But me? I had so much. Weeks earlier, a ditty had been going through my mind, over and over, "A boy, so intent on death, met a girl so intent on life, he needed to destroy himself in order to feel worthy." It was more than that, however, more than some kind of Freudian, death urge.

I had had a dream. In my best moments, it had been a good one. Holding hands with all of mankind, I had realized that we're all in this huge, incomprehensible movie ***together***. I had seen worlds beyond my imagination, sights and sounds too incredible to ever verbalize. Coming down from my flights of fancy, I was always amazed by the world to which I returned. How could hate, confusion, and pollution be the real world? Like so many of us who had popped a pill and watched a sunset, I knew better. I had realized that we live in a world plagued with **Maya**. Better my dreams and visions, better the symmetry of expanding and contracting energy. Delving ever deeper into myself, I had had the vain yearning of becoming a bodhisattva, a here and now together one that had experienced eternity. I would realize **truth**; find **peace** and travel with **love**. It had all been so simple when I first turned on. It had been all so new and so beautiful. Impossible to convey to the straights, let them see if they had eyes, let them hear if they had ears. Somehow, I had lost it all. First, buried in depression, I had run back to Chicago. I had then forgotten the dream, with Linda being the stimulus for an explosion into ecstasy.

Then, somehow, it had all gotten so impossible. Enough was enough.

Jamming to a stop in that hospital parking lot, I only knew that it had to be over, that whatever was happening to me must end. Even then, something was tugging at me, trying to stop me. Linda had withdrawn into herself, frightened, unable to figure out what was happening. I was still trying to stop myself; call it a touch of sanity or the self-preservation instinct of a screwed up, jaded me. Perhaps memories of better times and places. Nothing was going to stop me, however. I was determined. This must end.

With a rush, I was out of the car, slamming the door, running up the steps, bursting into the hospital. I stopped. I had entered a classroom. It was an empty classroom, done in green. I strode to the dark green, portable chalkboard. I stopped, looking over the empty chairs, the kind that had the thickened arm that allowed note taking. Me, the former teacher; no matter what I had done or become, my forte was still teaching. Now was my chance at immortality, a chance for some famous last words before falling into insanity so thick and deep that I would never totally recover.

I felt a confused Linda straggle into the classroom behind me. What could I say? Who would understand? I quickly scrawled, "Juice is safer--thus 'quoth' the preacher." Oh well. I had blown it once again. Why couldn't I have written some head logic gem, an obscure Latin phrase, a Russian proverb or perhaps, a quote from the Tao-Te-Ching? Juice is safer. Sure. If you want to run from reality, find it in a bottle. Booze is easier.

A sick liver, dulled senses and a slowly, rotting mind have to better than... Oh well, even now, I don't buy it. It was a shame that I needed anything to protect me from the joy of life.

Enough. I ran out of the classroom, bursting into the night air. Linda was somewhere behind me. I stood there, trying to breathe. Waiting. My attention was caught up in a flickering, neon sign. I headed toward it, jumping a metal guard railing. I stopped. I stood there, reeling, not knowing quite what to do. Linda was forced to come down the steps and walk around the ramp and the railing that I had jumped over. Her dimly heard, "I can't follow you," catapulted me into action. At this angle, I could read the neon sign. With a surge of energy and purpose, I headed for the bright yellow of the beckoning, "Emergency Entrance." Linda, some 20 feet behind me, was forgotten.

Once inside, I didn't really know what to do. I knew that I couldn't discuss drugs with the enemy. I found myself standing in front of a glass, reception window. Several people stood behind the glass, watching me. On the spur of the moment, I drawled, "Ahm drunk, ahm drunk and I need a place to stay. Ahm really drunk. Ah really am." They just stood there, watching me. One of them perfunctorily asked me a couple of questions. "How much have you had to drink? What have you been drinking?" They were just putting up with me. My act wasn't playing very well. I wasn't coming across. It looked as though they were going to pat me on the head and send me home.

I disregarded their questions. Using some of my excess energy, I projected a picture of a drunk standing in front of me. I could see and feel the faint lines of the energy field that I had projected. Ah, that was better. Concern crossed their features. I was making it.

There were four of them. Two nurses, an intern, and a cop. The four of them became a portrait, or rather, a still picture. I had gotten their attention, the shutter had clicked and now they were frozen into a picture of concern.

The nurse who was standing there: Wasn't she Mary Evelyn? Mary Evelyn and Ben, they were two lovely people, a beautiful, happily married couple. That first time around, believing in the search for knowledge, I had been "best friends" with Ben. He had had a hang-up with statistics. I had spent hour after hour tutoring him, although he still ended up with a

C. Although he received two Cs that first quarter (a third C would have dumped him out of graduate school), he had gone on to become one of the most successful graduate students in our class. Hard work and perseverance had paid off for him. When I returned to school for that second try at the doctorate, he had haltingly asked me if I would read his thesis on autistic children, as if my interest or approval would mean something. Hah! He and some of the professors had actually remembered my promise, my dreams, and my academic skills that had come so easily. If only they could have understood that this time I was fighting to walk and talk at the same time, caught in a perceptual world that I didn't understand.

Mary Evelyn, cute in her nurse's uniform, looked at me with true compassion. It was sweet, this joke that I was playing. I was acting just like her son, Todd, and his five year old games. Although she held back her laughter, her eyes had a humorous twinkle. When I had first left graduate school, I had gone over to say goodbye to her and Ben on my next to last night there. After an evening of talking to them and one of the younger professors, he had left, leaving the three of us alone. We had not seen much of each other for the last six months or so, as they were straight and I wasn't. We had stood in a circle hugging each other. They had wished me well. Mary Evelyn had looked at me with love and respect, "Thank you so much for spending this night with us. I know that you have so many friends. Thank you so much for taking the time to spend these hours with us." She really meant it. My last night had been spent alone. I had finally gone to a fast food place with a girl that had been staying with Bobby. My friends had problems of their own, be it finals or head hassles. After a summer spent slightly strung out, if I wanted to return to Chicago, it was fine. Heads only did what was best for them. Everyone was into his or her own thing.

I projected harder. And, of course, it wasn't Mary Evelyn. She could have given me a hot drink and sent for Ben. The three of us could have talked about statistics and autistic children, reminiscing about those first, mind-bending courses. We could have laughed and joked and then I could have gone home and tried to study. Perhaps, with a good night's rest, I would have awakened as if from a bad dream.

It was a clever picture. It had movable parts. I was led into the emergency room and told to lie down on an examination table. I was told to wait for the doctor. I felt both ashamed and determined. They came in and out, poking and prodding, asking me useless questions. Thorough incompetents, they used large, plastic, play utensils. There was a huge, plastic, blue thermometer that looked like something out of a small child's, "let's play doctor," game. The whole thing was silly. One of the nurses' kept screwing up. It took her several attempts before she was able to take my blood pressure. This was absurd. Ridiculous. At least they could make it more realistic. If they couldn't play the game any better, if they couldn't use real instruments, why then, someone should call time out and tell me that the drunk game, a silly game to begin with, was over and that I should just go on home.

Worse than their play-acting and incompetence was the fact that I was in a real emergency room. There were people that really needed help. While I was lying there, a redneck had been brought in, all beaten and bloody, staring at me through bloodshot eyes. I began getting upset to my stomach, sick in the fact that I wasn't sick. I felt like someone crying over a hangnail, meeting someone with no foot. The thought dawned that they were trying to shame me. I was making a fool out of myself. It was time to leave. At the same time, however, I had a strong urge to see the charade through to the end. Enough was enough. Whatever had been happening to me must end.

The doctor had my father-uncle-grandfather's eyes. Our last names were similar. I knew that he knew me and that he knew that I knew that he knew me. Neither of us was letting on. A pat on the head, a few pills and a, "go on home, fella," would have sufficed. Instead, he mumbled something and asked me to wait.

Left alone, my shame overcame my determination. I became perfectly straight with no hallucinations or problems. I felt stupid. It was as though a wrathful, must be insane, trip would provide me with that moment of truth, that ultimate confrontation that would let me prove once and for all, that, indeed, I was a man. Let's face it. There was the December of exploding ecstasy when something had popped in my brain. Now, there was the pressure of having returned to graduate school, with me trying to make it with both my head friends and with the straights that I had known, when I was neither. There was the fear of not knowing or remembering as much as the other graduate students, of not being able to live up to my professors' expectations, especially when I had been such a bright bundle of promise. There was my changing relationship with Linda. Hell, the change in climate, roles and surroundings had all combined to completely screw up my metabolism. A few nights of solid sleep, some good rest and some sunshine was all that I needed. I was okay, just feeling foolish and ashamed of myself.

I got up to leave. I made it to the open door. Flash. Looking through the doorway into the waiting room, I stopped, totally shocked. It was filled with dull, flat people holding large dolls. I began shaking. Oh no. I had come to the right place. These dull automons were being sent home with fake children. This was some kind of an Exchange Center, some kind of reprocessing plant. Those bundled dolls were probably little robots hooked to a central computer. They probably emitted a certain frequency that was used to control the masses. Trembling, feeling quite ill, I laid back down. I realized that I was lost forever. Flash. I was back. I no longer had the resolve to leave, however.

Later, they led me into the waiting room. It was now empty except for Liam, Bobby, Linda and myself. Frightened, Linda had called my friends. Liam, with his long, floppy hair, checkered shirt and tight Levi's, was, as always, together and right on. Bobby stood off to the side, looking austere in his long, brown hair and beard. Liam kept talking to me, looking me in the eye, not afraid of the crazy. Like a complete ass, I kept on saying, "I don't know, man, I just don't know. Ya know what I mean? I just don't know." He told me that he knew how it was, that I just needed to find a handle, if I could find a handle, everything would be okay. I shouldn't worry. All I needed to do was find that handle and everything would be okay. My rage and anger were gone. The bubbling madness that needed to be satisfied was gone. All I could say, though, all I could keep on saying was, "I don't know. I just don't know."

I was so stupid. I was so close to getting out of there. All I had to do was straighten up and say something to Liam like, "Look man, I'm okay. I'm screwed up, but I'm okay. I'm just kind of light tripping–some kind of paranoid, acid residual or some such. Look, just get me out of here. Tell them that I took some bad acid or something. Just get me out of here."

Maybe it would have worked. Maybe he could have done it.

Hell, we could have left, gone back to their place, blown some weed and laughed about my silly hospital trip. It could have become a happening. Hey, you remember when we had to come and get ya? Boy, were you screwed up. Hah. It never happened. All I could do was mutter, "I don't know."

Talking to Liam, with Linda there at my side, I was basically straight. Only briefly, did I go altered. Liam, Linda and I were caught up in an energy circle, caught up in my hospital trip, in my madness. The portion of the room that we were standing in started to spin. Bobby, first standing, and then sitting against the wall of the room, was aloof, on more stationary ground. He just dispassionately watched us. He became some kind of an angel or judge. It would be his decision as to whether or not I could leave. This quickly passed, with the room leveling out. Dizzy, part of me wanted to break away from Liam and Linda, go up to Bobby and say, "Look, Bob, I'm frazzled, but this is stupid. Look, get me out of here." This too, passed.

The last thing that I remember is that I was given a shot. I was in a new room with two interns. One of them was bent over my outstretched forearm with a hypodermic in his hand. I don't remember leaving my friends. I do remember the insertion of the needle. After that, it's a mystery. I fell away from wherever I had been. Extended white forearm. Hypodermic needle. Thick clouds of oranges and reds, falling away from me in swirling bands of energy. Thick, coagulated blood. Things spun. The last vestige of my rational, cognitive self disappeared. I was no more.

Much later, I would find out that I was given a shot of Thorazine in order to stabilize my metabolism. I guess that I had projected being drunk and crazy much better than I had thought. Much better. I woke up on a closed psychiatric ward.

In the 1960s, as a new teacher, I can remember telling my high school psychology class, "Statistics tell us that one out of every ten Americans will be hospitalized for mental illness at some time in their lives." Well, only two more in that class of thirty will have to worry about it. The teacher had made it.

My quest was over. I woke up totally insane.

SATURDAY

SATURDAY

I woke up in a hospital bed. Weak but calm, I had no idea where I was or I how I had gotten there. I knew, however, that I was in a hospital room. My only thought was that ***they*** had gotten me.

It was a typical hospital room. There were two beds with a metal, nightstand table between them. There were some closets with metallic doors and a sink with a rectangular mirror above it. A partially opened door led to the toilet. Large drapes covered the windows. The room was done in light pastels and was fairly bright. It was a neutral room, even tranquil.

Nearly a decade earlier, as a young, undergraduate student in psychology, I had visited the back ward of a mental hospital in Chicago. One corridor, the furthest back of the back, had been eerie. Each room (or cell, to be more precise) had had a large, metal door with a 3" by 8" slit at eye level. This slit was the room's only ventilation. Each room contained a single, wrought iron bed and a wooden nightstand. The light source was a bare bulb hanging on a frayed cord from the center of the ceiling. The windows were thick, frosted glass. They were frozen shut and they were barred. There was an abundance of chipped paint and rotting wood. Patients were strapped to their beds (right arm and left leg). My visit had confirmed my worst suspicions of what a mental hospital was like. I had been both amazed and shocked.

My present surroundings were quite different. It was simply a modern hospital room, relatively new, clean and unemotional.

I was lying there, neither tripping nor freaking on my environment. Not totally realizing, confronting nor concerned with it, I simply accepted the fact that I was in a hospital room.

I was terribly weak. Although uneasy and disorganized, I maintained a certain calm. Thoughts wandered in and out of my head, not staying long enough for me to grab hold of them. THEY had gotten me. My only coherent thought.

Lying there weak and scattered, with my mind acting like a switchboard randomly starting but never completing a myriad of calls coming in and going out, I began with a, "How did I get here?" My mind merry-go-round was momentarily forgotten as I went deeper inside of myself. Oooops. Psychedelic flashes of thick clotted blood falling away from me… Deep orange clouds with circular bands of pulsating energy… White forearm, deep reds and oranges…

I shivered away from this dizzying pocket of memory. My attention went to my body. I couldn't feel my insides; I couldn't hear my heart. Surprisingly calm, I began trying to hear or feel my insides, my heartbeat. I found myself looking at the wall. I began scanning the physical objects in the room. I remembered that I was trying to remember how I had gotten into the room. Oh no. I quickly shied away from even starting to recall the psychedelic remembrance of my injection. I realized that my left foot was numb. Concentrating on this, I found myself listening for my heartbeat. My attention strayed to the wall. Thirty seconds of this went by every hour or two.

I went from weakness to exhaustion. Unable to hold a constant thought, I rolled on to my side and tried to fall asleep. This too, was impossible. After what seemed like hours of trying-to-sleep frustration, I would be back, once again trying to hold a thought, trying to hold my attention to one subject.

My situation may have been similar to someone coming out of deep sedation. Only occasionally would I trip into an altered awareness. I have very dim memories of the baby blue, plastic water jug and the baby blue, plastic bedpan now becoming huge, much like the light blue thermometer of my admittance. When something like this would happen, my mind would delve inward, with me moving toward becoming some small, doll-like figure surrounded by large, play, light blue, plastic objects. Was this some kind of a regression to infancy? Perhaps. Too scattered to retain any thoughts, even paranoid ones, this would be later fuel for my ***change*** theories.

It was in this weak, no insides, drifting thoughts, wandering attention state, that I had my first interaction with a member of the staff. A black intern or aide came into my room. The nametag on his crisp, white uniform said, "Jerry." He showed me my closet, pointing out that my clothes were in it. He talked and moved quickly, almost choppily. He was of medium height, stocky and very dark, although his features were not especially Negroid.

He was a bundle of energy, moving this way and that, here and there. He had large eyes, with deep brown pupils set in reddish whites. His eyes darted back and forth, not meeting mine. His speech, with long pauses between phrases, came quickly out of the side of his mouth. His words hung in the air long enough for me to catch their meaning after the fact. (Literally. I could see/feel his words in the air and sort of read/listen to them as they disappeared.) It was like listening to a tape recorder that you're always behind. Due to the pauses between words and sentences, you're able to stay with it, responding to what has previously been heard while trying to listen to what is presently being said. Looking back, he was probably neither hyper nor especially quick. Rather, it was as if my movie had been speeded up. He was reaching me in 1½ or double time.

He asked me how much money I had; informing me that everything over two dollars would have to be kept in the ward safe. At his direction, I groped through the top drawer of the nightstand, finally finding my wallet. I was able to fumble through it, slowly counting out $1.50. While I did this in slow motion, he stood back, similar to a policeman waiting for you to produce your license, but not about to be tricked into looking through your wallet and being accused of theft or bribery. I carefully stated that I had less than two dollars. I was pleased at the normalcy of my speech. I could talk. Although my movements were slow, I had been able to keep my hands from shaking. I had been able to count. I waited expectantly, expecting a reward, a pat on the back or at least an exclamation of wonder at my cleverness. My accomplishments went unnoticed, however. He simply said, "Okay," and left.

Lying there, I felt as if my first test had been passed. I could still interact with another human being. I lay back, once again attempting to get it together. Horribly weak, my scattered energy sifted through my system. My thoughts ran away from me, much too quick for me to keep up with them. I felt exposed and vulnerable. Unable to figure out what had happened to me or to even complete a single train of thought, I lay there in a total daze. I was terribly uneasy, being so very weak, passive, unthinking, helpless and dependent. Sleep wouldn't come. Thoughts wouldn't stay. Time passed. Slowly.

My mind was like a spinning roulette wheel. It would stop, but before I could see where it had stopped, it was in motion once more. I tried as hard as I was able to concentrate, to think, to meditate. The thought was triggered: Yoga. Mind, body discipline. The spinning wheels of my mind ground to a halt. Yoga. Sweet, blessed yoga. It would work. I would break through or out of this weak stupor. I would be able to gather my strength and control my energy. I now had a purpose, something that I could do. No longer just a weak victim, I would once again be able to control my thoughts and direct my body. Yoga. Ah, sweet yoga.

Slowly, shaking slightly, I managed to get out of bed. The blue ward pajamas, although loose fitting, were too restrictive for my exercises. I struggled out of them, my mind idly wondering where they had come from, how I had gotten into them. The door to the hallway was open; I kept my jockey shorts on for the sake of decorum. I tried to sit on the linoleum floor between the beds. The floor was too hard; I didn't have enough room to stretch. I managed to get back in bed. Much too stiff to assume a half-lotus, I ended up sitting cross-legged in the middle of the bed. The bed was too soft, sagging in the middle. It was like sitting in a shallow hole. It would have to do.

I attempted to do some stretching exercises. Gawd, did it hurt. I was so very stiff and weak. Many times, attempting to do yoga after a long absence, I would be so stiff that I would quickly give up. Not this time, however. Nope. I was determined. Instinctively, I knew that I had to do something. Yoga was the only thing that I could think of. The stretching and breathing of yoga would settle me, allow me to make it to some familiar reference points. So many times we forget what we need, what we have to do in order to get back on beam, back on focus. I knew that I needed to stretch and to breathe, needed to relax and resettle into a more familiar me. I had just started my stretching when Jerry burst in on me.

"What are you doing?!?" all excited, shouting loudly.

"Huh?"

Just what are you doing? There are women and children on this ward. Just what do you think you're doing? Get your clothes back on. You should be ashamed of yourself."

His shouting didn't bother me. It was just excited babble. It was to the wind, to the air, not really directed at me. It was as though Jerry were playing to an invisible audience, perhaps flashing on repeating the incident around coffee. "Ya know what this crazy was doing? No really, he was sitting there nude, ah mean nude an' he had his fingers up his nose or some such thing." He ran to my side, looking like he wanted to grab and shake me. He stood there, open-mouthed, twitching, as if he wanted to jump up and down, needing to release all of that energy.

All of his noise and commotion didn't bother me. He did. He was bright, alive, mobile and energetic. His eyes were quick, his awareness of self and surroundings together. He was strong and sure of himself. While I was struggling to sit up straight, attempting to clear my head sufficiently just in order to be able to think, he was able to run around, shout and carry on. He acted superior to me; he was superior to me, much stronger, higher and more together. I didn't like him. Not a little.

"Stawh?!? Po-kneemayesh po-rooski?" (What! Do you understand Russian? In Russian.) I began shouting at him in Russian as loudly as I could. Startled, he stopped. No longer shouting, he just stood there with his mouth open. Hah! I had him. I continued yelling at him in Russian. He just stood there, looking confused. My level of awareness began to rise, rising almost to his level. His eyes bulged, all confused and wandering.

Wait a minute. He had cocked his head and appeared to be listening to what I was saying, trying to understand what I was shouting. Could it be that he recognized my speech? Had he heard Russian before? Perhaps I was just speaking too quickly. Was it possible that the Russians had a hand in this? Pop. In an instantaneous mind trip, I began to understand the implications of the entire, horrifying plot. The Russians were definitely in on this. Pop. I was back.

Jerry had noticeably slowed in awareness, thought and movement. My words petered out. My torrent of Russian was over. Jerry, who had been drifting off, started pulling himself together. His startled confusion was replaced by his former sureness. He did not appear anywhere near as cocky as before, however.

With a lingering trace of confusion and a tinge of something else (Was that respect I heard in his voice? Did he know that I was part of the real power struggle?), he began again, this time in a normal, even subdued voice. "Uh, sir, excuse me, but we have certain rules. Uh, you'll have to get your clothes back on. We do have women and children on this floor. Come on now. Get your clothes back on."

I complied. Who knows? I didn't want him to become violent, didn't want anyone to get physical with me before I could get to someone in authority. I moved with difficulty, slowly struggling back into my blue, ward clothes. Jerry waited, watching. At last, he seemed satisfied and left without saying anything. He appeared mollified and left shaking his head. My only reaction, "This is going to be more difficult than I thought. No yoga. *They're* not going to let me do any yoga. No yoga. I'll show them. I have a few tricks up my sleeve. I'll show them. They'll see."

The confrontation had actually strengthened me ever so slightly. I still knew some things. I could speak Russian. This would help. I quickly fell back into weakened exhaustion, however.

Weakness. All I knew was an all-pervading weakness. Slipping in and out of fantasies, my only real memory is of an all-consuming weakness. The fantasies, themselves, came and went. Each would be perfectly obvious as it happened. A single thought and there I was, with the rest of my mind hurriedly picking up bits and pieces, fragments of a shattered mind, forming them into a history reinforcing whichever fantasy had crossed my mind. Almost instantaneously, I would be in a new fantasy and then another one and so on.

Deep in my head, attempting to figure out what was happening to me, I met and swept through a whole series of basic bipolarities, conflicts and paranoia. Black-white, male-female, life-death confrontations... at a more surface level: I was dead, I was a prisoner of war, and I had been caught up in an Exchange Center... On and on and on...

One of the earliest, strongest and most persistent fantasies was that I was in a Change Center. Since I was a male, I would be reborn a female. Changing is. Were these unresolved, homosexual tendencies? Sure. Why not? I had read an article by some psychologists who hypothesized that rather than castration complex in the male or penis envy in the female, a source of many of our basic, sexual problems is womb envy in the male.

The male is beset by the desire to return to the womb and is envious of the woman who has one. Hah. I got to live out both fantasies as the ward was my meta-womb and I would be changed to a female.

My Change theory started innocuously enough. Tired of trying to figure things out, I slowly, cautiously got out of bed. I made my way to the hall door and timidly stood there, looking out into the corridor. I was afraid to leave my room, to interact with anyone, similar to a small boy afraid to meet the new kids in the just-moved-to neighborhood. The corridor was quiet and empty except for one other person. She walked, tall and stately, up and down the corridor, looking neither to the right nor to the left. She wore a flowing blue negligee, a blue housecoat, dark, movie star sunglasses and a platinum blonde wig. She was quite a picture, this majestic figure, striding up and down, back and forth. I would forget her and then she would be back in my range of vision. Although she passed my room several times, she paid me no heed. Even though she never turned her head, it was as though she was aware of me, but chose not to acknowledge me. Oh hell. I had her number. She was obviously a male.

Oooops. I was back in a Change Center. I had no feeling in my mid-section. The Change was already starting. Standing there in the doorway, not having met or spoken to anyone except Jerry, I tried to face the facts. After a microsecond of horror, I quickly accepted this new information. I was to be changed.

I rubbed my hand over my day-old, beginning to get thick beard. Here I was in these grungy, ward clothes. Sweat was dripping from my armpits with my shirt/smock already wet to the waist. I wasn't very pretty. I dropped away and began thinking, "Oh dear, I need new clothes, some make-up and I just must do something with this hair." I stood there, looking out into the corridor, staring across at the rooms opposite mine. Several doors were open. I could see several hanging negligees. "Oh, how unfair. I have nothing to wear. Here I am, with only these terrible clothes and nothing pretty to wear. I must have some of those." And yes, my imagination came up with this trite, little girl language.

I stood there, unable to move, wanting to race across the hall and grab as many clothes as I could. I could "see" myself snatching a negligee, wrapping myself in it, rolling around on the floor, becoming... I couldn't move. My consciousness shifted. I centered on the fact that I was always afraid to do anything, that I was never spontaneous. I was such a coward. My change trip was forgotten as I castigated myself for being such a spineless idiot. I needed to be able to move, to be spontaneous, to stop being so afraid of everything inside and outside of me. Yet, I couldn't cross that hallway, couldn't snatch those clothes. Defeated, I returned to my bed. I had been unable to leave my room and meet the kids in the new neighborhood.

Returning to my bed, completely defeated, unable to launch into my transvestite trip, I was totally exhausted. Sleep would not come. I completely spaced out of my Change Center routine. Then it started. A voice began echoing in my brain, "You're afraid, afraid to make a fool out of yourself, afraid to let people laugh at you. You don't bring laughter or joy to anyone." The voice changed. It became cajoling, "Come on, now. Don't be afraid. Come on. Make people laugh. Be a clown. Do something crazy. Come on." The thought of me actually doing something far out, something hilariously crazy and funny was almost too much. I had spent years disciplining myself to appear sober and serious regardless of what was happening to me. Mustn't let them others know you get high, you know. The voice kept on and on, first reprimanding me, then pleading with me, tempting me, seducing me. I couldn't sleep, couldn't shut the voice off. Finally, I knew that it would be over, that I would be able to find rest, if only I could do something really bizarre and funny. Giving in to the voice, I straightened up and got out of bed. I went to the door of my room, firmly resolved to really let go and do it. I would completely flip out, would bring laughter and happiness to them others. By making a complete fool out of myself, I would be able to find peace, would be able to shut off that insistent voice. I prepared to jump right into it.

The woman in the room next to mine had beaten me to it. She was a slightly heavy black woman lying on the floor half in and half out of her room. To my eyes, it looked like she was wearing some kind of green, ballet costume with all of this fluff sticking out at her waist. There was a micro second of horror. Her features changed ever so slightly. When Linda and I had been popped on that absurd marijuana bust, we had spent the night in jail. Separated from the girls, my buddy and I had spent the night together in a cell. Very early in the morning, we had been handcuffed and herded into a van. There had been this huge, black guy whose wrists were so thick and swollen that they weren't even able to handcuff him. I momentarily flipped out and wondered how he had gotten here. Obviously, all of us hard nuts to crack had been thrown in together for our reconditioning and reprogramming. My Change Center fantasy was gaining depth. Pop. I was back, watching her.

"Ah didn't do nothing wrong, yassir, yassir, ah believe, ah seen Jesus, yassir. Ooooooooohhhhh, Satan, don't you bother me, oh no, oh get away from me devil, ah didn't do nothing, oooh, please." She was screaming and squirming, looking this way and that. The devil, I guess, was only feet away. I couldn't really take her seriously. I didn't feel the devil, or for that matter, anything evil or sinister. There didn't seem to be any discordant vibrations or any bad energy.

I also couldn't feel any pain emanating from her. When our eyes met, hers appeared to be a lot saner than mine (I had caught a glimpse of myself in the mirror in my room—a glimpse had been enough and I had quickly turned away). No, she didn't seem to be in trouble. Rather than worry about her, I was amazed that she was doing such a great job of appearing completely foolish. Although a little overawed, I was tempted to get into the act. I came close to trying to help her out. I could have bent over and whispered instructions to her, "A little more saliva, that's it, drool. Ah now, let's see, try looking a little more afraid, hmmm, well, okay..." I held back. She was certainly doing a good job all by herself. I could never have come close.

And then she was looking at me. "Ah know you, yassir, yassir, you're the Holy Ghost, yassir, ah know you, oooh!!!" Her eyes became more real, focusing on mine. She recognized me. Ah hah! Someone knew me. I became quite excited. I gathered myself together and fell right in with her routine. She knew me. I realized that I was supposed to do something. I could help her. I could be necessary. I could do some good. I waited expectantly, waiting for my cue.

She kept on getting sidetracked, however, screaming about the devil or about how she hadn't done anything wrong. I kept waiting, all keyed up about getting into the act. I started to get upset. Come on now; let's stick to the script, the one where I have a part. Every once in a while, though, she would get back to me, lower her voice and say, "Ah know you, yasser, ah's knows youse the Holy Ghost." When this would happen, I could feel the energy flow between us. I fell right in with her. She needed me. I could help her. I should do something. Should I bless her, kneel down with her and do some "aums," or should I slug her, or... It was disconcerting, however, as she would continually leave me, getting into her own thing. I wasn't quick enough. She kept leaping around, doing her writhing and screaming, with me only an occasional part of the scene.

And then Jerry was there. The woman dropped completely back into her original routine, yelling and moaning about the devil. I was completely forgotten by her. Some other people came to help Jerry. He gave me a perturbed, disgusted look; I was in the way. Discouraged, no longer expectant and excited, I was drearily tired. I went back into my room. Although disappointed and let down, I idly noticed that the voice in my head was gone. Lying down, I fell into a deep sleep.

They woke me up for lunch. Everyone ate in the television room or in the kitchenette adjacent to it. On the way to lunch, half-asleep, straggling down the hall, I heard one of the aides refer to the television room as the computer room. He was laughing and said something to someone about somebody to the effect that, "We'll settle him down. We'll just get him to sit in the old computer room." Ack. One of my strongest fantasies was thus triggered. Each of us, unique and separate, suffering from scattered vibrations would be sent to the Computer Room where we would be mesmerized by the Master Controller. Each of us would be leveled out, brought to the same vibrational frequency by the all-powerful boob tube. It seemed to actually happen. The television set was on a shelf that protruded out of the wall, some eight feet off of the ground. Sitting there, under the television's spell, the strong would get weaker (tired, bored?) while the weak would get stronger (alert, attentive?). To my hypersensitivity, it was evident that everyone would get caught up in the television. While our attention was on it, the energy levels of each of us would sift and level out, bringing each of us to relatively the same place.

Those first couple of days, the television was worse than a mere leveler. Occasionally, I would realize that it was a two-way device. The characters would come on, observe us, and report our progress, or lack of it, to the Master. Not only would the television modify us, sucking us into its peculiar vibrations, it would also spy on us. Every so often, I would observe television characters, usually those on live, talk shows, watching me. I would usually freeze, attempting to remain neutral in thought and action. Very rarely, filmed characters would flash me knowing looks. Were they the captured ones?

That first meal was a strain. While I was weakly putting my tray of food on the table, one of the other patients, a white male in his teens, became manic and began shouting at his food, "Eat me!" He was ignored. As other patients began to eat their food, he began shouting even louder at them, "Go ahead. Eat me. Go ahead. It's okay. Eat me!" Still mostly ignored, a black girl in a heavily sedated, zombie-like state, froze and stopped eating, only staring at her food. One of the help was at her side, cooing and assisting her. The boy's shouting was obviously disturbing her and starting to get on everyone's nerves. They began quieting him. He started to spin out and then was off, pacing around the ward while the rest of us continued to eat. There was a mumbled "Oh that Jack. He's always acting up." from one of the other patients. "I know, but he gets on my nerves." from another. And then he was forgotten.

There were three women, the strongest of the patients, who sat together and ate off to the side in the kitchenette. Their lunch was normal and it could have been in any lunchroom. I was in the television room with a couple of the other patients, including the dark girl who appeared to be only partially aware of her surroundings. I noted that these normal-type, strong ladies had broken the spell of the Computer Room and were able to stay out from under its influence.

I was very tired, very exhausted. Still half-asleep, I was too tired to build any fantasies. After I finished my meal, I sat bent over, with my head in my hands, eyes covered. I stayed that way for some time. I became slightly clairvoyant. Even though my eyes were both shut and covered by my hands, I had the illusion that I could see everything around me. My reverie was broken by one of the women in the kitchenette. In a loud, knowing voice she stated, "Humph, he's pretending that he can't see!" Startled, I wondered how she could know that I could see in this different way. Although I didn't move or acknowledge her comment, a part of me realized how very difficult this was going to be. ***They*** could even know about this.

Later, while I was just sitting there, horribly tired, the three women tried to interact with me. They had adjusted well to ward life. Elaine appeared immature; she was physically thin with small breasts and had acne. She was the most quiet of the three. Bertha looked a little like a truck driver. Not that bad, but really masculine. She was the most dominant person and the one who knew about my being able to see with my eyes closed. Lillian, the parading blonde of that morning, was always hidden behind sunglasses and wigs. They would all add fuel to my Change theory. Although, I would usually see the three of them as males becoming females, it would occasionally be the other way. Whether going from male to female, or from female to male, it just didn't matter. What was important was that they were being changed.

Lillian and Bertha tried to kid with me, even flirt. I was new meat on the ward. Bertha went so far as to ask me if she could touch me. I was instantly horrified and felt complete terror. If she would have touched me, I would have probably screamed. Thankfully, with my glazed eyes and lack of response, she left me alone.

Too dazed and disoriented to interact with them, I made my way back to my room. My interactions with the staff had been little better than my weak interactions with the patients. My hearing was completely screwed up. I never knew if someone was talking to me or if I was hearing voices. The staff took to calling me, "Mr. Douglas, sir." I wanted to tell them that it was okay, that they could call me by my first name, but was never able to get it out. I became, "Mr. Douglas, sir."

On the way back to my room, I knew that I was in trouble. My brief interactions with the staff and other patients had only convinced me that I was truly in trouble. I needed some kind of handle, something to hold on to, a train of thought that would stay with me for more than a few moments. I needed a rational explanation of what was happening to me. One moment I would be totally blitzed, the next instant I would be fairly straight, wondering how I gotten into this whole thing. The only thing that was constant was the incredible weakness. Weakness. Always weakness.

Back in my room, isolated from the staff and other patients (I had no roommate), I made my way to the window. Oooops. The windows on the other side of the corridor, which included those of the television room, kitchenette and reception desk, looked out on the hospital parking lot. The view on this side of the corridor, however, was a view of the area that I had never known. There were thick trees, a forest if you will, and a water tower. I counted the floors. Ohmigod, I was on the fifth floor. At a very deep level of mind (a near trance state) in Mind Control, I had learned a very powerful, visual mnemonic trick. Numbers were paired with visual images. The letter 5 was paired with *law*. Arggh. Was I being run on Course 5? Of course, why else would I be on the <u>fifth</u> floor?

The world tilted ever so slightly and I was, indeed, a Prisoner of War. I could see, feel and live it. Weren't those soldiers there? Why else would there be soldiers? Wasn't that really a gun tower? Were these the rain forests of Nam? Tortured prisoners: Couldn't I hear and feel them? Didn't I merge with them?

I pulled away from the window, shaken and exhausted. Back to bed. Back to blur. Back to weakness and frustration at not being able to sleep.

I would slowly orient myself to the ward. The ward, itself, consisted of a single corridor. My room was at the far end, away from the large, swinging double-door entrance. The entrance to the ward was kept locked; one could buzz people in from the reception desk, which was about a third of the way down the corridor. Between the entrance and the reception desk, there were, in order, a conference room containing a stereo and some old records, the television/sitting room that served as the major meeting place of staff and patients, and a small kitchenette/supply room. After the reception desk, there was a small passageway that led to a padded observation room and then, a series of double occupancy hospital rooms. On my side of the hall, across from the reception desk, there was a conference room followed by regular rooms. The showers were directly opposite the reception desk. The rest of that side of the corridor was filled with regular rooms. The far end of the corridor, my end, was marked by a large fire exit. It would take me some time (days after my admittance) before I could map the above.

Later that afternoon, a cart filled with goodies was buzzed in through the ward entrance. There were all kinds of candy, some magazines and even a stack of comic books. I excitedly found out that I could indeed buy something. I hurried to my room, remembering that I had some money in the nightstand. I bought a comic book, the top one on the stack. At last, here was something that would get my mind off of myself. I could forget my problems, stop trying to figure everything out, ignore the mind-blowing trips. I would read a comic book. Sure. It was a mistake.

I have always loved to read. Back in my room, out of deep habit, near normal except for the weakness, I settled into the bed, propping up the pillows, wrapping myself in the sheets and blankets, preparing to get engrossed in my comic. In my ward state of mind, however, anything could have happened. Have you ever read a comic book after having a case of beer, while taking a roller coaster ride, or just plain stoned out of your gourd? I don't know where I was at, but reading the comic book became very strange, very quickly.

The comic book, itself, was some intricate, science fiction story about a Mr. Atom. He had numerous, bizarre adventures, became microscopic, ran into an anti-self and so on. Whew. I, of course, took everything literally. Concentrating on each word, watching the cartoon figures blur, I went so far as to believe that the comic was some secret set of instructions. If I could only follow them, I would be able to space out of the maze in which I found myself. I became totally engrossed in my reading, flipping out several times as I continued reading. Finally, completely exhausted, I attempted to sleep.

As I tried to sleep, I began getting into the comic book. I realized that my real fear, my real confrontation, would be with myself. My ultimate challenge, the climax of my existence, would be running into myself. The primal split. In order to get myself back together, my two halves would have to meet, merge together into a new whole, or attempt to destroy each other, with only one victor. I fell into a feverish, half-sleep, tossing and turning, with psychedelic images of the comic book character and myself all confused and swirling.

When I woke up, my comic book adventures were forgotten. Once again, I began trying to figure out what was happening to me. Nothing held together. I just spaced back and forth into countless starts at **the solution**. My emphasis changed, however. From a constant, "How did I get here?" I was consumed with, "How do I get out of here?"

I had already noticed several strange things that were happening on the ward. Seeds of the ultimate, conspiracy trip had already been planted. Coming in and out of a daze, I noticed that people were continually coming and going, on and off of the ward. It seemed that everyone had their own method, their own secret as to how to get on and off of the ward. I had started to identify several groups or levels of people. There were the dupes (the permanent staff, most of whom were white) who thought they were in charge but didn't really know what was going on. There were the help (aides and other workers, most of whom were black) who may or may not have been in on things—some definitely were. And then there were the patients, with some of them definitely in on it. Everyone, even some of the other patients, seemed to have their own way of leaving the ward. I knew that I had to find a key, a handle, a way—my way, to get off of the ward. Bertha, for example, was quicker than most of the help and intimidated them. I had to find some way to do the same thing. How could I get on top of it, find my own handle, my own way of dealing with the staff? I had to stop being so chicken shit. I must get off of the ward. This obsession held me together; it gave me purpose. I must find a way to get off of the ward.

Not able to dwell on it, I could dimly remember how I had gotten on the ward. No, not the psychedelic injection or emergency room horrors. I had pretended to be drunk. I could remember the pretending to be drunk. Hah. The thought dawned. I would get off of the ward the same way that I had gotten there. I would simply leave. I got to my feet and went to the closet. I put on my bulky, fur parka. It was a relic from Chicago. Dark green, with a fur-lined hood, it was out of place in Florida, even in the northern Florida winter. Putting it on, feeling together, I would simply bluff myself off of the ward. Hell, I would just tell them that I was no longer drunk. Thank you all very much, but I'm okay. Please buzz me out. Yes, of course, it would work.

Wearing this huge parka, I started walking to the reception desk. It didn't dawn on me that I was still wearing the blue, ward pajamas and that I was barefoot. I took huge breaths, breathing through my nose, calming myself, steeling myself for the bluff of my life.

Danny, a thin, high-yellow, Afro-American male nurse or aide and Mrs. U., an Asian nurse with whom I was to get emotionally involved, were stationed at the desk. I came spacing along, bundled in the parka, barefoot, with glazed eyes, messy hair and growing thick stubble on my chin. They didn't hear me coming. I hunched over the counter; still, no reaction. I loudly cleared my voice. Startled, the seated Mrs. U. looked up. Danny, who had been studying some forms, simply stood there, blankly looking at me.

Mrs. U. was the first to recover. In a composed, friendly, even cheerful voice (her eyes were still doubtful), she said, "Oh, Mr. Douglas, we were looking for you. We have to put your nametag on. Danny, please get Mr. Douglas' name tag."

Danny fumbled around, coming up with a thin strip of plastic that had my name and date of admittance on it. I shivered. Although it was probably a typical, hospital identification band, it was similar to those put on newborn babies. Was I indeed to be changed, to be erased, and to be reborn in this place? By this time I was completely confused and had forgotten why I had gone to the reception desk. I knew, however, that they weren't going to put any wristband on me.

Danny, who had still not spoken, but kept looking at me ever so strangely, fitted the plastic band around my wrist. He attempted to punch it closed; this required a small, metal tool. I just stood there, hunched over the counter, completely upset. They weren't going to tag me. I sent energy, tons of it. I could have lifted a car, bent steel bars, and been able to do just about anything. Although I made no overt, physical move (I could have crushed him like a grape), he wasn't able to punch it closed. He kept on trying, looking at me shyly, even apologetically. Finally, he took it off of my wrist, trying to punch it closed on the counter top. Mrs. U. tried it. They both tried it. I kept sending energy; no one was going to tag me. I became exasperated watching them and almost snatched it up, doing it for them. Nope. Not that. They weren't going to tag me.

They started trying to make light of it, embarrassingly giggling. The absurd scene went on. Finally, Mrs. U., still giggling, said, "Well, I guess we won't be putting it on just now." Looking grim, with my face set in stone, I just nodded. (I was never tagged. Even after I stopped hallucinating and had some rational recall of my ward experience, I would still think that some funny things had been going on although most of what happened to me was basically in my own head. Still, the staff were a little weak.)

Satisfied, feeling strong, I walked back to my room in a manner similar to that of a gunfighter returning from a high noon that he had not found to be terribly difficult. Back in my room, discarding the parka, I crawled into bed. Lying in bed, I drifted back into a weak fuzziness. A thought nudged my consciousness: I was still on the ward. My strength and energy totally disappeared, leaving only a weak, tired, defeated shell. I had to get off of this ward. Not angry, manic or clever, I knew that I must get off of the ward. I needed to get outside, needed to get off by myself and get my thoughts together. Nothing made any sense. I had to get off of this ward, out of this entire situation.

Restless, unable to sleep, I once again got out of bed. I had no plan, no ideas. My only purpose was a deep-seated urge to get off of the ward. I stood at my door. I slowly wandered out into the corridor. I drifted over to the far end of the hallway, the one away from the entrance, the reception desk and the television room. I found myself staring at a door; it was an emergency exit or fire door. Was it or was it not locked? I had no will, strength or purpose. I simply stood there, staring at the door. After countless, mind-time of just standing there, a thought broke through. An alarm would probably go off if I pushed open that door. Alarm? My head snapped around and I found myself staring at a fire alarm.

I had not known that it was there. With no conscious volition or purpose, I found myself pulling the alarm. Perhaps I thought that in the resulting confusion, I would slip out of the fire exit. Perhaps I thought that the ward would be cleared. I don't know.

Suddenly, there was an immediate loud clanging and all kinds of commotion. I stood stunned and frozen. As if from a great distance, I watched several doll-like figures running back and forth, crisscrossing from one side of the corridor to the other. My world went sideways. It was as though I were watching all of this running and activity from a great height, perhaps as much as from 4 or 5 stories up. Caught up in this unreal, out of perspective world, thoroughly entranced by the running figures and all of the commotion caused by the alarm, I completely forgot about slipping through the fire exit. I had become a non-thinking straw dolly. Eventually, I was led back to my room.

Looking back, although seemingly continuous, each of these incidents is like a vignette, a happening out of an eternity of fuzzy, never-ending weakness. Out of this jelly like weakness, I can recall these isolated incidents quite clearly. The real horror, however, wasn't in these bizarre incidents, but rather, the endless hours of not being able to think or to cope. My predominant state of being was not a series of trip experiences, but rather, an all-pervading, low energy, impotence. Each time that I would really get into trying to figure something out, something would happen to sidetrack me into something else. Perhaps a blessing in disguise, as I still had little or no memory and almost no cognitive powers.

After my fire alarm incident, as I was lying in bed, I dropped into a whole new shtick. I realized that I was completely worthless. I was haunted by my worthlessness. Everything that I had ever tried to do had backfired. I was a worthless fool. A dud. After hours (moments?) of castigating myself, I started to gear myself up. I must shape up. All of these people waiting on me, taking care of me. Oh no. I must do my part. I had to be worth something. I must do my part.

With a sudden, unexpected burst of energy, I jumped up. I would do my part. Earlier, at the reception desk, I had had some strength. This was the first time since coming to the ward, however, that I was able to move, really move. With a manic burst of energy, I ran down the corridor to the television room, to the kitchenette, to the reception desk. I began emptying all of the ashtrays, clearing the tables, dumping my room wastebasket into the larger one at the reception desk and so on. I was completely hyper, working quickly and efficiently. No longer would people have to wait on me. I would show them; I could do my part. I wasn't worthless. I could help. I was a big guy.

They tried to stop me. "Come on now, come on, you don't have to do that. Come on now." I ignored them. I was doing my part. I worked feverishly. Hah! I would show them. Sweat began dripping from my forehead and armpits as I continued working, all hyper and intent. They continued trying to stop me, trying to reason with me, but not using any physical force.

Very suddenly, my energy petered out. I allowed them to walk me back to my room. I was quite subdued for you see, a voice was pounding over and over in my head: "You're taking work away from others. This is someone else's job. You're taking work away from others. Find your own work. You're taking work away from others." Exhausted, tired, and defeated once again (When would I be able to do something right?), I allowed them to lead me to my room. Days later, Lillian would tell me how cute I had been, running around the ward, dumping all of my clothes and belongings into the trash and so on. Oh well. C'est la vie.

Back in my room, I was half asleep when they came for me. It was Danny and Mrs. U., that dynamic duo. They kind of milled around my room, moving furniture. I finally realized that they wanted to move my bed out of the room. Groggily, I tried to get up, wanting to help or at least get out of the way. I tried to tell them that I was okay, that I could walk, but I wasn't able to get the words out. Half asleep, with them completely ignoring me, I became confused and tongue-tied. I tried to show them that I was okay by starting to get out of bed, but they would have none of it. I did manage to get out a half-hearted, "I'm okay. I can walk." Other than a, "No, that's okay." they continued to completely ignore me. Still spaced and disoriented, I simply laid back, relaxing completely, falling into a "whatever happens, happens" head.

They continued to mill around. They were having some real problems. The situation took on a Laurel and Hardy aspect with them appearing to be incompetent buffoons. Not spun out, but weak and disoriented, I waited as patiently serious and passive as possible. They continued trying to move the furniture and maneuver my bed out into the hall. The problem was a simple one, requiring them to first move my bed away from the door. After moving the other bed out of the way, they could then move my bed toward and through the door. They were not able to figure this out and continually tried to squeeze my bed past the one nearer to the door. As I write this, I'm reminded of an old joke. A guy gets a flat tire outside of an insane asylum. Attempting to change the tire, all of the nuts and bolts that he had removed from the flat tire, roll down into a sewer. Perplexed, not knowing what to do, he just stands there. A crazy with glazed eyes, standing behind the wrought iron fence of the asylum tells him to take a nut off of each of the other tires and to use them to temporarily secure the fourth tire. The motorist looks at him with shocked surprise, "B-but how did you know that?" The inmate answers, "I may be crazy, but I'm not stupid." Although too shattered to have those kinds of insights at the time, their actions were similar to someone not being able to figure out that you could have one less bolt for each tire, at least temporarily.

Danny and Mrs. U. finally took to giggling, making much ado about their ineptness. They finally figured it out. At last, we were in the hall. By this time, I had grown quite bored with the whole thing and was once again half-asleep, lying flat on my back, open and passive. Perhaps Danny was trying to be cute. Maybe he was just trying to be friends. Maybe he was just an idiot. Whatever.

I peered up at him from my highly vulnerable position. He stood at the foot of my bed, out of perspective. Looking at me, he suddenly had an idea; his features changed, taking on a set, determined, even devilish expression. My mind took it further, with his face becoming some kind of devil's head. Leering intently at me, he bent over and began pushing. He pushed as hard and fast as he could, shouting, "Wheeeee!" We raced down the hall with his now grotesque head always staring at me. The walls, rooms and reception desk went whirling by in blurred swirls.

He put on the brakes. We slid to a stop, coasting to a halt in front of a room halfway between the double door entrance and the reception desk. The room was directly across from the television room. It was the most observable room on the floor. Getting my bed into position was an easy matter as it was to be the one closest to the door. Having positioned my bed, Danny stood there, grinning down at me. It wasn't a malicious grin. Perhaps he was just having fun, just goofing around, just trying to have some fun with me. Whatever his intention, the effect had been creepy. In the days to follow, still trying to figure everything out, I would have psychedelic flashes of that trip down the corridor. It would only strengthen my conviction that something strange was happening on the ward. I may not be playing with a full deck, but everything weird wasn't just a product of my imagination.

I guessed that they moved me due to the fire alarm incident or because of my Mr. Clean routine. I was now in the hub of activity, surrounded by mirrors and motion. I had a roommate, Jack, another person who bore watching.

Jack was a little strange. In his late teens, perhaps 17 or so, he was a thin, six footer. He had thick, dark, wavy hair and a pinched, pinkish face. Tremendously immature, he would always be bothering someone and would occasionally throw temper tantrums. The staff and the other patients either put up with him or babied him. He was also the kind of person that had done everything, or rather, had to have you believe that he had done everything. His, "oh yeah, I've done that," or his, "sure, I've been into that," were kind of irritating, especially when you knew that he didn't know what you were talking about. A nice guy, he was just impossibly immature and childish, with very easy breaking points.

Meeting him that first afternoon of mine on the ward, I was more spun out than he was. He came across as tremendously open and friendly. He had adjusted somewhat to ward life, having all kinds of entertainments, including a guitar. He told me that if I ever wanted to play his guitar or use any of his things, I should just go ahead and do it. I was disorganized and confused, especially after my ride down the corridor, but felt as though I had arrived at summer camp. Luckily, I had gotten someone nice with whom to share my cabin.

It was right around this time that I would occasionally pop into a Prisoner of War fantasy. Ironically, a simple question by a passing nurse triggered me into this delusion. Having been moved and having met Jack, I was standing in the hall. A nurse, walking by, suddenly stopped and turned, asking me, "You know where you are, don't you?" I just looked at her and said, "Of course. Yes." She nodded and continued on her way.

At that moment, I could have told her that I was on a psychiatric ward in a hospital in northern Florida. I could have told her much more, however. In that momentary exchange, I had also flashed on that brief, nightmarish glance out of the window, when I had swirled into Prisoner of War. Shivering away from that vivid, psychedelic remembrance, my mind quickly built a P.O.W. fantasy, taking isolated facts and fancies, building them into a network that would support that mind set.

For example, Jack was the typical, young G.I., who had cracked early. Some of the young blacks who served as aides and workers were obviously captured soldiers now in the employ of the enemy. Mrs. U., an Asian, and one of ***them***, was in on it. Not being rational, my mind would go even further. We were all prisoners, even the doctors and nurses. These professionals (the dupes) unwittingly served the enemy, not really realizing what they were doing. Over the next few days, I would spend endless mind time attempting to figure out who the Master Controller really was. My usual guess was a Quasimodo type hidden away in the bowels of the hospital. I would get psychedelic flashes of him moving all of us like chess pieces.

Yes, I could have told her where I was. I even knew what floor we were on, having counted them in my brief glimpse out of that window. I could have probably told her how far we were from my college's campus. At the same time, however, I knew so much more, including the fact that I was a prisoner of war. My P.O.W. trip was instantaneous and at least as real as being able to say that I was in a hospital in Florida. Sure, I knew where I was and what was happening. I wasn't about to let the enemy know that I knew, however.

The ward toilets fit in well with my prisoner of war fantasy. Each hospital room had a small cubicle, containing only a toilet. Showers were in a separate room across from the reception desk. Sinks were in the individual rooms, proper. In the small bathroom (actually a toilet room, I guess) there was a knob on the cubicle wall calling attention to the intercom system by which you could call a nurse if you needed help. The knob was the size of a 50-cent piece and was illuminated by a pulsating, orange light.

Late that afternoon, I tried to use the toilet. In addition to my mind terror, I also had a number of physical problems while on the ward, including constipation. So there I was, squatting on the stool in this small, austere, closed-in cubicle with its tiled walls and floor and this ominous, pulsating orange light. Constipated, grunting, the room went tilt. The screen of the intercom waited for my confession. Images of hopelessness filled my head.

Occasionally, I would view the toilets as observation rooms, other times I would fear that gas would be pumped in. I even got into the possibility that they were elevators and that I would be taken to a new level of horror. I would always leave the door cracked slightly open so that the elevator wouldn't work. As with everything else, however, my mind was too melted to consistently maintain a prisoner of war fantasy.

Supper approached. I would try my last escape attempt. A large, steel cabinet containing our dinner was wheeled onto the ward. Trays of drinks were set on top of it, with our food trays on shelves inside. It was a large cabinet, some 3 by 6 feet and about 4 feet high. A kid wheeled it in, plugged it in and left. Food and drink were dispensed from the cabinet by the regular staff.

As I ate, the thought dawned on me. It would be simple to escape. I could simply pretend that I was one of the help and just push the cart off of the ward. I would be buzzed out of the maze of horror.

I hurried through my meal and carried my empty tray out to the waiting cabinet. Putting my tray on top of it, I realized that no one was around. It would be so simple. I would just unplug it, push it the twenty feet or so to the double-door, entrance to the ward and yell, "Yo!" like the others did. Once the unlocking buzz came, I would push it on through, remembering to take the service and not the passenger elevator. Both elevators were side-by-side, right next to the ward door; I had seen them when they had buzzed the cabinet in. Once out of sight, on the elevator, I would further plan my escape. Once outside, I would run like hell. It seemed simple enough.

I approached the plug. It was a large industrial one and gave off a slight hum. As I bent to unplug it, my world went mad. The slight, electrical hum became a huge roar. The cabinet, itself, became a huge, menacing device with robot like awareness. Actually, rather than the metallic cabinet becoming huge, it was more as though I became quite small, about two feet tall or so. I saw and heard this device from the perspective of an infant or toddler, a hypersensitive, learning-how-to-walk child. I stopped, completely terrified. As soon as I was able, I got out of there. I returned to my room, completely shaken.

For the rest of my time on the ward, I would approach the cabinet warily, like a puppy approaching a stationary, model train that starts up every time the small dog gets close to it. The cabinet never changed on me again, however. Seeing it in its true size relative to my near six feet, I would vaguely wonder about what had happened. The experience became similar to a bad dream that I had had while on the ward, just as the entire ward experience has become an unreal, bad dream to my present self.

The cabinet incident was my last escape attempt on the ward. I would fall into my most predominant thought pattern while on the ward. Simply, I was lost. It was hopeless. I would be on the ward forever. I would never leave the ward. Ever.

That evening is mostly lost to me. Visiting hours (after dinner, from 6 to 8) are completely lost. Shaken from my cabinet incident, I may have slept through them. I did, however, have some interactions with the other patients after visiting hours were over. They were slowly becoming familiar to me.

There were the three women, Bertha, Lillian and Elaine. There was my roommate, Jack. Beth, an impossibly cute, small teenager about 15 or 16 was a little doll, usually showing high energy, and always sweet and cute. There was Cynthia, a black girl of about 14, who sat frozen in her own world, unable or unwilling to communicate with the rest of us. There was the black woman who had thrown the fit outside of the room next to mine, who was rarely seen and usually in the presence of a nurse or aide. There was Martha, a petite woman in her 30's or 40's, who had very fine features.

Martha sat like a porcelain figurine, neither acknowledging nor interacting with the rest of us. Within a day or two, she was released to her family or transferred to another location. Whatever the case, she was soon gone. There were a few others, some of whom stayed mostly in their own rooms. The ward wasn't very large; it would hold, perhaps, a couple of dozen people, if filled to capacity.

After visiting hours, most patients would gather in the kitchenette or sitting room. There was a natural letdown from the tension generated by the visitors. Although not noticeable to me that first night, it was also the time that we would start coming on to our evening medication.

That first night is a blur. My main contribution to the conversation was a, "I'm never going to get off of the ward. I'll be here forever." I said it often. Reactions varied. One of the other patients might say virtually anything in response. It didn't matter if their response was a, "No one ever leaves," or a, "I can leave anytime I want to." I knew that I was lost. The three women had all kinds of "in" jokes, double meanings, witticisms and so forth. The conversation would move quickly, up and down, back and forth. I was not able to keep up. I would take everything literally, getting totally lost, while they hurried on to their next statement.

For example, one of them might say something like, "I think I'll just walk right out that door and take a stroll." Flash. I would see an energy door, outlined in whitish gold. In my head, I would try and space through it. Failing, I would resurface. I would sit there dumb, not knowing what anyone was talking about. If I did get into the conversation, I would almost immediately be spaced right out of it once more. Occasionally, it would be as if we were on a drug high, the three women and myself. It was as though we were in a circle of vibration. If I could only get in tune, the four of us would be able to space off of the ward on some kind of an energy ledge.

The conversation, itself, was schizophrenic. Some talk about rocket ships, time warps and more. I didn't really know what was going on, simply sitting there, attempting to interact, with my only contribution an occasional, "I'll never leave the ward." It would be days later that I would find out that the three women had been playing with my head. It made little difference, as I had been almost completely gone and it didn't make much difference if they were playing with me.

Later that night, Jack and I were alone in the television room. One wall was lined with couches with draped windows above them. The couches sat facing the corridor wall that held the mounted television. There were two small, rectangular mirrors that faced each other on the two other walls. Standing in the middle of the room, I happened to look into one of the mirrors.

My gaze settled on a darkened, shadowy, ghostlike apparition. Due to the placement of the two mirrors, I saw this ghostly caricature of myself reflected in a mirror, reflected in a mirror, reflected in a mirror... growing ever smaller, ad infinitum. My world stopped. For a moment, I was beyond life and death, caught in an endless horror of gray mists and ghostly apparitions that went on forever, both before me and behind me. Time stood still. Totally spaced out, caught in an endless moment, buried in the senseless, non-ending repetition of my weird, mirror image, I simply stood there.

Hopeless despair. Never-ending regret. Terror beyond time. I was nudged to the side. Call it the Hand of God, or my inability to continue to stand motionless. It was over. No longer between the mirrors, it was over. A shiver passed through me. A convulsive squeezing of the shoulder blades and I was away from it. It had passed. Thank you dear Lord. Oh sweet Jesus, thank you so very much.

It must have been late. Jack was spacing around, doing his thing. Not sleepy, I decided to go to bed. Crossing the hall to my room, I ran into Bertha. She wanted to talk. Confused by my mirror episode, I was easily led to a table in the kitchenette. We sat down, hunched over the black, metallic tabletop. It was good to see another human being, good to get my mind off of where I had just been. We didn't really have anything to say to each other, however. At her suggestion, we began to play some cards.

She taught me a simple card game that was similar to what I knew as War. It was new to me. She was very nice, even solicitous, treating me like a small child. I had trouble focusing. I dimly remember that the tattoo on her arm (did she really have one?) went psychedelic with its reds and blues becoming similar to the oranges and reds of my remembrance of the shot of Thorazine. At one point, her face started to change into that of my dead stepfather's (he was a former Marine and had had a bulldog tattooed on his arm), but didn't make it.

Weak, tired and feeling as though I were underwater, I had difficulty in understanding the game. Shuffling, dealing and even holding the cards was a difficult endeavor. My physical coordination had been coming and going all day, mostly going. In both my head and body, I struggled to stay with the game. Flash. I was relatively clear and lucid, feeling good, really good. The simple child's game was just that, a simple child's game. I remembered that I loved to play cards. Energy flowed into my fingertips. I felt like speeding up the game, doing some fancy shuffles. Bertha didn't notice my change and continued to mother me, showing me when and how to play, cooing the instructions. She was obviously enjoying her Big Sister role. A portion of me wanted to shout, "Look, this is simple. I know what to do. Let's get on with it." On the other hand, I hated to hurt her feelings and I didn't want to break in on her helping me.

I held back and continued to play slowly. I waited for her instructions, trying not to win, and, of course, kept on winning. As a child, I used to play dice with my grandmother. It was an Old Country game that we had played for pennies. Seemingly, my grandmother would always get the best roll of the dice. She would take to cheating in my favor. If I caught her, I would get tremendously angry. Although I desperately wanted to win, I needed to win fairly. Playing with Bertha, I wanted her to win, but was not able to misplay or otherwise slant the odds in her favor. She really got into the game, concentrating on the cards, making faces when she lost, taking everything very seriously. I began to worry about her, began to worry about my winning hurting her. Over the next week, this would become an obsession with me. I would always be worrying about hurting the other patients.

Bertha kind of saved the day. At least, she quickly got me out of any worry or guilt about being a superior card player. Simply, she asked me questions. Trying to answer them opened me to my head and its fuzzy, thoughts and images. My feeble attempts at verbalization quickly dropped me back into, "Huh?" I didn't have to fake anything. Sitting and playing cards, any kind of cards, was an achievement in and of itself.

I dimly remember that I tried to explain energy ledges to her. (What in the world is an energy ledge?) I told her that if I could only get it together that we could space out of there. Together, on an energy ledge, we could do it. She urged me to try it. Images of her face, large, blocky and masculine, inches from mine, set in concentration, waiting for me to do it. I tried. My effort allowed me to lose it. I lost it almost completely. I was finally able to admit defeat. She leaned back, satisfied that I couldn't do it. Did she know? About energy ledges? About moving through time and space? About getting caught between universes? About waking up with no memory on a psychiatric ward? I don't know. Maybe she entered my craziness. Maybe I tapped a vein of fear in her. Perhaps she was just humoring or funning me. She always seemed so strong and so straight. I don't think that she knew what I was talking about. Coming so soon after the mirror episode, our entire time of playing cards was surrealistic. Her questions and my efforts at answering them and trying to play cards had totally fatigued me. It was time for bed. Mumbling good night, I left her there.

It must have been quite late. Except for Jack, who had a tendency to be everywhere, Bertha and I had been the only two patients that were still awake and out of our rooms. Jack was spacing around the television room, making a little noise. Neither Bertha nor I paid him any attention. Totally exhausted, I straggled back to my room, ready to collapse in sleep. Jack came into the room, also ready to turn in for the night.

I started to strip, getting bare to the waist. Jack looked at me with open-mouthed amazement.

"You're going to sleep like that?"

"Uh, sure."

There were strong energy rushes with the room starting to spin. What was going on? Was he some kind of sexual deviate? I continued stripping, keeping my jockey shorts on. Jack just continued to stare at me. Finally, as if out of some kind of bravado, he also stripped to the waist. He stood there, defiantly looking at me, as if to say, "Hey man, I'm okay, I can strip to the waist too." He just stood there, wavering ever so slightly, looking at me out of his pinched and puckered face. No animosity, just a, "look at me, I can do it" expression on his face. I got into bed.

Jack remained standing, still looking at me. He picked up a can of shaving cream, eyes still on me, and began slowly, purposely, smearing it all over himself. He started with his face, got some in his nose and mouth (ohmigod, was he going to eat it?), on his chest, on the back of his head, all over. His look stayed twisted and defiant. At times, he looked as though he wanted to break into some kind of manic laughter.

I almost got into it. I almost got up and grabbed the can from him. I could have stood tall, smeared some in my hair, then had him smear some in his, and then we could have gone back and forth, smearing each other, and then ending our smearing with manic laughter. It almost happened. It didn't.

"Hey man. C'mon, what are you doing? C'mon now."

"Umpfgh."

It was over as quickly as it began. Some of these other patients must have been traveling through trips as quickly as I was. Without a word, he stopped, put the can down and washed himself off. He took off his pants and climbed into bed. We were both completely out of the shaving cream trip. An observer, questioning us, may have been surprised that we could hardly remember that it had happened, even though only moments had passed.

One of us shut off the lights. Instead of remembering the shaving cream incident or talking about it, we just continued lying in bed, rapping about drugs and other things. It was like getting high with a stranger and finding out that you had all kinds of similar experiences. At the time, I was beyond duplicity. I had enough difficulty interacting with another human being, let alone trying to put on a false face for them. I quickly realized, however, that Jack was mostly full of it. No matter what I brought up, and in that comfort of fatigue and talking in the dark, I mentioned all kinds of esoteric happenings, Jack just kept on saying, "Oh yeah. Yeah, I've been there. Oh yeah, I did that. I know what you mean." It did seem as if he had experienced a number of things that I had. When I brought up transcendental meditation, which was met with a "yeah, yeah," I finally realized that, for the most part, he didn't know what I was talking about.

While we rapped, with me doing most of the talking, and Jack doing a lot of saying "yeah," he would occasionally break into a hyper, singsong burst of slang and whistling. He would make all kinds of weird noises, with it impossible for me to follow him. In addition to not being able to follow him, I would be so easy that I had trouble remembering what we (I) had been talking about.

I thought that Jack was weird. I also liked him a lot. Occasionally, he just got a little too irritating. Otherwise, he was okay. We stopped talking right around transcendental meditation, with him falling off into a restless, turning sleep.

Left alone and still awake, I decided to try and practice it. Perhaps this is what I needed to do in order to find some peace and begin to figure out what was happening to me. I had never really gotten into transcendental meditation, did not have a mantra and did not really know the technique. As I understood it, however, the idea was to follow the bubbles of awareness as deeply as possible, with them getting smaller and smaller, until one gets to the source or center of one's thought. This process reportedly results in an expanded awareness and a transcending, "Aha!" experience.

I went deep inside of my head, hoping to follow the bubbles of my awareness to a deeper level of consciousness. Uh-huh. Nope. My thoughts were speeding missiles, going helter-skelter. There were no bubbles. Rather, the inside of my head was like a thick, jelly-like mass with gaping holes in it. Bright pockets of memory, still inaccessible to me, were everywhere. It was like standing in the middle of a huge lump of Swiss cheese (made out of jelly) and at the same time, being in the middle of a crossing or intersection of the most complex subway, train station or airport in the world. Whew. Nope. I quickly withdrew from inside of my head. Uh-huh. Grand Central Station encased in jelly with trains at their peak, rush hour traffic was not for me.

Lying there, unable to sleep, afraid to get back inside of my head, I didn't know what to do. Jack's shock at my partially, bare body gave me an idea. I would masturbate. By playing with myself, I would be able to get my energy together. The resulting climax, a catharsis of released energy, would clear my head, allow me to sleep, enable me to get some rest. My hand snaked down to my genitals. My breath grew shallow. I felt terribly wicked, yet justified. This was necessary. Neither shame nor guilt entered my consciousness.

Nothing. There was no feeling, whatsoever, in my penis or testicles. Nothing. Not a thing. My genitals were limp, unfeeling pieces of rubber. They may as well have belonged to a rubber statue or to a doll. There was neither life, nor energy nor movement. There was nothing at all, just a growing fear as I wondered if I had already lost my manhood.

Determined, I continued to massage my genitals for several minutes (or was it seconds?). There was no life or feeling in them, whatsoever. Except for the nerve endings in my hands, I felt nothing. My genitals were missing in action. Would I, indeed, become female? Had it already started? Was it too late for me to salvage my manhood? I stopped. I slowly fell asleep, quite afraid.

Thus ended my first day on the ward.

SUNDAY

My head was a bowl of whipped egg whites with gaping holes everywhere. My body was encased in a thick, palpable, immobile sea of Jell-O.

As a child, I had spent a year in bed with tuberculosis. Throughout my life, I have been prone to high fevers and physical breakdowns of short duration. In addition, there had been the depression and bad trips of my late 20's. Nothing I had ever experienced, however, could compare to the weakness and lethargy of those early days on the ward. Helplessness. Total helplessness.

Buried in physical and mental weakness, unable to rationally explain my situation, frustrated in my escape attempts, only occasionally allowed rest from the terror of my external environment (subject to change from the mundane to the mad at any moment) or from the voices and horror within, I constantly called on a higher being for help. I would increasingly call on someone or something to save me as *pain*, both mental and physical, was beginning to become the predominant aspect of my life. From weakness to pain; from lethargy to turmoil as I twisted and turned against whatever it was that was crunching my body and mind.

I had been a religious youth and an adult seeker after truth, at least my version of the truth. Confirmed a Lutheran; I had joined a fundamentalist church as a teenager. The Evangelical church forbid drinking and frowned on just about everything else (Billy Graham is okay but his wife wore makeup). As a young adult, although no longer religious in a church-going sense, I had continued my search for truth and meaning. In addition to my academic studies, this had led me to heavy reading of religions other than

Christianity, including Hinduism, Buddhism and Taoism. Increasingly, I was led to introspection, yoga and meditation, and long discussions into the night about the meaning of it all. I had a strong desire to figure it all out, to increase my awareness, to understand what all of these philosophers and religious leaders were talking about.

That morning, tossing and turning in my bed, I prayed constantly. It wouldn't hold together. My mind jumped from mystic to saint to Buddha to Christ. I went from this religion to that one to yet another. Going from this method to that belief to this practice to that command, I was unable to hold a thought. I was unable to meditate, unable to concentrate. Even in my cry for help, I was not able to hold to a consistent train of thought.

This went on forever, with a half-asleep, feverish me calling on first, this one and then, that one. Crying here, struggling there. The inside of my head was similar to my wandering attention state of the previous morning. My head was filled with pain, frustration, and weakness.

Later that morning, I found myself surprisingly alone in the television room on a quiet, Sunday morning. The truth dawned on me. I was cross-programmed. I was praying to a series of entities, attempting to follow a variety of faiths and methods. I must remain constant in my plea for help. I realized that I must turn to my source, to my upbringing. I had been, first of all, a Christian. At one time, I had even been a devout, Bible-carrying fundamentalist.

The Lord's Prayer. That's it. The Lord's Prayer. I would repent of all of the bullshit of a wasted life. I would repeat the Lord's Prayer with reverence and sincerity. My faith would set me free. I would repeat it over and over. God would hear me and help me out of my misery. The Lord's Prayer. That would do it.

"Our Father, glory to thy name. Amen." What the...? "Our Father, who art..." Uh? What was going on? I knew the Lord's Prayer. "Our Father, who art in heaven, give us this day our daily bread, forever and ever. Amen." Uh? No, wait a minute. That's not it. "Our Father, our Father, our Father, who..." What's going on here?

I tried. I really tried. I began to cry lightly, salty tears running down my cheeks. Although not realizing it, this was the first time that I had tried to remember something from my past while on the ward. "Our Father..." My thoughts continued to run away from me. I couldn't even remember the Lord's Prayer. I kept on blanking. Persistence is? I needed to know the Lord's Prayer.

Defeated, I slowly got up. Shuffling along, like a small, repentant child, I timidly approached one of the black nurses. Not able to get her attention, I stood waiting. She finally noticed me.

"Uh, nurse."

"Yes, honey."

"Uh, do you know the Lord's Prayer?"

Slightly miffed, with a concentrated brow, "Well, uh, do ya mean the 'Our Father' one?"

"Yes."

"Well, let's see..." Turning to another nurse, talking to me, "Gee, it's been so long. Let me just see."

And then there were several nurses around, each giving their comments, trying to remember how the Lord's Prayer went. They were tremendously nice and kind, each one of them trying to figure out how the prayer went. One of them recited it to me, but it didn't sound exactly right. I needed to know **the** Lord's Prayer. No approximation would do. Only by repeating the real one, could I free myself from this pain.

"No-o, I remember it different."

And then one of the nurses, a thickset, black woman, winked at me. "Just a minute, honey, just a minute. We'll get it for you." And then she was off, holding up a finger for me to wait. The other nurses milled around, waiting for her to return. She was back almost immediately. She had found a Bible. The other nurses wandered off. She stood there, leafing through the Bible, assuring me that it would be okay. "Now don't you worry, honey, we'll find it for you." Talking to herself, "Now, let's see, it should be somewhere around here."

With an, "Aha, here it is!" she led me back to the television room. Gently sitting me down, she handed me the open Bible.

I blankly stared at the pages. The Bible had been opened to St. Matthew, chapter five. The "5" had been circled. My world went, "Oooops." The Master Controller had anticipated me. I was being run on course five. Was there no way back to reality? I shrugged off the growing feeling of loneliness and despair. I nervously began to read. I was no longer sure, however, that the Lord's Prayer was **the** answer. (Thankfully, I didn't build a whole philosophy of life on the letter five. Years later, curious, looking it up as I rewrote my ward experience, I would discover that the Lord's Prayer was in chapter six, not chapter five.)

This wasn't it. This wasn't it. This wasn't the way that I remembered the Lord's Prayer. Then I dimly remembered that there were different versions of the Lord's Prayer. One read, "And forgive us our trespasses as we forgive those who trespass against us," while another version used, "debts," and "debtors." In my ward frame of mind, "trespass" conjured up images of cartoon-like people shooting through space, each on their own voyage. To trespass, would be to cut them off, making them slow down or alter their path. The worst form of trespass would be an actual collision. "Debts" had a completely different connotation. As a religious teenager, I had been shocked to discover that there is no *the* Ten Commandments with Catholics and various Protestant sects having different wordings. On the ward, a minor change in translation was not just a simple change, but a mind-blowing event.

What was *the* Lord's Prayer? How could I be saved? I had to know and repeat the correct one. I drifted into hopelessness. I was never going to be okay. I was never going to leave the ward. My attention drifted away from the Bible in my lap.

The television was going. I passively sat there, idly aware of it spewing forth Sunday morning church music. Eventually, it caught me. I realized that the members of the choir, especially those singers on the left, were watching me. Did they know the Lord's Prayer?

There, that tall one on the left, arching his eyebrows at me. Who the hell did he think he was? Did he know the Lord's Prayer? In a moment of bravado, I jumped up and turned off the television. Remembering the nurse's kindness, I returned the Bible.

With nothing to do, I returned to the "Computer Room." A few other patients started to drift in, sitting here and there. Someone turned the television set back on. Once again, choir music and Bible-thumping Christians telling the world how to be saved filled the air. Did they know the Lord's Prayer?

In order to shut out the now grown sour taste of religion, I went to the far side of the sitting room and sat perpendicular to the television. Although I could still hear it, I would not be exposed to its rays. There were some magazines on the small table next to my chair. I eagerly picked up a sports magazine. I had always loved sports and followed all of the major spectator sports. It was difficult to read. I still couldn't maintain a train of thought. I began scanning the magazine, flipping through the pages.

Wait a second. What's going on here? The magazine was from the previous fall. The magazine listed the final rankings of college football teams and showed the bowl game winners. Neither the ranked teams nor the bowl game winners rang a bell. I simply didn't remember them. None of them. I didn't remember them! Ongoing pro basketball… how in the world could these teams have these records? Uh-huh. Nope. It couldn't be. The thought dawned: someone had tampered with the magazines. They were gimmicked. It's easy to prove your sanity. Just remember facts. Of course, Ohio State (or was it Michigan?) won the Big Ten. What do you mean, they didn't. It says so right here in this magazine. It doesn't? But it did, didn't it?

And then I was frightened. It was my first realistic horror while on the ward. With shift changes, there had been a constant coming and going of staff. The only way that I knew any of the staff was by reading their nametags. I did not or could not remember their names from moment to moment. What if someone starting changing nametags? It's easy to prove your sanity. Sure, unless someone has changed persons, places and things on you. All someone would have to do is switch the clock every once in a while, change some nametags, and doctor some magazines. Whoosh, they've got you. There you were, a melted ball of wax, talking to yourself, maybe drooling a little. I could not remember things at all clearly, my time perception was completely screwed up and I was on a psychiatric ward. Who would listen to me? Who would vouch for me?

If they wanted to erase my identity or destroy me, it would be a simple matter. My identification, locked in the ward safe for safekeeping, had several different addresses on it. I had lied about Linda being my wife. Many of my closest, straight friends knew that I had been getting high. By their standards, I had been acting quite strangely. I had no fair witness, no one who could vouch for me. I was totally helpless. They (whoever they were) could do with me as they will, taking away my identity or pinning theft, treason or murder on me. I was totally at someone else's mercy.

Even if I were not the victim of some malicious, maddening, diabolical scheme to destroy me, I was still totally helpless. I had no control over the food that I ate or over the medication that I received. My physical surroundings were severely delimited. I had only partial control over my mind and body, not even able to control my thoughts or memory. From not finding *the* Lord's Prayer to not remembering sports information to the realization that I was helpless, subject to the capricious will of others.

It was too much. I stopped worrying about the sports information, could no longer dwell on my helplessness. I began to do virtually anything to make the time pass. Read, walk, and sleep—I would do anything to take up time and have it mercifully pass. Anything to get me off of my situation and let me forget about myself and my situation; I would do anything, just anything.

That morning is virtually lost to me. One microsecond of horror stands out, however. One of the nurses, maybe an aide, someone that I didn't recognize and would not see again, was some seven or eight months pregnant. She was working away at the desk. She seemed pleasant enough. She had short, curly hair and a very pinkish, puckered face. I found myself watching her. Oooops. My world changed. I realized that while she was real, her big stomach was not. It was as though she were growing one of those robot dolls of my emergency room flip-out. This big belly was fake, maybe a robot doll disguised with padding to make it appear as though she were pregnant. I had a momentary urge to go and smash her in the stomach. The thought was neither mean nor malicious. Perhaps I would get a prize for figuring out that she wasn't really pregnant. Maybe bells would go off and a new game would be started, since that puzzle had been solved. Too fatigued to act on my perceptions, the urge to expose the fake pregnancy quickly passed. Whew. Yes. Oh thank you. Thank you Lord for not allowing me to hurt her. Thank you very much. Thank you. Amen.

Later, about noon, I began to very timidly and politely make requests of the nurses. Could I go outside? Could I make a phone call? Could I join the patients that go off of the ward?

No matter what my request, the answer was invariably, "Ask your doctor. Your doctor will answer that. Have you seen your doctor yet?"

"Who is my doctor?"

"Hmm, let's see." The nurse bent over and began going through some file cards. "Your doctor is Dr. D."

Arggh. Ack. I had known a "D" in Chicago. He was in his mid-30s, Avant Garde as opposed to hip. In the process of divorcing his second wife, he had been living with a beautiful, young woman with whom I had been briefly involved. He was a moderately, successful intellectual who had begun experimenting with drugs. "D" was difficult to know, always wise cracking and glib. Also, he was a good looking guy who had won one of my ladies. Well, actually, it was a lady who had chosen him over me. I had been a tripster and he had been married. With his divorce, I had no longer had any chance with her.

The last time that I had seen him, however, we had gotten high together. Together, we had stood looking at a large, modern painting that filled his dining room wall. It was a sunburst (?), all yellow, orange and red with a white background. Momentarily, glib bullshit forgotten, he and I had been together, enjoying the near psychedelic painting. It had been a good moment and the first and only time that I had been close to "D."

Standing there at the reception desk, I drifted into reverie, seeing the now swirling and ever-deepening sun of that painting.

"Have you seen your doctor yet?"

"Huh? No."

Oh my, I had to see "D". What did it mean? Almost immediately, I was back to energy and vibration games. Psychedelic suns began exploding in my head. Yellows, oranges, and reds, images of images, and shadows of my Thorazine shot filled my head. I had to see "D." What did this cryptic message mean? Must I attain a certain vibrational frequency, a certain high in order to see him? Was that it? What kind of intricate game was this? Was I the only one that was lost, the only one that didn't know the rules? Was that it?

"H-how do I see Dr. D?"

"Hmm, he'll be here in a couple of hours at two o'clock."

With no time perception, whatsoever, and flashing suns in my head, I had to see "D." Not knowing how to reach the correct vibrational frequency, I had been given a clue. Two o'clock. I could not miss two o'clock. Shaken, I didn't trust myself and surely did not trust THEM. I must not miss two o'clock.

I would wander off, returning to the reception desk, first to verify who my doctor was, and then to find out what time he would be on the ward. I would always check with different staff, hoping that they weren't all in on it together. After several verifications, I began returning to the reception desk in order to check the time. Hours of mind time would pass, but only minutes according to that clock on the wall. I began freaking out. Would the Master Controller allow that big, old clock march ever so slowly to say, 1:45, and then let it jump to three or so? I began hanging out at the reception desk.

And then he was on the ward. Finally, after forever, "D" was on the ward. My doctor had arrived. I could only see him at a distance, however, as he kept disappearing behind closed doors with different patients. He was using the stereo room for his conferences. It was right next to the ward entrance. My questioning of the staff changed from asking when I could see Dr. D to, "Is Dr. D still here?

I must not miss "D." I kept an eye on the closed stereo room door, continually watched the clock over the reception desk, listened for the buzzer that would open the ward entrance and allow him to depart without seeing me. Nervous anticipation.

And then it was my turn. Nervous and hyper, with constrictions in my back and neck, I entered the stereo sitting room. It was icy cold. I was fairly together, just totally nervous. This was important. I had to hit him with the right words. Mind racing along, I rehearsed my plan. We sat down together.

He was tired looking, nearly bald, and had a weak chin. Reds and blues were predominant in his recently shaved face. He was slow and southern. Laconic, with slightly sunken eyes, he reminded me of a lizard. Thankfully, he didn't turn into one. I didn't like him.

"Well, how are you getting along?"

His question triggered my head. How should I play this? What should I tell him? Possibilities raced through my head. Momentarily, I felt rational, energetic and even sane. Would he wonder why I was there? I had requests. Would I be able to con him into letting me outside? I needed some sympathy for the pain and terror of my ward experiences. Would I get it? I had to show him that I was in need of some help. On the other hand, I couldn't be too open or too honest. If I attempted to tell him about the head terror that I was experiencing, I instinctively knew that I would fall right back into it. Appearing too intellectual and obviously disoriented, I didn't want a paranoid schizophrenic label. I decided on a middle approach. I would be polite and rely on his authority and benevolence. I would blame it all on drugs. Doctors could understand drugs. I would leave out Mind Control and psychic phenomena. Yes, that's it. Drugs would work.

"Well, uh, I'm, uh, not too sure. I can't really, uh, trust my senses. Like that couch, what would you say the color of that couch is?"

I had it all planned. As soon as he told me the color of the couch (it was brown, red and green striped), I would tell him that that was how I saw it. I would then try to explain to him how sometimes, however, it would go psychedelic, becoming wavy and blurred, breathing and writhing. As soon as he was able to understand this, I would briefly explain tripping and mention how I was being exposed to temporary hallucinations. He could blame it all on an acid residual or some such. If he could follow me, showed any sympathy, I would then go into self-diagnosis. Maybe, I could even get him to agree to rest, sunshine and the outside world. It just may work.

"I never pay attention to it."

Huh? What the…? He sat there, solid and stolid, unmoving, staring off at the wall. Was he just an automaton, a weak pawn like the rest of us? That stereo was obviously a listening device. Who was in control? Was this just another scheme, just one more plot to break me? My plans and quick thinking were immediately lost in terror and disorientation. What was going on here?

He mentioned Linda. His features changed ever so slightly. Now I knew who this son of a bitch was. Upon arriving in Florida, Linda had almost immediately found a high paying job as a cocktail waitress. It was like a miracle, as jobs are always difficult to find in a college town. According to her, she had "just been led to it." Already beginning to spin out, I occasionally thought she was some type of witch (then again, I sometimes thought of myself as a warlock suffering from amnesia). She had started on a Friday night and was to have had that first Saturday night off, as we had tickets for a play. A married couple owned the restaurant lounge where she worked. Linda had been hired by the wife and had been promised the night off. The husband, however, had insisted that she work.

It had been a major disappointment. It would have been our celebration night out. Disgusted, I had gotten thoroughly wrecked, arriving to pick her up early. Although I was dressed well, my starting to get long hair and sunken red eyes labeled me as one of those hippie types. Waiting for Linda, I had been hassled by the owners for waiting for Linda inside. I moved to the bar and had a couple of drinks; customers could wait where they pleased.

Getting angrier, I decided to talk with the husband, a Mr. M. Talking to him, he had been polite but cool towards me. I was just about to start my complaints, when his wife and Linda came over. It was quitting time. She could leave. I never did say anything to him about her having to work that night. Instead, he and his wife raved about how well she was working out. His last comment as we left was, "Wait until you see what we make out of your wife, you'll be surprised."

Instant rage. Linda was young and beautiful. She had a sensational wardrobe, having worked in a fashionable clothing store while in Chicago. She had a college education, and was sweet, innocent and cultured. What was this dumb bigot going to make out of her? Swallowing my rage, Linda and I had mumbled our thanks and left.

A week or two later, spinning out more and more, I had made her quit the job. I didn't like what he was making out of her. On the morning before my hospital entry (how many years ago was that?), totally spun out and disoriented, I had found myself accidentally trying to get a job at the same place. The wife's, "You can't take her place" had led to all kinds of insanity.

Yeah, Dr. D., you phony, I know who you are. Mr. M., Dr. D., man of a thousand faces, I know who you are. Spoiler of the fresh and innocent. You son of a bitch. If you hurt Linda, if you touch my love, if you...

Bang. Crash. Oooops. It was the first time on the ward that I had thought of Linda. Oh nooo... Oh my God! Oh, dear sweet Jesus, what have I done? Oh shit, oh please, oh no. I was on a psychiatric ward! I had left my woman, my love, *alone*!!! I was hopelessly lost, locked away forever. She, a defenseless innocent, was exposed to all of the mesmerizing insanities of an unfair world. I had deserted her. I was on a locked ward. I could neither help her nor myself. This wasn't some intricately, fantastic head game. This wasn't just a bad dream or some mental contest. This was *reality*! I was on a closed ward, locked away from my love forever and ever. No. Please no. Oh dear Lord, please no.

I began to cry. I cried. I bawled. Tears spilled down my face. I could not stop crying. Apologetically, I tried to smile, tried to stop crying, tried to excuse myself. I cried and cried, unable to stop the tears. This was too much.

Dr. D. allowed me to cry myself out. I was eventually able to stop. Finally, when I was almost settled down, wiping my tears away, we were able to talk.

We agreed that I had a drug problem. Doctors did understand drugs. I had no will to attempt to explain that I had had about a hit and a half of acid in some 3 months, with no psychedelics for many months before that. Rather than a drug problem, I felt that I had broken something in my brain, fallen through into some world that started out as ecstasy with Linda and then changed into an increasingly bizarre hell. I guess that I was hyper; Dr. D said something about giving me some medication to bring me down. Linda and Liam (yes, I knew him) would be able to visit me later that day. Thus ended my talk with my doctor. Even with my crying, it had been only a few minutes. I never did get the chance to try to explain my situation or symptoms. I made no requests. All the things that I had wanted to ask him were forgotten. It didn't matter anymore.

Liam and Linda were coming. Linda, I would get to see Linda once again. I would get to see my love and my close friend once again. Linda, Linda, Linda, I would get to see Linda. They were coming; they really were. Liam and Linda. Warm sunshine. Linda. Glow. Linda, my sweet Linda was coming.

The afternoon was a haze. Crippled and sick, occasionally hallucinating, I just didn't care. My loved ones were coming to see me. Have you ever seen a freaked squirrel? Oh. Wait. Have you ever seen an unmoving, freaked squirrel? Imagine a freaked squirrel inside of a weak, depressed, unmoving, 180 lb. body, or rather, 180 lb. of freaked, not-able-to-move squirrel. The afternoon was a blur filled with nervous anticipation. I was together, yeah, together like an 18 year old soldier about to step on a land mine and somehow knowing it but unable to keep from putting that foot down. Still buried in Jell-O, I was sitting on a precipice with rippling energy surging up and down my spine, ripping my insides apart. Linda. Linda and Liam were coming. It took forever.

Then, unexpectedly, they were there. They had arrived. Nervous pacing, uneven waiting, and then they were there. The visit was a disaster. It started out okay.

Nervously falling over each other, exchanging a babble of forgotten words as we tried to find somewhere to sit, we all kept trying to say hello at the same time. We finally found an empty sitting room. It was across the hall from the stereo room, adjacent to my wardroom. Metallic gray, it had a tiled floor (off white mixed with beige) and plastic couches.

We sat down. Linda huddled against me, our hands tightly squeezed together. She was so very beautiful. She was dressed hippie-like, with a bright yellow, leather sun sewn on the seat of her jeans. Long, dark, flowing hair framed her clear, innocent, trusting face. Although her face was a mixture of sadness and sympathy, it also glowed with joy at seeing her man once again. I was playing some game that she didn't understand, but as soon as I got it together again, we could go on being totally in love and happy once more. Liam sat off to the side, to the right of us. He was relaxed and together, wearing blue Levi's and a checkered shirt. His long, floppy, blonde hair was clean and brushed.

Have you ever waited, really waited, for something to happen and then when it was happening, you were so nervous, tense and excited, that it was almost as though it wasn't happening? That first date, the prom, your first time on stage, the first game of the year or whatever. So much anticipation and nervous energy that you couldn't slow down and enjoy what you had been waiting for. Our visit started out like that. A lot of "How are you?" with looks of concern mixed with joy at seeing each other again. I kind of waited for the crackling energy to quiet down enough so that we could begin to talk. Finally, I began getting into the visit. It was so very good being with these two loved ones.

Just as the three of us began to really talk and share, an elderly, black man came in. Bent over his mop, gray fuzz on his chin, he was cleaning the floor. My two friends and I were center stage, with this old man miles away, part of a distant tableau. Change. Then he was right there, in our energy circle, soaking up our vibrations, monitoring our discussion. With his eyes on the floor, apparently just doing his job and not paying any attention to us, the son of a bitch was listening in. Then, he and I were together, with Linda and Liam dropping to a different level of frequency.

I lowered my voice, talking more softly, trying to signal Liam and Linda. They didn't seem to notice him, apparently didn't feel him, and didn't share my perception of what was going on. I began getting agitated. Concern swept their features.

Perhaps it would have been okay, except for the voice that began pounding inside of my head, rattling my eardrums. "We gave you Liam and Linda. Remember, we gave you Liam and Linda. You owe us. Remember, we gave them to you. You owe us. Don't forget, you owe us. We gave you Liam and Linda." Listening to the voice echoing inside of my head, unable to shut it out, I became increasingly hesitant in my speech. The old man and I were together. Although it wasn't his voice, he knew what was going on. My loved ones remained an unknowing pair.

"Honey, what's wrong, what's the matter with you? Are you okay?" Linda turned toward me, facing me, grasping both of my hands. We sat there, our knees touching, hands clasped, staring at each other. Her face was a mask of love and concern.

Sitting there, with our knees pressed together, our hands so very tightly squeezed together, I looked deep into her eyes. Oh my love, as I look into your eyes, I see... Hah! As I stared into her eyes, I saw two huge, shadowy black, devil's heads, one in each eye, staring back at me. They were mirror images of an ominous and foreboding entity. Pictures of me; it was a parody of a parody. Yes, sweet love, as I stare into your eyes, I see... The room went, "***tilt***!" I knew that I was in trouble.

Finally, after an interminable time, the elderly black man left. I can remember Liam changing his seat so that the old man could mop more easily. I remember Linda and I raising our feet so that he could mop underneath our couch. I remember the voice pounding over and over in my head. I remember hate and determination. I remember thinking that they could do whatever they wanted to do with me but that they had better leave my friends alone.

I was back into Change theory. I suspected that I owed ***them*** something, namely Linda and Liam. "Oh gods and devils that be, do with me as you please, but don't, oh don't, fuck with the lovely, the beautiful, the innocent, the naive. For in that moment, I, the AVENGER, riding to hell and back, with the strength of ten thousand or ten thousand ten thousands, will surely crush and destroy thee." I became impossibly strong, tapping and gathering untold energy and power. No one, nothing, was going to hurt my loved ones. Let them, if they dare, confront me, attempt to destroy me, but never ever touch those deserving of better.

The room leveled out. A nurse began bothering us, insisting that it was time for Linda and Liam to leave. We left the room on a scattered note. How could I tell them what I saw, felt and heard? Liam would understand, but there wasn't time to rap it down. Besides, the enemy was everywhere. As we walked out into the corridor, I was twisted into some kind of all-powerful entity. I blocked the bad vibrations from my friends and cleared an energy trail for them to the ward entrance/exit. Walking them to the door, I glanced over my shoulder. There were three or four blacks positioned strategically along the corridor. One to the right, one further down on the left and so on. Their black faces stared at me, as if waiting for payment. Wasn't that also shocked surprise that I saw on one of the faces? The voice kept on pounding over and over in my head, "We gave you Liam and Linda. Don't forget, we gave you your friends. You owe us. What are you going to do for us? You owe us." The hell with the voice, the hell with them. My friends, heaven help me, would be safe.

As Liam and Linda were buzzed out, I realized that I could follow them. I was in street clothes, having been allowed to dress for the visit. I could make it. Walk tall. Just pretend. Get outside. Burst into fresh air and sunshine. I almost tried it, but I was afraid that either Liam or Linda would blow it. If they tried to restrain me, it would get really bad. As they left, however, I had a purpose. I would give the devil his due. This did not mean sacrificing my friends or loved ones, however. I would die first, if that were my karma.

With Liam and Linda gone, I was suddenly drained of my strength, feeling tired and broken, yet hyper. Once again, I would have to try and get it together. Another fantasy had been born, however. Sides were being taken. Factions were solidifying. Some force that I identified as the master controller was manipulating all of us, even the poor dupes who thought that they could trick me into giving them my friends. He would have to be met. This was, indeed, some kind of Change center, some kind of reconditioning center.

In Mind Control, I had been trained to do health cases (faith healing at a distance), sending love and energy to those in need. At a deep level of mind, while in a near trance, meditative state, I had also been programmed to be a force for good, to send my essence wherever it was needed for the good of mankind. I was, indeed, in the right place. I had fulfilled the purpose drilled into my subconscious. I had managed to get into the world of bad vibrations. Many strange things were happening in this squirrel factory. In the tradition of Achilles and mighty Ulysses, I was charged with action. Time to get it on. Broken on the way, I had better start getting it together in order to exert a positive influence on my sick environment.

My crusade against the forces of evil would have to wait, however. The visit had left me shaken and confused. Nervously tired, exhausted and sticky with sweat, I needed to clean up my act. I was together enough to inquire about a shower. They were available. I could take one. It would be my first real washing in days. This was a good thing as I was beginning to reek of body odor.

Going back to my room in order to get my things, I ran into Bertha. It was a little awkward. She obviously wanted to talk. Expectant and eager, she blocked my way, looking at me, waiting for what I was going to tell her, as if I had asked for a meeting.

"Uh, I was just going to take a shower. I haven't had one for a while. Uh, probably see you later."

Acting surprised, she reared back her head. It was as though she had withdrawn her head to the far end of some large, vibrational funnel. Her head changed in size and according to my perspective, it became small and far away. Regarding me from this deep, distant perspective, she suddenly brought her head forward. It came sharply into focus, now looming large at my end of the funnel. Her face had acquired a knowing look.

"Ya already had a shower today."

"Uh, how's that?" I, of course, instantly knew what she meant, replaying the movie of my bawling in my mind.

"Ya know. Earlier. Earlier, ya had a shower." She concluded this with a knowing laugh, cackling over my confusion.

She knew. For God's sake, she knew. She knew about my crying episode with Dr. D., about my uncontrollable shower. She knew, just as she had known about my being able to see with my eyes closed. Another subplot. Bertha was in the power hierarchy. She had to be. She could go off of the ward. She knew what when on in my mind. Maybe she did know about energy ledges. Maybe she was just wearing a clever disguise. Who was this person? What was her role in the master controller's Machiavellian plans?

As in most hospitals, doctors and nurses were constantly being paged over the loudspeaker system on the ward. "Dr. Randolph, Dr. Randolph, please report to room 227. Dr. Randolph, please report to room 227." Increasingly, the paging voice would be Bertha's and the doctor being paged would be Dr. Douglas. There was, of course, no Dr. Douglas in the hospital. Whatever was going on (was she really on the speaker system paging me?), I began suspecting that Bertha was one of the real powers behind the phony, superficial, power structure.

Standing there in the middle of the hallway, confused by her superior knowing, I had no choice but to walk away from her. I went to my room in order to gather my things. She just stood there, continuing to look at me. Aware of her watching me, I was not up to any kind of confrontation.

I have known ecstasy. Taking a hot shower after two days of sweating desperation on a psycho ward is where it is at. Going to the shower room, stripping down, I gingerly poked around, hesitantly stepping onto the cold, tiled, floor of the shower. With no door to lock, I was nervous about someone coming in and seeing my nudity. I was also worried about getting hit with splashing cold. Standing off to the side, I was able to get the shower on. With a minimum of difficulty, I was able to get the water temperature set right. No mean achievement, as my physical coordination would come and go. I moved under the heavy torrent and pummel of the strong current of hot water. It was good, even magnificent.

Basking in the heat, luxuriating in the warmth of the hot water, soaping myself, I felt great. It was my first moment of feeling normal, of forgetting that I was crazy, that I spent while on the ward. There were no thoughts, no trips, no figuring out, no vibes, no voices, and no fantasies. There was just beautiful hot water and me, coming together in a good, old, familiar shower. Wow. Double wow. I soaped myself down several times, not wanting to leave the warmth, comfort and normality of this pleasant, even blissful experience. Finally, after quite some time of peace, I shut off the water and toweled myself down. Even the toweling was a beautiful experience with the towel's rough cloth rubbing against my warm, clean body. I put on some fresh, clean clothes. From Linda? I had dressed in street clothes for my visit with Liam and Linda. They were probably the ones that I had worn when I was admitted. I would now wear regular clothes for the rest of my stay. I felt good. I felt great. I stepped back into insanity.

It was difficult to sit around and let time pass. Perceived hours would be only minutes according to the clock. It was too exhausting to continually try and figure out what was happening to me. Although interactions with the staff and the other patients would pass the time, these brief interludes would often prove to be too disconcerting, even terrifying. A short attention span, tense, bruised nerves and the fear of an impending trip fantasy led to a boring, jumpy-type existence. I would start to read something (too hard to concentrate, too tiring), go to watch television (oops, starting to get eerie), change my shirt (have to do something), look in the mirror (oops), walk to the kitchenette, sit and listen or talk to someone (hmm, getting kind of crowded and troublesome), space off, try to read (not again) and inadvertently start to think (ouch!). Time passed ever so slowly.

Sunday was the first day that I tried to write. Hearing my name being paged, caught in a Change center, realizing that my identity was being erased, not wanting to disappear without a trace, I attempted to write down my history. The problem was a simple one. My memory was an empty vacuum with mists and colors sweeping through it, with random rockets coming and going, not stopping long enough for me to recognize them. Sitting, pencil in hand, staring at a sheet of paper, I remembered my name. "My name is Vincent Blade Douglas." Blank. Mist. Swirl. Blinking back the tears, pencil shaking, I swore that I would remember. There was the incident with Jerry. Ah, I know Russian. Stop. Blank. Wait. Being programmed by the television. Ah, I know Alpha Mind Control. I'm acting like a paranoid schizophrenic. Ah, I know psychology. Where did I go to school? Where did I go to school? Ah, I've got it. Slowly, shaking, I put it down on paper in a weak, babyish scrawl.

The worst part of trying to remember was the voice. It was wickedly sarcastic. "Oh, that's so cute, back to pencil and paper. Can't take the movie, huh boy." Over and over, growing stronger and more insistent, the voice was first mocking, then cajoling and then angry. Echoing continually in my head, the voice both ridiculed and hurt me. Shit. I knew what it was saying. Spun out in my worlds of esoteric wonder, I had developed whole theories about it. The movie, that is.

Simply and sketchily, one of my many interpretations goes something like this. Visualization is an important key. One can, by being able to hold images in one's head, assume physical positions such as a yoga asana that are normally very difficult to assume. One can direct oneself to numerous paths by being able to hold firm images of oneself getting a promotion, losing weight and so on. The theory is that if one can get a firm picture of what one wants to do or to be, then this image will trigger one's subconscious resources to attain that picture or manifestation of self. The theory is somewhat explicit and can be found in Mind Control, eastern philosophy and numerous religious writings. I have discovered it in print ranging from newspaper articles to heavy, philosophical tomes.

Acidheads and speed freaks aren't into still pictures, but rather, into movies. Instead of picturing themselves in a certain position, meditating on it and working toward it, they're into movies. It's a question of speed. This life is a trip, a movie. Shakespeare had his, "All life's a stage with us but actors on it," while the head generation has its movies.

Dopers (grass heads/marijuana users), or so it seemed, heard new things in new ways. Heads saw new things in new ways. It was a matter of speed, with the eye tuned to a much faster vibrational frequency than the ear. The above is the start of what I (we) called a head game.

On the ward, I knew what the voice was saying. No longer a head, no longer into the movie, I was a cop-out. Back to the drawing board, back to cumbersome words, back to pencil and paper, back to slow motion. I managed to get a page or so of history down. It was muddled and an effort. I was torn between terror at not being able to remember things and a guilty shame at no longer being in the movie. All in all, my autobiography was not very successful. I would try again.

Liam and Linda had come to see me during late afternoon on a special visit. Normal visiting hours began at six o'clock. As the visitors began pouring in, I felt uncomfortable and out of place. Bertha, bright, alive and animated, was walking around, arms linked with a dull, placid, tired looking, male automaton. She glanced furtively around and led him to a private sitting room, the one that Liam, Linda and I had used, the one adjacent to my and Jack's room. I idly wondered when he would be on the ward. He was obviously marked for **change**.

Jack's mother was there. She was a tired looking, physically trim, middle-aged woman with very nice legs. She and Jack went into the stereo sitting room. She was too strong, too dominant for him. He would never be able to trick her into taking his place on the ward. A whole host of black visitors, bright and alive, filled the television room.

Those first few days on the ward, I seemed to be more on a level with the blacks. They appeared to be more relaxed and quicker than the whites. The whites came across as tired, not living in the present, hassled individuals while the blacks seemed a little more with it, more flowing and less uptight. This became increasingly noticeable over the next few days as the regular staff, mostly tired whites, filtered on to the ward. These whites, with noticeable sacks around their eyes and worry lines in their faces seemed to pay only partial attention to their surroundings. The blacks were more involved with their immediate environment. Their faces seemed normal to me, while my super sensitivity picked up and emphasized flaws in the faces of the whites. This was especially true for staff and visitors, as white patients such as Bertha and Jack looked normal to me.

Feeling uncomfortable, with noise and people everywhere, I retreated to my room. I was exhausted as, in many ways, it had been a trying day. Lying down, I attempted to go to sleep. I tossed and turned, falling into a psychedelic half-sleep. Half awake, half asleep, I began having a nightmarish illusion of thoughts and vibrations coming through the wall. Too dim and near sleep to adequately verbalize what I felt, I realized that I was being fed Bertha's automaton through the wall separating the head of my bed and the neighboring sitting room. I could see, albeit dimly and surrealistically, him lying on a bed, in a trance. He was being linked to me. Too dopily asleep to actively resist it, I highly resented the intrusion into my consciousness. It was as if a tape of Bertha's husband were being run into my brain. Although I was not on top of it or in control, it was as though I was being exposed to his problems and hang-ups.

Looking back, I suspect that Bertha and the man that I would later find out was her husband, had gone off into the sitting room in order to be alone and to make out. Whatever the reality, experientially I could feel strong emanations coming through the wall. Somehow, I was becoming mixed up with him. It would become increasingly evident that not only was I a helpless victim of my own hang-ups and problems, but that I was being exposed to the hang-ups and problems of the other patients. The shell of my being was cracked wide open, allowing the inanities of my environment direct access to a deep level of me.

I was finally able to shiver away from the episode. I tore myself away from the happening, rising out of my subdued, spaced out, half-asleep, weakened condition. Splashing cold water in my face, I, as with so many of my early ward experiences, quickly forgot what had just happened. I prepared to rejoin the milling patients and visitors once again. Walking around my room, however, I felt too weak and crawled back into bed.

Depressed, attempting to mull over the day's activities, nothing would hold together. One of the staff came in, a black nurse that I didn't recognize. Seeing my dazed condition, she looked at me and carefully said that it was time for my medication. First, she took my temperature and pulse. She then got my pills. There were several of them. Not only was I personally in trouble, I knew that I was being confined in a very strange place. I innocently accepted the pills, politely saying, "Thank you." The taking of my temperature had given me an idea. I quickly got the pills under my tongue, pretending to swallow them. The nurse was almost immediately gone.

I now had a problem. It was a delicate one. How would I get rid of these pills? I was in the bed closest to the door leading out into the corridor. The door was on my left at the foot of my bed. I was in a direct line with the reception desk. The way that my room was positioned, staff at the reception desk could either look at me directly or watch me in the observation mirrors while their backs were turned. The cubicle containing the toilet was directly in front of me. The room sink and the mirror above it were slightly to the right of the door to the toilet. It was obviously a two-way mirror. Hidden cameras and listening devices were everywhere.

I wasn't worried about my thoughts being monitored. They switched often enough that even I had trouble keeping up with them. Just in case, however, I thought neutral thoughts, not centering their attention on what I was doing. I slowly got out of bed. I realized that my room and the toilet cubicle operated on different frequencies. As I passed from my room into the john, framed in the doorway, I palmed the medication into my palm.

Sitting on the toilet, I casually dropped the dissolving mess between my legs. I carefully thought about how nice everyone was while I disposed of the drugs. After attempting to relieve myself, I flushed the toilet while still sitting on it. Even though I was in one of his control booths, I thought that I was safe. If the Master Controller could catch me at this, he was only playing with my head and could end me at any time.

Visiting hours were over. As the guests began straggling out, I left my room. Patients milled around in the natural letdown that occurred after the visitors left. As per usual, a group gathered in the kitchenette, as in a coffee clutch, talking down their tensions.

I was often impressed with how kind the other patients were to each other. Everyone was solicitous of each other. Each of the patients, except, possibly, for Jack, appeared to be sensitive to the needs of others. Jack, although a nice guy, was too wrapped up in his own problems to be able to really worry about others. Cigarettes were shared, goodies received from the outside were distributed, and favors were done. We were all in this together.

Jack, however, occasionally tried the god-like acceptance of the other patients. He would become a nuisance. That night, several of us (Beth and the three ladies were there) were sitting around sipping juice or coffee. Some chocolate cake received from a visitor was passed around. Jack went manic, running around, stuffing his face, and doing a, "Umpfgh!" He ruined several cups of coffee, spilling some, sampling others. He bumped into a table, almost hurting another patient. Lillian cringed, saying, "I wish he wouldn't do that." This was answered by Bertha's, "I guess he's kind of tense." Mostly ignored, talked of in the third person, no one became vindictive or confronted him.

With a burst of energy, he ran off to his room. While his, "Look at me!" behavior was boring and irritating, everyone seemed to accept him. Later, when he came back to the group, no one particularly noticed him or brought up his earlier behavior.

Perhaps the attention span of the other patients was as short as mine.

We were sitting around, quietly sipping our drink, when, "Bzzzzz", the buzzer went off. Elaine's head snapped up, fear clouding her eyes, words and thoughts forgotten. Other than Lillian watching her to see if she was okay, no one paid any attention. When she was able, Elaine rejoined the conversation as if nothing had happened. Instead of making fun of each other, the patients constantly comforted each other and were almost always gentle and understanding. In my lucid moments, I would be impressed.

The conversation was a blur, although once again, as with the previous evening, all kinds of games were being played. My major contribution was still, "I'll never get better. I'll never leave the ward."

Later that evening, Beth and Jack began goofing around with each other. They began running back and forth, occasionally bumping into each other, almost wrestling with each other. Their slight physical contact made me cringe. Except for Linda, the thought of any physical contact was totally abhorrent to me. Also, whenever any of the patients got this closely involved with each other, just as in any kind of serious conversation, there was an underlying current of tension. At any moment, one or both of the participants could flip out. Interacting this strongly was like walking on eggshells or very thin, cracking ice. Anything could happen. Nervous, I sat there, squeezing my arms together.

Jack and Beth were both hyper. Although not completely free (there would be quick stops with glances at both each other and possible observers) and not completely enjoying themselves (at times their behavior was forced), they were able to have some fun, goofing and fooling around with each other. Finally, out of breath, they stopped for a while. A pizza. It would be great to have a pizza. They began to get all hyper and excited again. A pizza would be great.

I was included in the scheme. The three of us would get a pizza. Beth, young, fragile and so very cute, was especially excited. Jack, who took every opportunity possible to act up, was also excited. I couldn't tell, however, if he was really excited about the pizza, or just wanted to jump up and down, letting off energy. More reserved, I also started to get excited about the thought of a pizza. The three of us decided to definitely get a pizza. We split up, going to our rooms in order to get some money. Beth ran off down the hall, while Jack and I walked across the hall to our room.

In our room, Jack and I started to dig around, looking for our money. Searching for my money, I stopped and turned to Jack, asking him if it was okay, if we could really get a pizza. He just continued to look through his things, absently mindedly saying, "Sure."

"No, I mean, is it okay, can we get one, will they let us?" Momentarily rational, I wondered if he knew that we were on a closed ward. Did he know that we would have to send out for the pizza? Would we be permitted to do that?

He stopped what he was doing. He turned and looked at me, his mouth twisted open in surprise, his eyes large and unblinking. "You know that you're the devil. You know that you can have anything you want."

Oooops. Moment of stillness. Dark shadows. Psychedelic flashes. My face pulled back in a contour-changing grimace. Swirling mists. Subliminal roar. Voice in my head. Yes, of course, we would have our pizza. In my head, "We shall have our pizza, thus speaketh the lord of the night. The prince of darkness shall have his due." The moment passed.

Back in the hall, the three of us ran up to the reception desk. The nurse on duty was amused. She quickly agreed to our plan and began looking up pizza places in the telephone book. While she made the phone call, Jack, Beth and I were busy counting out our money, trying to see how much we had. The nurse got the price over the phone. Let's see, now, that means each of us owes... Still confused by the devil experience in my room, I had difficulty in handling and counting the money. Beth and Jack were equally inadequate. Flash. It was simple. These poor innocents couldn't even count. For the moment, calculus, statistics with its normal curve and analysis of variance, all mathematics, were once again mine. Not wanting to hurt their feelings or butt in and do their counting for them, I continued to fumble with my money. I made sure, however, that the final total and our separate contributions were what they should be.

Waiting for the pizza, we were like three little kids, all excited, talking about how good it was going to be. It was fun.

It was something to do. The hell with all of the head trips, all of the trying to figure out what was happening to me. This was real. We sat around, huddling together, talking about how good the pizza was going to be. Still hyper and disjointed, every once in a while, one of us would jump up and go and do something, just walk or run to our rooms or space around for a while. Eventually, we would all be back together again, talking about the pizza.

When the pizza came, it was exciting. We took it to the kitchenette, opening it as though it were a very special birthday or Christmas present.

Smelling it, anticipating the taste, we hurriedly opened the cardboard box. We attacked it like three starving animals. It was so good, that it immediately had to be shared. It was too good to keep to just us. "Hey, c'mon, have a piece. It's so good. C'mon now. Are you sure that one piece is enough? Hey, help yourself. It's great." It was the great pizza feast. Although it was getting a little late, there were still a few patients around. We all dug in, rapping between bites about how good it was.

All in all, Sunday was one of the haziest and fuzziest days of my ward experience. It was basically spent in waiting, with me spurred to action either by an occasional fantasy trip, severe physical or mental discomfort or just plain boredom. The big happenings, my visits with Dr. D. and with Liam and Linda had helped the time to pass. Time had been taken up in the actual visits, in the anticipation of the visits, and also, in the nervous letdown after the visits were over. The day had not been anywhere near as psychedelic as Saturday had been. There had even been a few moments of near normalcy: taking a shower, sharing a pizza, chatting over coffee. These were moments when I would forget my situation, my hopelessness, my head and body terror, and function almost normally.

I guess that I was getting better. I thought that I was getting better. My mind and body were becoming increasingly sensitive to the possibility of pain, however. Increasingly, I would cringe away from the beginnings of pain in either my head or in my body. There were long periods of time when I knew that the most blessed thing in the whole world was simply, to sleep. How fantastic to be able to turn off, shut down and crawl into a deep, restful, dreamless sleep. To be able to cut off the now constant body ache, to quiet the constant whir in my head, to be able to just lie down and sleep was all that I wanted to do. Yes that was where it was at; a poor man's peace.

But as Shakespeare said, even in that sleep of death, what dreams may come? To be denied peaceful sleep, to be constantly buffeted by physical ache and mental anguish, to awaken scared shitless in the night with my rational ego, my conscious controller too dimmed, tired, and broken to sort things out. To be the victim of a constant, ever changing, always the same nightmare, grown more believable due to its constancy, to sink further and further into fright and fear... Ah yes, sweet Hindu's, to be released from this endless cycle of life and death, to be released from the constant wheel of birth, growth, decline and destruction. To be able to space into the bliss of an all-consuming, ever restful Nirvana seemed the highest good. Perhaps that is where it is at. Sometimes.

I guess that I was getting better. First, I would get much worse, however. Jack had been too manic to sleep. He kept spacing around and finally gathered his bedding and took it with him to the stereo sitting room. I was left alone, trying to sleep.

The night was fearsome. Absolutely fearsome. I prayed to Buddha, to Christ, to the kid. The kid. A 14 year old perfect master, or so they said. He was coming to town. A few days before my ward entry I had attempted to go to a meeting held by one of his forerunners. It had been one of my eeriest, pre-ward experiences. Walking across campus, stoned out of my skull, wearing my Alpha hat, going wherever I was needed, wherever humanity was in danger, I had tried to attend the meeting.

The auditorium had become a large, golden womb that acted as a magnet, drawing the robot-like youth of the university. Walking alone, in pairs and in groups, they appeared to be unknowing zombies heeding a call that no one else could hear. Literally. I still remember walking across campus, being drawn to the meeting, seeing groups of others slowly making their way there. Instead of laughter or movement as in going to a concert or ball game, those drawn to the meeting appeared to be in a trance-like state.

As I entered the lobby of the auditorium, I experienced my first audio hallucinations. Someone seemed to be calling Dr. Douglas although I was only a student. As I slowly made my way into the building, there were several helpers or initiates or whatever, who had red crosses painted on their foreheads. They seemed to be guiding people. Did they really have red crosses on their foreheads, did they really know my name? I don't know anymore. You keep count.

Inside the building were a handful of steps leading to the actual auditorium. As I walked down the steps, thick, palpable energy rose to my chin. It was golden and appeared to be somewhat substantial. It was almost as though I would be baptized in this golden energy as opposed to the water of Christianity.

I got out of there. It would be a few days before I would sense myself actually drowning in this energy. (Hmm. Let's see. Unable to be reborn in this new religion that I didn't trust, with a screwed up metabolism, I had instinctively turned to a hospital that was more in tune with my middle class upbringing. The medico's would shatter me with their Thorazine and other medication, allowing me to be reconstructed. It makes some sense. Sure. Why not?)

Trying to meditate on the kid only triggered these memories of my eerie walk across campus and my inability to attend the meeting with the others who had been drawn there.

Praying, struggling, too jumbled to meditate or to think clearly, I tossed back and forth, sweating and uncomfortable. I began to mumble, "Anything. I'll do anything. I'll do anything to get rid of this pain. Anything." I fell into Orwell's *1984*. I jumped into the part where the couple that had been having a secret love affair is captured. The male undergoes a number of tortures. Finally, he is confronted with his ultimate, mind-bending horror. He had a lifelong fear of rats. A cage full of rats would be fitted over his face. Faced with deathly terror, he realized that the only way to save himself was to sacrifice his love. Let it be her face. Fit the cage of rats over her face. Let her head be torn and maimed by the rats.

As soon as the thought that I would do anything to stop my pain entered my head, I realized that it was Linda or me. One of us would be destroyed. I had already died a thousand deaths for her. Although the culmination of several trends, a major reason that I had so fiercely tried to break out of what was happening to me and had accidentally landed on the ward, was an ever-growing fear that I would become violent and do actual physical damage to her.

Linda or me? It was an easy choice. My love was fresh and innocent. I was not. If one of us had to be destroyed, if one of us had to die, it would, of course, be me.

I first curled down under the covers with pillows over my head. I then made a cocoon, covering the pillows and myself with the blankets and sheet. I buried my head under the pillows, tightening the covers around me, attempting to cut off all possible oxygen.

Warning screams sounded deep inside of my head. It was dark. It was lonely. My breath became warm and thick. I started to flip out but held on. The screams inside of my head began becoming somewhat muffled. The darkness, an all-pervading blackness, began becoming comfortable.

I buried myself deeper in the coverings. The screams inside of my head stopped.

My breathing, now consisting almost entirely of carbon dioxide, became labored and then easily shallow. I was covered with a deep, feathery caress. It was a gentle, soothing touch. I became impossibly light headed. A growing warm, comfortable feeling sprang up in my head and in my chest. I curled down deeper and more tightly in my bedding.

All pain slowly receded. Everything became blacker and then lighter. My head was filled with a light gray color, almost like a film or television that was turned on but with no picture. Then, as though someone were using a large felt pen, thick black ink slowly filled in my grayish consciousness. I blacked out. Literally.

Thus ended my second day on the ward.

MONDAY

MONDAY

It was so good. I felt all warm and soft, so very weak and helpless. There was no pain or worry. Curled against my pillow, I felt as if an impossibly soft blanket of light awareness covered me. Snuggled deep in my covers, I felt safe and warm. Soft, warm, light and comfortable, I was dimly aware of a large, gentle something nudging my consciousness.

I was aware of something on my shoulder. A deep voice was cooing, "C'mon honey, c'mon, time to wake up. C'mon honey." I managed to open my eyes. My field of vision was filled with a large, white blur. It slowly took form. The whiteness sharpened into a clean, crisp, recently starched nurse's uniform. There was a large, black hand gently shaking me. A large, kindly looking, black woman filled the uniform. She was softly crooning, rocking back and forth. I felt deep warmth emanating from her. Off to the side, behind her, there was another black nurse, much slimmer, who stood there, abstractly looking at me.

I just wanted to lay curled up in my little ball forever, with this large, friendly, warm being pressed up against me. I wanted to suckle her breast and have her strong, gentle sureness protect me forever and ever. I felt so very good.

Not resisting, a large, blue thermometer was pressed into my mouth, reminiscent of the large blue utensils of my admittance. The nurse was doing something to my arm, taking my blood pressure and feeling my pulse. I liked her warm, strong, thick fingers on my arm. They were so very warm and sure. It was all very beautiful.

"I think we've got him now," the large, close one was talking to the slim, far away one.

Yes, of course, you've got me. If I would have only known that it would feel so good, be so painless, I would have given in sooner. I wouldn't have fought or resisted so hard. I wouldn't have tried to dredge up all of those old memories or continually figure out what was happening to me. I would have simply given in. Yes, of course, you've got me. It was okay. It was so very good.

The two nurses began laughing and talking with each other. It was as though they were making fun of me. Was it my weak body curled in a fetal position or my stupid, dreamy, silly ass grin? I slowly fought to keep my eyes open. I began to realize that I wasn't dead. I began realizing that I wasn't a Changed baby girl, but rather, a weak, fuzzy me.

The two nurses must have thought that I was cute, lying there all curled up in a ball. They took to baby talking me, while laughing and rapping with each other in loose, singsong voices. I began to get angry, but was far too weak to do anything about it. Damn. I was still on this absurd, inane, hospital ward.

After they were finally able to get me to sit up, the two nurses left. After some time, I was able to struggle into some clothes. Morning cleanup was virtually impossible; I did manage to half-heartedly brush my teeth and splash some cold water on my face. I straggled out into the hall, more asleep than awake. Breakfast was waiting with all of the other patients nearly finished. I was too weak to carry my breakfast tray. Mr. Sam, one of the male aides, carried it for me into the television room.

Thus began my third day on the ward. Monday was to prove to be an event filled day. I would meet and become acquainted with the regular staff, some of whom had seen weekend duty. In some ways, I would become stronger; in other ways, I would actually grow weaker. My earlier impressions would only gain depth: there was something very strange and wrong with this place.

I finally woke up during breakfast. Still weak and tired, little was happening. After breakfast, I wandered back and forth between my room and the television sitting room. Nothing was going on. More to make the time pass than for any other reason, I began trying to write.

It was a struggle. I still had little or no memory. One of the nurses came over to see what I was doing. She showed surprise and took my first history in order to show it to my doctor. It was the 10 or so incomplete sentences that I had done the previous day. I became totally caught up in my writing, oblivious to all else. I wrote for several hours, or rather, spent several hours trying to write, as I only came up with a page or two. If nothing else, the effort took up time.

Slowly, but surely, the memories came back. Each was resurrected from a deep grave of sludge and slime. More and more easily, I was able to face the swirls and gaping holes of my torn and broken mind without fear of falling into psychedelic horror. I finally had something to do. Not able to figure out what was happening to me, not able to get off of the ward, not able to be worth something, not able to actively resist or go along with the Change, I was still able to do something. I could, with considerable effort and a certain amount of pain, regain my memory. I could not, however, recall or dwell on memories of the ward and recent, pre-ward experiences. These were still lost to me. They were speeding missiles of oddly spliced together film. I would not remember being a Prisoner of War. I would either be a P.O.W., caught up in that fantasy, or I would be something else. I was able to access, however, that still whole, protected in the vaults of my mind, memory of my more distant past.

Attempting to write in the television room, I was eyed suspiciously by the other patients. I began feeling uneasy. Both patients and staff would shoot me quick, sidelong glances. Cynthia, a withdrawn, nonverbal black girl in her early teens, blankly stared at me with clouded, unseeing eyes. I began hearing my movie voice once more. I retreated to my room.

In my room, still buried in my work, I would occasionally notice that staff were watching me through the observation mirrors. Although I was sensitive to their observing me, the room did not change into a bugged cell as in my prisoner fantasy. Increasingly nervous and worried, I continued to write. At any time, the patients, the staff or even myself, could fall into a roving reporter game, thinking that I was writing about them. I almost did get into observing and writing about them. My present, however, was still too shaky and mind blowing for me to live in it. I delved, instead, into the memories of my distant past, hoping to somehow rebuild a functioning me.

Mrs. H., one of the white day nurses, suddenly burst into my room. Agitated, excited, out of breath from having run down the hall, she burst in on my now calm, totally involved writing. She stood there; pink faced and distraught, catching her breath. "You'll have to give me that... Oh!?!

I'm sorry. It's a pencil." Turning quickly away from me, she began walking back to the reception desk, shaking her head and muttering to herself, "Humph. They said it was a knife." My fears had been justified. Someone was flipping out over my writing.

They had taken yoga away from me. They had taken freedom and sunshine from me. I had been condemned to a room and a corridor, filled with broken people and an incompetent staff. But, damn, the writing was helping me. They weren't going to take that away. Over the next half hour, taking pains not to be seen, I hid some paper away. I also hid a pencil. To do this, I broke the pencil that I had been using in two (Where had I gotten it from?), gnawing the wood away with my teeth in order to make a second point. I also concealed a note, describing my predicament. I worded it carefully, hoping that it would not simply be dismissed as the work of a paranoid schizophrenic. Every time that I finished a page, with my total effort of several days resulting in only a very few pages, I also hid that away. I hid everything in a different place. The extra pencil was tucked away under some innocuous articles on the shelf in my closet. Extra paper was buried in a bottom drawer of the nightstand that separated the two beds. The note describing my situation was tucked in one of the many pockets of my parka. Completed pages were put in a variety of places. Just in case.

Mrs. H. looked incredibly similar to the wife of one of my professors. They had the same last name. Later that day, gathering my courage, I would timidly ask her about it. She would lightly dismiss me with a, "That's funny. Someone else just asked me about that. Oh well, I'm not." I wondered why she wouldn't admit that she was Sonia. Although Sonia hadn't particularly liked me, the least she could do was admit who she was. Then again, Mrs. H. occasionally reminded me of my professor's little girl, who was about 8 or so. Maybe this nurse wasn't Sonia. I thought, though that she had to be at least a relative or one of *them*. It was just one more game to figure out.

That morning, even relative to my other ward experiences, I had one of the most bizarre experiences of my life. I would think about it for hours on end, both there on the ward and afterwards. I know that I was hearing things. I know that I was subject to hallucinations. Trying to figure things out, I was also falling into the web of delusion. Even so, I cannot sort out what was real and what was not. I call it my x-ray trip.

I was lying in bed, still weak from the previous night and exhausted from my efforts at writing. Attempting to sleep, I could only toss and turn in unrest. Although uncomfortable, my pain was not extreme. I began rationalizing my experience. With everything that had happened to me, I began thinking that the worst was over. Although weak and underwater, my discomfort in no way approached the pain of the previous night. I could hold on. I could make it.

I began thinking, however, about x-rays. Why would I think about x-rays? "As long as they don't give me any x-rays. Anything but x-rays. If only they don't force me to have x-rays. I'll be okay if they don't make me have x-rays." I use the word, "thinking," as opposed to saying that I was hearing voices as the voice in my head had my sound and intonation.

I have been distrustful of x-rays for a long time. Due to having had tuberculosis as a child, I have had numerous x-rays throughout my life. As a child going to grammar school in the 50's, I remember the warnings about radiation poisoning in case of nuclear attack. As a teen, I remember reading about how radiation never leaves us, building up in our tissues throughout our lives. With the increasing use of nuclear energy, I still have some anxiety regarding x-rays. Additionally, as a child I had read a comic book about a scientist who stepped through a time warp and found himself in a world of intelligent apes. Humans were the lower primates in that world. The apes had been amazed that he could wiggle his thumbs; they prepared to x-ray him, unknowingly about to use a powerful machine that would inadvertently kill the scientist. The rest of the story traced his escape back to his own world and his own time. I didn't like x-rays. I have a long history of being afraid of them.

Mr. Sam walked in on me. I recognized him from earlier that morning when he had helped me with my breakfast tray. He would become a regular. He was a short, stocky, affable black with grayish black stubble on his chin. He was friendly, came across as mentally slow and was the chief instigator of calling me, "Mr. Douglas, sir." In turn, I would always address him as politely as possible, tacking a "sir" on to his name. He came bouncing into my room, looking jovial, laughing and humming to himself.

"Ah, Mr. Douglas, sir, we going to get you an x-ray. Yes sir, time to get you an x-ray."

Arggh. The enemy could read my thoughts. What can I say? What can you say? What can we say? Coincidence? Sure, why not. What difference does it make? Subliminal hearing? Nurses talking about the need for me to have an x-ray at the desk and good old rabbit ears picking up on their conversation some 40 feet or more away. Maybe yes, and then again, maybe just one more, "Can you believe it?"

Terror. The weakened caricature of myself that I was while on the ward, simply nodded mutely. Yes, of course, time for my x-ray. I was forced to change from my street clothes into my blue, ward pajamas. "Just the rules, Mr. Douglas, sir, just the rules." Finally ready, I managed to get out into the hall. A wheelchair was waiting for me. "Sir, why do I have to sit in a wheelchair? I can walk."

"Just the rules, Mr. Douglas, sir, just the rules."

I obediently sat in the wheelchair. As he pushed me off of the ward and on to the service elevator, I sat there in mute horror. What was happening to me? In my mind's eye, I began getting into inkblots. Rorschach ink blots.

Prior to my commitment, I had been studying projective techniques used in psychological assessment. Curious, I had self-administered myself a Rorschach inkblot test. It was kind of dumb. It was common knowledge among graduate students: Don't give the inkblot test to someone who has recently tripped. You'll get too many responses. It will be impossible to score. In my increasingly spun out state, the blots had gone multi-dimensional on me. Each blot is symmetrical with one half the mirror image of the other half. In effect, they had acted as an energy lure to my weakened essence. I had had nightmares of a cartoon like image of myself falling into the center of these huge energy-pulling blots. On the ward, that very first morning, stopped by Jerry from doing yoga, not being able to feel my insides, I had attempted to flash on my innards using the third eye of my mind. Blots. I had only come up with psychedelic inkblots.

A common response to a number of the blots is that they look like x-rays. Huddled in my wheelchair, bent over in fear, being pushed by Mr. Sam toward the great x-ray machine, my head once again became filled with energy sucking inkblots. I became increasingly helpless.

We reached the first floor. Leaving the service elevator, we entered the hospital proper. It was quite busy. Moving slowly down the hall, Mr. Sam and I passed the old, the crippled and the really sick. Shriveled women looked at me out of deep pools of sadness. I was torn between heart rendering sympathy and complete terror. This was obviously an Exchange Center. Would I be exchanged for one of them?

We passed the main entrance to the hospital. I could see outside. It was sunny. The outside was only a few yards away. I was a doorway away from freedom. I was so very tempted to run for it. The tightness in my gut, together with the weakness in my knees and the fear in my head kept me from running like hell. We continued on past the entrance. Turning in my chair, I took one last look backward at that doorway to freedom. A uniformed guard was sitting there. Where had he come from? (Why would there be a uniformed guard in the lobby of a hospital?) I would have been caught even before I could get outside. Oh well.

As we approached our destination, it was like approaching the edge of the Grand Canyon. I began feeling that this was it. That policeman, wasn't he there the night that I had been committed? That nurse. Surely, she had been there. This then, would be the climax of my entire hospital trip. It was as though everyone had been gathered, all waiting in anticipation. I had thought that the worst had been over, that I was getting better, but now!?!

We finally reached our destination. Mr. Sam left me sitting in my wheelchair in the middle of the corridor. There was a waiting room filled with people off to the side. Left alone, too weak to run, I got up and went into the waiting room, walking stiffly and slowly. No one said anything to me. The seated people just looked at me oddly. I was dimly aware of how I must look to them. I had been too weak to shave that morning, I was back in the ward pajamas, and I had deep, sunken eyes (only momentarily glimpsed when I would accidentally look into a mirror). I wanted to warn them. I almost went hysterical. In my mind's eye, I could see myself shouting to them that sure I was crazy, but "Ohmigod. Run for your lives. This is a terrible, evil place. Get out while you can. Please, oh please, believe me. Run for your lives." In my mind's eye, however, I could also see myself breaking down and crying hysterically. I knew that I would go completely out of control, if I tried to warn them. I held my tongue. I went back out into the corridor and sat defeated in my wheelchair.

I began hearing voices. Mr. Sam was off somewhere, probably making arrangements for my x-ray. I could, however, hear his voice in my head talking to someone, "Ah don't know, ah don't know why he didn't run.

Ah don't know as we went by the doorway real slow. Ah don't know. He could of. Do ah still get one?" The hell with them! No, I wouldn't run. It wouldn't be any two-for-one nonsense. Let them do their thing. I'm not cracking. I instantly knew what this was all about. ***They*** were trying to collect and annihilate all of the undesirable aspects of me, and they were the ones who decided what was undesirable. If I had attempted to run, they would have gotten one for me, the crazy and also, one for me the attempted escapee. Mr. Sam was worried about getting at least one for me, as their plan hadn't worked.

When I was finally led into the x-ray room, this all passed. The new terror was too strong and too immediate. A black nurse met me. She was slim, alert and alive. Her eyes met mine; she seemed to know me. She was incredibly beautiful. I had a strong, masochistic urge to be dominated by her. There was also a young white nurse or nurse's aide there. She appeared to be completely dazed and stupid looking, with her light, blue eyes and pink nose going out of focus as she stared at me in a confused and befuddled manner. It was as though the black nurse and I were standing in the center of a very strong, stationary energy field, the edges of which were rotating in a large circle. The white aide was outside of our energy field; she had trouble staying with us. Her features blurred to one side similar to how a spectator would look as seen from a very fast merry-go-round.

It happened then. I know that I was confused. I know that I was hallucinating. Okay, I was a totally psychotic, paranoid schizophrenic. Who cares? After hours of pondering, I still don't know what really happened. I can even rationalize Mr. Sam walking in on me during the terror of my thoughts of being given an x-ray as subliminal hearing on my part. They had probably been talking about me getting an x-ray, with me overhearing the conversation without my being consciously aware of it. I have no idea, however, about what really happened in that x-ray room.

The black nurse, calm and competent, got an x-ray plate and positioned it on the platform used for taking pictures from above. She placed my right hand and arm on the x-ray plate. Why? I was supposed to be getting a chest x-ray. Why would she be x-raying my arm? Next to my arm, she carefully positioned what looked like a huge, light blue mitten. It was large and insulated, looking similar to what a person wears in order to take something out of the oven. It was a good 10 to 12 inches long. Docile, I complied with the nurse's wishes, keeping still as instructed, in order not to ruin the x-ray. She seemed very pleased. Stepping behind the radiation screen, she gave me a big smile and said, "We're going to make a model patient out of you." She flipped the switch, taking a picture of my right hand and arm.

Ohmigod! My hand. It was the right hand and my right arm. It was the power arm. My strength. What was going on here? I had had missing insides or so it seemed that first morning on the ward. And then there were the inkblots, swirling and consuming my consciousness. They were going to make me into a *model* patient. I would be photographed, duplicated and replaced with magnetic controls. I would become a stupid robot, totally under the control of some unknown entity.

Frozen, I stayed where I was, bent over with my hand and arm on the x-ray plate. The black nurse came and took the plate away, very confident and happy over my cooperation. While she was positioning a plate for my chest x-ray, I straightened up and began wandering around the room, as if in a daze. Through my now tear-filled eyes, I took a look at my x-ray order sheet. It blurred. I saw an order for x-ray # lebbenty-lebben. I was truly lost. Having fallen through a time warp, they were x-raying me over and over again, until finally, I would be totally and inexorably destroyed. The mesmerized white nurse just stood there, looking confused, probably an innocent dupe in this terrible game.

The black nurse positioned me for my chest x-ray. I weakly let her. Having had dozens of chest x-rays, I knew the routine. I could only think, "The hell with them." I wasn't as easy as all of that. At precisely the moment that she pulled the switch, I purposely moved. Let the Master Controller figure that out. They could blow away my head with their terrible drugs, take away my power with their confinement and secret doings, but they weren't going to fuck with my heart.

Finished, I was led back out into the corridor, helped into my wheelchair. Mr. Sam began pushing me back to my room, back to that god-awful corridor. Shaken and terrified, I had to do something. I had to get out of there. This was just too much. Duplicating my arm. Replacing my insides. Whatever was going on, it had to end.

I began pitching Mr. Sam, "Sir, please, oh please sir, just let me see the outside. Just let me sit in the sun for a minute. Oh please, sir, please. Just let me smell some fresh air and feel some sunshine on my face. Oh please. Please, sir, just for a minute."

"Uh, Ahm sorry, Mr. Douglas, sir, Ahm really sorry, but it's against the rules."

He was blanking, however, growing confused, and feeling sorry for me. I must be free. Once outside, I would run like hell. Let them shoot me and feed me to the dogs. I must be free. I continued pleading with Mr. Sam, hoping to con him into giving me that chance to be free. He seemed to be wavering. I was getting through to him.

"Poor, poor boy," clucked an elderly nurse, overhearing my begging. She was walking by us with some difficulty as she was wearing high, black, buttoned, therapeutic looking shoes. The spell was broken. Mr. Sam came back to earth. Shaking his head, clearing it, he squared his shoulders and took on a firmer disposition. There was no longer a chance for me to trick him.

It really didn't make any difference. My resolve had been broken. Linda's roommate had had superman comics all over the bathroom wall in their apartment. One strip had had a futuristic setting. Criminals were forced to wear special shoes that dropped them to a lower, slower vibrational frequency. Normal people who were able to move much more quickly, had been able to recognize, avoid and censor these criminals. This matron, obviously an authority figure in the hospital, was just another captive, another dupe, like all of the rest. She had been forced to wear the special shoes, forced to move slowly. She still thought she was in control, but she wasn't close. Where would it end? How could I, one frightened little absurdity, have any chance against Quasimodo and all of his insidious devices and hypnotized dupes. How could I ever hope to be free? Something was very wrong with this place. It would get worse.

By the time that we got back to the ward, I was totally freaked. Weak and tired, I retreated to my bed. In a weakened, dreamlike state, eyes closed, I began getting flashes of a deliciously beautiful, slim, black nurse bent over a partially hidden object in the brightly tiled basement of the hospital. In amazement, I watched this movie going on in my head. Flash. It became ungodly real, as vivid as my world with my eyes open. I looked on in amazement. This beautiful creature was playing with some small doll like figure. As she manipulated this doll, my world changed.

I was forced to action. I sat up and got out of bed. The movie was forgotten, I had a constriction and magnetic tugging in my stomach. I needed to move. I was being pulled and tugged around the ward, feeling this strong force in my stomach. I let it happen, confused and amazed.

It changed. As a child, I had played with Scotty dog magnets. I had had two small magnets with plastic dogs (one black, one white) glued on top of the magnets. Using a thin surface such as a piece of paper, one could move the top one by moving the one underneath the paper. It was like that. I became a huge magnet, tugged this way and that through my neutral surroundings by some incredible force. Similar to skating without moving one's legs, I was being pulled around the ward.

Certain paths or routes felt better than others. If I went in the wrong direction, pain would rack my insides. Turning, going in another direction, if it was the right one, I would only feel a slight tugging, now in my stomach, now in my feet. I first moved only when it was necessary in order to stop the pain. Then, not fighting it, I gave myself up to it, moving whenever I felt a slight pull. I would occasionally catch psychedelic flashes of a beautiful black woman manipulating some small object in the bowels of the hospital. I was led, pulled and pushed this way and that around the ward.

I was finally led to the shower room. Shuffling past the showers, I began feeling a glowing force just ahead. Although I still had no feelings, whatsoever, in my genitals, I began getting almost sexually excited with warmth in my chest, head and hands. An aware, rational portion of my mind just kept watching me, not attempting to censor my actions. Walking around, behind the showers, I came upon a bathtub. It was filled with incredibly dirty, grayish water. I stopped. Standing there, it seemed right. Was this to be a baptism of death with me crawling into this filth? I began feeling drawn to the water. My fingers idly wandered to my shirt buttons. Part of me wanted to get rid of my clothes and crawl into this stagnant pool of gray.

I jumped. Someone was coming. I quickly came together, bursting into a sweaty nervousness, similar to a male youth surprised in the early stages of masturbation. Sweating, feeling guilty, I turned around and started to get out of there. A black nurse, one of the nicer ones, was leading a black woman to her bath. The patient was the woman who had flipped out on my first day on the ward. The one who had cried out about the devil and the Holy Ghost. Seeing me, not noticing my confusion and guilt, the black nurse crooned, "Oh my, Mrs. X, someone else may be ahead of us. We just might have to take our bath later?" With this, she looked questioningly at me. I managed to mumble a, "No-o." I got out of there.

Back in my room, my magnet trip was still not over. Jack walked in. We looked at each other. We both started to laugh. It was a compulsive, hysterical laughter. Uncontrollable. Flash. Zip. We were two magnets with opposite polarity, existing in the same horizontal plane. We were bound together in some very strong, electro-magnetic field. Polarities would switch. We would be drawn together and then pushed or repulsed apart. We were somehow tied together on a horizontal plane with me also controlled on a vertical one.

We both seemed to know what was going on. Then again, Jack would play anyone's game as long as he got the chance to act up and get rid of some of his manic energy. We tried to talk, but could only laugh and laugh. Momentarily able to stop laughing, a glance at each other, and we would be off into riotous laughter once more. If I remained stationary, Jack was forced to move. If he came to a halt, I would be catapulted into action.

With considerable effort, fighting the rising laughter and magnetic tugging, I was able to get out, "Uh, Jack, uh, it's as if we're, uh..." Hysterical, mind-blowing laughter. Grasping a thread of strength, "Huh, I can't stop laughing when I'm near you." Laughter. Space. Movement.

"I know," was his only reply and then he was off running around the ward.

For the next twenty minutes or so, we were similar to some kind of vaudeville act or a skit at an ice show. We were like two clowns skating around, trying to avoid each other, but inadvertently running into each other with a bang. For example, I would be lying in bed, aware of Jack spacing around the kitchenette. I would be aware of him in both a head and a body sense. I would be drawn to the television room. So would Jack. Entering by different doors, he would see me and be propelled backward. Occasionally drawn together and then repelled apart. Continually, one or both of us would break out in manic laughter.

Finally, saying the hell with it, I decided to break the programming. I remained in bed, resisting the tugs and pulls. The pain was unbelievable. I doubled up gasping, first biting my blanket and then stuffing the pillow in my mouth. I grabbed my gut, digging my fingers into my stomach. I would have done anything to stop the incredible pain.

For the rest of that morning, I had a truly magnetic persona. I don't know the cause. Perhaps it was my radiating fear and the metal wheelchair. It was probably just my head. On Sunday, I had used Jack's electric shaver. Now, trying to plug it in, I almost zapped myself. Just getting the plug next to the wall socket had produced a violent reaction of electric shock.

Bertha, who had been across the hall, was instantly standing beside me. I guess that I skipped time frames as she seemingly made 20 feet in about a tenth of a second. She had been off of the ward and had brought me a gift of cigarettes. Maternally, she took the shaver from me and plugged it in with no difficulty. She gave me a superior but friendly smirk as she handed it to me. Standing away from the wall socket, I carefully took the shaver, mumbling my thanks. Gingerly holding its plastic cover, I was able to shave, although I continued to get slight electric shocks along my chin, neck and cheeks.

Things became conductors or receivers for me. As a fledgling hippie, I had turned people on to wood and metal. Wood is a symbol of life and in the Hindu system, a fifth element to earth, fire, air and water. If you're tired, weak or depressed, go hug a tree. If relaxed and sensitive to it, you'll be able to feel a faint but vibrant life force. Conversely, if you have all kinds of excess, scattered, nervous energy, use a large metal object that's grounded such as a hot water radiator or metal lamp post to drain off scattered energy. Relax, imagining your excess energy draining off into the metal. It seemed to work. On the ward, however, I was too scattered to attempt this, although I would have loved to have been able to hug a tree.

I had long been sensitive to vibrations but never before anything like this. I was truly electromagnetic, with all kinds of positive and negative poles attracting and repulsing me. There were sparks and slight shocks. The experience was probably similar to how someone would feel who had built up static electricity by rubbing his or her feet on a thick carpet on a damp day. It was so very intense, however. My electric personality lasted several hours.

Increasingly, I was falling into either of two mind sets. On the one hand, I was a prisoner in a Change center, subject to some diabolical scheme. On a more realistic level, this would translate to a restricted environment and a perceived strangeness in some of the staff. On the other hand, I was hurting the other patients. Although I was getting better, I was like some kind of a bull in a china shop or an odd sized piece in a puzzle. I didn't know how to play the games of the other patients. I was hurting them.

Getting over my magnet episode, I was lying down in my room, feeling sorry for myself. I was hurting other people. I couldn't play their games. My writing was bothering the other patients. I had ended the magnet game with Jack. I had also ended another game. I had found a calendar. Gone was the metaphysical mind boggling of Saturday and Sunday.

A calendar. Wandering around the ward, I had found a calendar. It was tacked to the wall next to the reception desk. It was clear. I could read it. It was February. Days were crossed out. It was Monday. I had been on the ward 2 ½ days!!! Amazing. If somebody had asked me how long I had been on the ward, I would have answered, "forever." If pressed, I would have continued to say forever, flashing on the thought that a part of me was always on the ward as a portion of me was always insane. If someone could have gotten me to real time, I don't know what I would have said. A month? A year? Weeks? Subjectively, it had been a very, very long time. This brief description of my stay on the ward does not do justice to the incredible amount of mind time that I spent there. Not even three days! Difficult to believe. It would take several more days before the reality would start to set in. I had only been on the ward for 2 ½ days. It was absolutely amazing.

In those first couple of days, there had been a number of riddled, trippy, not really remembered interactions with Bertha, Lillian and Elaine. They were the chief instigators, taking the rest of us for a ride. It hadn't been malicious. More like grownups playing with children. Sitting around, having coffee, we were in a rocket ship. Vavoom, going to a different time. I don't really remember what it was all about. I did, however, take everything very literally. A, "for ages," meant exactly that, not just a few weeks but a very long time.

Although I can't remember the content, I know that a game was being played. Later in the week, Lillian would start in on me about something to do with time. I would tell her that I knew what day it was. I had found a calendar. She would be very surprised and answer with a, "Oh, then you know that we were only funning, that we weren't serious." I was unable to analyze the situation on Monday. It would only be Lillian's surprise later in the week that would allow me to hazily remember the three women playing with my head. The information that I had only been on the ward for a couple of days was enough. To be able to think, "Well, then, that means...," was still beyond me. I sat amazed. A couple of days!?!

Sitting alone in my room, I became increasingly sad. I couldn't play the games of the others; I didn't know the rules. I didn't want to hurt anyone but I didn't really know any games that all of us could play. Despondent, I picked up Jack's guitar and began plucking the strings. Hah! A warm, soft glow covered me. I would sing and be happy and entertain the others. I would start with myself, for if each of us isn't happy, we really can't bring happiness to others. That was it. By being happy, I would bring happiness to others. Excited, I picked a Bob Dylan song out of Jack's songbook. I began playing and singing. I can't read music, don't know how to play the guitar and have a voice that couldn't hold a note if my life depended on it. It didn't matter. No one would mind. I would be happy, sing well and spread my joy to all. I began to lose myself, playing and singing one song over and over. I just stroked the strings, letting my voice do its thing. It was a moment of lightness and joy. I was a traveling minstrel, spreading good tidings across the land. It was a good time.

I felt someone standing behind me. There was nothing sinister about it, just someone standing there. I stopped playing and turned to see who it was.

She jumped. "Oh, I thought it was Jack that was playing."

Reading the nametag on her nurse's uniform, "Hello, Mrs. U. How are you?" (I had no idea who she was. It wasn't until searching my memory to write about my ward experiences that I realized that this was the Mrs. U. of Saturday. The nurse who had helped Danny to move my bed.)

She broke into a big, bright, happy smile and started shouting in a joyous, laughing, surprised voice, "He knows me, he knows me; he's getting better!" With that, she was off, running down the hall to the reception desk with her legs going from side to side in that deliciously, provocative way of running that women have. Other than noticing her rump (pleasant) and her legs (sexy), my only thought was that some strange things were going on around here.

Her "getting better" bumped me into Mind Control. In a near trance (the alpha state), I had been programmed to repeat and believe, "Each and every day in each and every way, I'm getting better, better and better." Seemingly an innocuous, beneficial way to achieve a more positive mental attitude, I was and am excited by the possibilities of self-programming. On the ward, however, the "getting better" phrase bumped me into memories of psychic experiences and the heavies. Guitar and singing forgotten, I lay down and once again began trying to figure everything out. I not only wasn't able to function in the normal waking state, I also wasn't able to use slower brain waves indicative of a meditative state or the "third eye" of yoga. Attempting to go inside of my head brought the same swirls, fear and terror as before.

Ah though, I was learning. I could think of Mrs. U. and her not unpleasing Asian face, her naiveté and her sexy legs and posterior. When I had first met Jack, thinking of him as a fellow prisoner and a bunkmate at summer camp all at once, Mrs. U. had walked by. With a knowing leer, he had said, "That's yours." A portion of me had taken this to mean that it was my job to infiltrate, con and defeat this Asian, authority figure. Part of me had also caught the obvious meaning. She was an attractive lady.

Watching her undulating hips and white stocking legs, I had wanted her very much. If I were ever lured into one of those secret rooms in order to hurry the Change, it would be with Mrs. U. I truly desired her.

Later that Monday afternoon, I stopped Mrs. U. in the hall. We talked together for quite some time. In a male-female sense, she appeared to be both gullible and easy. She had an innocent, trusting, interested (really interested), pleasant manner about her. Together with her trying-to-understand openness, she had a body that exuded a strong sexuality. She reminded me of the type of woman, who, resisting sexual advances, would quickly be fighting her own body and her own body juices. She had a nicely rounded, sensual appearance. Standing there, talking with her with our bodies ever so close, she entranced me. My body could feel her warmth. Although I still didn't have any feeling in my groin and would not be able to have an erection until quite some time after I got off of the ward, I lusted after Mrs. U.

Mrs. U. didn't seem to notice my desire and would have probably been shocked at my thoughts. It didn't really matter. Just talking to her, standing close to her, was enough. Our discussion was a fantastic tonic for my shattered personality. Standing there, leaning against the wall, physically close to her, I began telling her about different eastern philosophies, about Buddhism and about the third eye. She listened attentively, not showing any shock or dismay at my words, commenting that she had a grandfather that had been a Buddhist priest so that she knew something of these matters, although not in any depth. She asked me what I saw in the third eye. Looking at her, now with love, I spaced. Using the third eye, I flashed and focused on a remembered poster of a small, Asian girl that a friend of mine had had hanging in his apartment. With love and tenderness, I told her, "I see a young Chinese girl, about three, very beautiful, running down a city street amidst falling leaves. She is very happy. She is very beautiful."

Mrs. U. seemed to space with me. Then, with her Asian face set in concentration, she replied, "Yes, then you know what is going on. You know where you are."

"Yes, of course."

Maybe she hadn't been listening to me. Maybe she was humoring me. Whatever the case, I was gone. I instantly knew about traveling through time and space, about projecting one's essence through the use of mental images, about the need to obtain coordinates and reference points in order to be able to be accurate. I knew so much more. Thoughts swirled through my head, "Hah! Have you had enough clues? Of course I know what's going on. Who the fuck do you think that you're messing around with, anyway? You think that you're part of the power elite. That you and the Chicoms are behind all of this. You don't even know that you're all puppets in Quasimodo's intricate game."

I was suddenly filled with worry. My thoughts changed. Had I given too much away? Did I have enough knowledge, enough aces up my sleeve, to bridge the next level of control? First, the blacks had tried to control me (Sunday and that morning), what with their silly voodoo dolls and superstitious trust. Now, I was trying to bridge another level of control, another gap in the mystery of the ward. It was exciting. Almost.

Mrs. U. left me standing there and went back to the reception desk, now assured that I was okay. She started talking to one of the black nurses. She began pointing to her forehead. They both started to laugh while sneaking glances at me. Oh, Mrs. U., how could you forsake my love and my trust? How could you make fun of me when I had tried so hard to tell you what was happening to me? I knew, however, that she was just putting the black woman on. Mrs. U. would tell the true story with all of its sinister implications to her superior. Things would start to get interesting.

That afternoon, Jack, Beth, Cynthia and I were taken to physical therapy. Mr. Sam and a large, heavy black nurse escorted us. On the elevator ride down to the therapy room, Jack and Beth, especially Beth, talked about how they hated physical therapy. Jack, as usual, just seemed to be going along with whatever was happening. Beth, however, seemed to have some real misgivings about the impending therapy. Cynthia stood mute and withdrawn in a corner of the elevator. At my deepest, most crippled state, our eyes had met. I had almost been able to communicate with her. She was weak, disoriented and totally withdrawn. I don't remember her ever talking. I didn't get into Jack's carping, Beth's fear or Cynthia's withdrawal. The ride in the elevator did not match my terror of that morning. If nothing else, I was just glad to get off of the ward.

The six of us, a weird group to be sure, made our way through the maze of corridors on the first floor. I noticed hallways, blind alleys and exits as we turned here and there. I needed to get oriented to the hospital and its layout. I had no real urge to break and run; that morning had squirreled my nerve. I was also starting to get involved with the intricacies of the situation, and I was lasting whole minutes as some kind of psychic secret agent. I kept alert, however, for if the opportunity ever presented itself, I knew that I had to be prepared. I was convinced that I was doomed to the ward forever. My only hope would be eventual escape.

The physical therapy room was a scene out of a health club ad. Brightly lit and modern, it was filled with intricate devices. There was a plethora of equipment. Several sets of springs, similar to what boxers use in training, hung from the walls. There was a large wheel that could be turned with a crank, foot and leg devices used to lift weights, levers to pull and squeeze. There was a large, elevated ramp on one side of the room. It was a couple of feet high and had a metal railing.

Mr. Sam spaced off. The black nurse positioned herself on the ramp and hunched over the railing, looking down at us. As instructed, the other patients and I were lying on the floor. A late middle-aged, physically trim, authoritarian nurse led us through a variety of stretching exercises.

Stiff and weak, it was a little difficult for me to do the exercises. I wasn't complaining, however, as the diversion was welcome.

Oooops. The room went in and out of focus and changed. I fell into a dimly remembered science fiction movie. Humans had been turned into pigs and other animals in a subterranean torture chamber. It all fit. There was the room with its intricate devices, the gloating pig-like overseer on the ramp (literal, as the features of this heavy black woman had changed), and us, helpless on our backs on the floor. After a moment of horror, the room changed back into a this-reality focus.

Facing us, leading us in calisthenics, the physical therapist kept on looking over her shoulder into another room that adjoined the therapy room. A green screen hid her view from us. I had caught a glimpse inside this other room, however, when we had come into the therapy room. It contained a very elderly woman who appeared to be quite ill. She was in bed being fed intravenously. As I did the exercises, I could feel waves of energy leaving me and flowing to this old woman. I was being drained. Oh sure. I understood what was happening. From the young and strong to the old and weak. Good old Change theory. I allowed it to happen, not bothering to try and resist. It was beginning not to make very much difference to me. I had no control over any of this and may as well suffer through it.

I was so very stiff that I enjoyed doing the exercises. Everyone seemed to get into them. Even Cynthia, mute and withdrawn, although she was almost always out of step, several beats behind the rest of us. There didn't seem to be any reason for Beth's worry and Jack's antics. I began feeling, however, that things would be quite different if I weren't there. Perhaps there would have been a party or a real reason for Beth being so hesitant about coming to do physical therapy. Something was wrong. I could feel it. It was as if the entire exercise session was a show for my benefit. As I slowly surfaced while on the ward, this would become an increasingly predominant theme. Things would be different when, I, the observer, was not there.

As we finished the exercises and prepared to leave, I tried to catch a glimpse of the old woman. I expected her to be much younger and stronger looking. She would have gotten a lot of good stuff from our group. With Mr. Sam's return, however, I lost my train of thought and forgot about trying to see whether or not the old woman had been rejuvenated. We returned to the fifth floor without incident. No one was letting on. No one was giving away the joke.

Back on the ward, I was in a neutral, near-normal frame of mind. The diversion, itself, as well as the physical movement involved in the exercises had been good for me. I was told that Dr. D. was waiting to see me. I was led to the stereo sitting room. With no opportunity to build anticipatory fear, I was only slightly nervous as I entered the room.

Not too surprisingly, Mrs. U. was there. I had bridged the next level of control. My face remained expressionless as her eyes met mine. Dr. D. paid me little attention. His eyes were on the first page of notes that I had written.

"Hmm, I see here that you've been doing some writing."

"Yes sir."

And then, very quickly, looking directly at me, he asked, "Po-knee-ma-yesh po-roose-ki?" ("Do you understand Russian?" in Russian.)

"Un peu." Without thinking, I inadvertently answered, "A little," but in French.

Dr. D., a smug look on his face, simply nodded. He flashed a knowing look at Mrs. U. It was a look of superior knowledge, a look of "Aha! We've got him." Her Asian face impassive, she nodded. I couldn't figure out if she controlled him, if he controlled her, or if they were both on the same team, controlled by someone else. For better or worse, I had cracked the Russian/Chicom bloc.

Compared to that first interchange, the rest of our session was bland. Dr. D. looked tired and acted bored. Mrs. U. remained attentive and silent. Basically, Dr. D. asked me to verify the contents of my letter. I was able to amplify some of it, explaining, for example, that I had taught. He asked me why I thought that I was hurting other patients on the ward. I shivered. This was too close for comfort. I mumbled something about not being able to understand or interact with the other patients. Dr. D. remained tired looking, seemingly neither interested nor impressed.

Stumbling in my speech, I knew that I was coming across as a little shaky. There was nothing that I could do about it, however. I hoped that Dr. D. would see me as an intelligent normal-type person, who had had a brief psychotic episode or drug flip-out and was getting better quite quickly. After that first meeting on Sunday, I had no desire to try and explain my condition to him. The hallucinations, psychic experiences, physical discomfort, fears and disorientation remained with me. All I wanted to do was to please him enough so that I could get off of the ward. In my brief encounters with him I was always nervous and uncomfortable. I had no faith in him and was always wary of stepping on his professional toes or southern ego. My numerous requests were always forgotten and went unasked during our brief sessions.

Our meeting was over quickly. Dr. D. and Mrs. U. seemed satisfied. They had only been into that very first encounter, testing my knowledge, seeing what I really knew. Not yet recovered enough to be into duplicity, I had automatically fallen into a subservient patient role. As I left, however, I began flashing on the intricacies of the situation. I wondered what new horrors were in store for me.

I spent the rest of the afternoon waiting for Linda and Liam. I kept on reflecting on what was happening to me. I could almost hold a train of thought. Although I would continually slip into and out of things, I was able to come back to and remember things that I had been thinking about. I kept on rehearsing a script of what was going on.

On a paranoid level: There were various factions. It was like coming to a new schoolyard. Instead of one gang, there were several. Each group vied for your submission and allegiance. First of all, there were the black staff, who were promised control if they would perform certain duties. I suspected that they weren't allowed to leave the premises and that they were forced to live in crowded dwellings hidden away in the bowels of the hospital. They had to get a certain number of replacements in order to leave the complex. At first, I had been controlled by the blacks (Sunday and that morning) with their voodoo dolls and superstitious trust. It seemed that the blacks mentally tried to get me to do things. I had heard them talking about me, "He just doesn't listen; he doesn't obey." Some secret power had promised them complete control if only they followed certain secret formulae. I was always totally polite to them and did whatever they said, as long as they met me straight on and called me by name. They could not control me mentally, however, though they seemed to try.

Then there were the white "in" patients, such as Bertha, Elaine, Lillian and Jack, although Jack kept on screwing up. They had to lure new initiates on to the ward, acting as bait for friends and relatives. They did this in order to obtain certain privileges and the promise of eventual release. The strong ones such as Bertha actually acted as ward bosses, intimidating both some of the staff and the other patients.

Then there were the dupes. Mostly white staff with a couple of blacks, they thought that they were in control. They were definitely allowed to leave the premises and return to their homes. They really didn't know what was going on. They had probably been hypnotized to serve ungodly ends. Perhaps each morning they would report for their daily mesmerizing.

On the bottom rung, there were the newbies. These were the patients such as myself, who did not yet serve any faction. We had not been let in on the game.

The entire hospital was some kind of Change center, sucking in the sick and the disoriented, together with their families and friends as well as concerned, but unknowing professionals. All of us were being used for some hidden purpose. Perhaps the sick were being used as lures with the well ones duplicated; perhaps the hospital was a great leveler with all us being brought to some hypothetical average. My perception and interpretations changed constantly. In the misguided battle for supremacy, I was being battled over by the caretaker, black staff and by the "in" patients, with the professional staff unaware. Certain factions, such as Dr. D. and Mrs. U. may know more than the others and think that they were part of the power structure, but this was only a delusion on their part. They were still only pawns in the puppet master's incredibly, intricate game. My conscious mind would continually note facts and incidents that would reinforce all of the above.

On a relatively straight level: I was sick. I was tripping. I had diminished control over my head and my body. I was scattered, delving both into my own fear and paranoia, but also, into other people's nightmares. I was picking up and getting into the terror of the other patients. In my weakened condition, I was exposed to both my own hells as well as those of others on the ward.

Either way I was lost. I was too exposed and too fragile. The staff was too unknowing. I would never ever leave the ward.

Tired and disoriented, I began wandering around the ward. It was too difficult, trying to keep all of these complex thoughts in my head, although

I knew that I needed to tell Liam about what was happening. He would understand. I wandered by Beth's room. She was asleep, curled in a ball. She looked quite ill. Her features had changed. She was much darker and looked East Indian. I had a microsecond of horror. That afternoon, a very elderly black man had been wheeled on to the ward on a stretcher. Seen only that one time, he had been crippled and in obvious pain. He had very white hair and looked to be in his 90s. His skin was a mottled, light brown or tan; he looked as if he had been much darker but lightly white washed.

I instantly knew what was happening with the images of Beth and the old man merging in my head. This was just another case of vibrational vampirism. Beth's health was being drained into him with his color going to her, just as the tape of Bertha's husband had been read into me. From the young to the old and from the strong to the weak; this refrain rang through my head. He was obviously in the room next to Beth's, the one with the closed door. Wheeled in for his fix, couldn't they see that it was destroying her! I shivered in horror, blanching at both my impotence and the injustice of it all. The innocents such as Beth and Linda should be protected. If ***they*** wanted to play their hideous games, let them try someone like me. Leave the weak and the innocent alone. Shaken, terrified at what was happening to Beth, I continued on my way.

Waiting. I was caught up in endless waiting, with only fear and fantasy to break the boredom and the now continual pain. Supper came and went. And then it was six o'clock. Liam and Linda were among the first visitors.

I was prepared. I was rehearsed. First, however, there were the hugs and joy at seeing each other again. It was so fantastic seeing them again. Linda had brought me a bag of goodies, including cigarettes, candy and more of my regular clothes. Surprise and joy quickly registered. Then, almost immediately, holding Linda's hand for dear life, I started in, "I'm never going to get well. I'm never going to get off of this ward. I'm never going to leave here."

In unison, they immediately responded with "Oh no. Come on now. You look much better. You'll be okay." They would have none of my talk. I couldn't stop, however. Small tears started in Linda's eyes.

I kept on about how I would never leave the ward. By now I sincerely believed that I was lost forever. In a distant sort of way, I was even beginning to accept it. I went so far as to suggest that Liam and Linda would be good for each other. I was about to suggest that he should live and sleep with her. Before I could get into that, Liam immediately cut me off at my, "You'd be good for each other." I desperately tried to get Liam into my paranoia and conspiracy theory. I told him about the Russian/French incident, the inept staff, some of the bizarre things that had happened.

Liam was beautiful. They both were. Linda held on to me, squeezing a "no" into my hand every time that I got into my "I'll never leave this place" rap. Tears filled her eyes with her voice coming out in heavy, emotional whispers. Liam, however, was prepared to blow me out of my delusions.

He listened to me. Totally relaxed and involved, he sat opposite me, looking straight into my eyes, not off to the side like Dr. D. or with his head cocked in quizzical amazement like Mrs. U. He had no judgments or ego analyses to make. He stayed with me. Not only listening to me, he was actually able to hear me.

When I told him about answering Dr. D's Russian in French, without him saying anything about it, Liam immediately came back with, "Yeah, so what, we both know that he's kind of squirrelly. Look, man, every time that I try to talk to him about you he just cuts me off and says that you've been on drugs for a real long time. We both know that that's not true."

"Yeah, well I kind of told him that I took drugs." Liam's face just wrinkled up but he let it pass.

When I would start giving him some paranoid explanations of what was happening to me, his face would just wrinkle up in a, "Who are you trying to kid? Hey, brother, this is Liam, come on, we've been there together."

I couldn't really con him. Hell, he certainly had been there. We had both been there, living through some heavy experiences together. He simply stayed with me, listening, not spacing off, not rehearsing what he wanted to say, and just waiting for me to say something that made some sense or conversely, something that didn't make any sense. He had no value judgments, just a "be straight with me" attitude. Gawd, what a therapist Liam would have made. He's so honest, open, straight on, and together. If a crazy happened to say something new to Liam, no matter how totally bizarre, he would probably stop him and say something like, "Hey, whew, hang on. Let's get into that. I think that I understand what you're talking about, but let's..."

I wasn't able to amaze, snow, shock or frighten him. I desperately began trying to hit on an honest approach that would let him know about the hopelessness of my situation. I sat facing him, staring into his eyes, watching for a reaction to my words. If he started to wrinkle up his features, it meant that I was spilling forth bullshit. If he looked at me askance, it meant that I wasn't getting through. I finally thought of a way to explain my situation that he could understand. "Hey man, look, you know about scattered vibes. Look, I'm scattered, apart, not in control. I can't do yoga or meditate or get off by myself. They give me pills that weaken me; pills that affect me in ways I don't understand. I don't know their effects or how to cope with them. Sick people surround me. I'm being caught in their dreams, in their bad vibes." I went on and on. Liam knew what I was talking about. Dreams and vibes. We had both been there. I didn't have to convince him or worry about whether or not he thought that I was crazy as we had both experienced some incredible things while on psychedelics. We had a common frame of reference.

As I told him about some of the things that were happening to me, his initial response was, "Are you digging it?" It's simple. You take this little pill and your world turns funny. No matter how crazy, wild or bizarre your perceptions, it is okay if you're able to dig it. If you're sensing people, places or things through walls or across distances, that's fine as long as you're enjoying it. If you're not, then you simply pass on it. Rationalize, switch tracks, shut down, think about something else, and get into the music or whatever. We had all kinds of sayings, techniques and logic to aid us to get higher than kites; we also had all kinds of methods to help us to get back down. We had been the explorers of our minds, attempting to see what we could see while covered in this veil of illusion.

When I explained to Liam that it wasn't cool, that I had no control over what was happening to me, that I was in pain, he registered surprise. He was used to having fun during his trips. He told me that I had to hang in there, hold on, relax and slowly but surely get a handle on what was happening to me.

I continued to pour out all of the nonsense that was happening to me. He simply accepted it, continued to listen and occasionally hit me with the right words, words that I needed to be able to live through what I was experiencing. The gist of his advice was that I was tripping and I might as well enjoy the movie. If I couldn't enjoy it, I needed to hold on and wait until it got better. Although I never got to it, telling Liam about the science fiction horror of the physical therapy room would have only produced envy or a joke. "Oh wow. No kidding? Hey, remember when we had to drop a half tab in order for that to happen? No kidding? Hey, what other movies are you into? Are you digging it?"

Eventually, Liam got me to laughing at myself. Then, the three of us were laughing at all of the bad numbers that I was doing to myself. In a moment of levity, I even let slip how I dumped my medication in the toilet. I told them how I had thought that I was a prisoner of war and had snuck into the john with it, holding it under my tongue. I would find out later that Liam would squeal on me. Although I received medication several times a day and only remember dumping it that one time, I would never have to worry about whether or not to take it again as I would be closely watched for the rest of my stay. Rapping down the bullshit with Liam, holding Linda's hand, laughing, I began to feel pretty good and also, pretty silly. Maybe, just maybe, I was going to get out of this god-forsaken place. During those couple of hours, I had my first glimmer of hope. Weak and distant, it was hope, nonetheless.

As visiting hours drew to a close and they were getting ready to leave, however, I spaced into some of my most serious paranoia. Not only were they concerned about me; I was also concerned about them. I kept on asking them if they were okay. Laughing, they mentioned that the day before they had gotten lost and that they had to be shown the way out of the hospital. I began to know fear. Was it possible? Was I, indeed, the lure with the two of them some new victims? Could they have been taken down into the basement and placed in front of that swirling wheel of lights? Were they in the first stage of the treatment that would lead to their total disintegration? Probably not. Hopefully not. Liam seemed too together and Linda was too warm, soft and just plain herself. I voiced my fears, however, and kept warning them. They had the sense to reassure me, rather than just dismissing my fears.

They were perfect. They told me that they would be taking my Volkswagen bug. Liam had gotten the car keys from the desk. Yes, they were sure that they could make it outside okay. No, I wasn't to worry. They led me to the windows in the sitting room. They pointed out my car. They told me to stand there and watch them leave with it. They even explained to me how they would leave the hospital, what turns they had to take and so on. Walking them to the ward entrance, I was filled with love and trust. What a pair! They were obviously worried about me, but not too concerned about my being crazy. Their love showed through. There were no judgments or analysis. I was simply a loved one in trouble. With friends like these, half of our mental patients could probably go home tomorrow.

They left. I went straight to the window and stood waiting for them. Time started to stretch into forever. I held on, however, overcoming my short attention span, remembering that I needed to wait and see them. Then they were there. At the car, they remembered to stop, turn, flash me the peace sign and vigorously wave. Linda blew me a kiss. They drove off. Whew. They had made it. But wait, that VW van, full of hippies, wasn't it following them out of the parking lot? I felt a brief spasm of fear, but smiled it away. Liam and Linda would be okay.

The ward after visiting hours was always a letdown. That Monday had been the start of the regular ward routine. The weekday staff had started their shifts. The staff, some of them having worked over the weekend, began becoming recognizable to me. Most patients, especially those who had received visitors, would continue to hang around the sitting room, unwilling to retreat to their rooms. We all received our medication during visiting hours; some were on heavy tranquilizers so we would all get a contact high. Each day, everything would slowly but surely become more mundane and less mind blowing.

Bojangles was at our coffee clutch. He was a large, light colored, black aide with a huge, protruding stomach. Balding, with the hair on the sides of his head sticking straight out, he looked like a fat, Clarabelle the Clown (or do my readers not remember the Howdy Doody show?). He would dance around, impossibly light on his feet for all of his bulk. Sensitive and deeply serious, he was, however, always laughing and making jokes, bouncing here and there. Woo, I'm the Bojangles man. Jack, particularly, seemed to like him and always joked around with him.

Bojangles seemed nice enough. I didn't trust him, however. He came across as phony to me, seemingly always putting on a show but not really into his antics. He would quickly shift from a big, old clown to a quietly serious hulk. He always seemed to be conning someone. That night I began picking up on a new phenomenon. It was the most evident with Bojangles.

Simply, the "in" patients were quicker and probably more intelligent than the caretaker staff. As mentioned before, they had all kinds of "in" jokes and sayings. They would put both the other patients and the staff on, with the aides not knowing when they were being kidded. By this time, I was caught in between. I began getting some of the jokes and understanding some of what was going on. I was still too slow with too short an attention span to really interact or be an "in" member, however. If one of the patients pretended to flip out in order to get a favor or just to play with someone's head, Bojangles would start to joke, waver, then get worried. I was too slow to pretend. Bojangles and some of the other staff began watching me to see what my reactions were. If I laughed, they would laugh; otherwise, they would start to take the patient seriously. On the other hand, if one of the staff started to bulldoze, and they would, I would be there, a second conscience staring hard. It became confusing, as no one knew whose side I was on, including me.

That night, observing the coffee clutch, I began building a theory regarding laughter. Simply, you could tell where a person was at by what they were able to laugh at. This would be amplified. I also realized that a number of the patients both conned and intimidated certain of the staff. It is well documented that there is a tendency of confined people to identify with their captors, serving in some cases as better guards than the actual guards. I never went so far as to try and police the other patients, however. I always identified with the other patients, although after those first few days of complete disorientation, I was perhaps the most well-behaved, subservient patient on the ward.

Becoming fatigued, I left the coffee clutch. It had been a fairly normal event with Bojangles running around, making jokes while the patients became involved in animated conversation. Danny had come on duty and had done a swish routine. I idly noted that both he and Bojangles were a little effeminate and probably gay. I did not, however, drop into any mind-boggling Change theory.

The visit with Liam and Linda had been a revelation. The normal coffee clutch had reinforced their visit. For the first time since landing on the ward, the thought dawned on me that maybe, just maybe, I wouldn't be there for the rest of my life. For the first time, I thought about the possibility of being allowed outside, of going home again, of living once more. My entire will had been consumed with trying to figure out what was happening to me while trying to still my head and body terror and regain my memory. This new shtick of actually leaving the ward and going home was too good to be true. It was too much hope for me. Of necessity, I spaced away from continuing to think about it.

I turned in early. Trying to go to sleep, I felt indescribably shaky. Nervous. Jumpy. Still my weakened, semi-depressed self, a new dimension had been added. The jumpiness seemed to be coming from within my bones. Sleep would not come.

Jack was too hyper to lay down. He kept on spacing around, doing this and that, with me dimly aware of him. He eventually gathered his things and went off to the stereo sitting room. I continued to try and fall asleep.

My head began filling with strange images. Colored mists and dimly heard voices swirled through my head. Tossing and turning, I fell into a half sleep. I began fixating on trying to figure out what was happening to me. What was going on? Who was in control? I needed to get to a level of mind where I was not subject to this ever changing swirl of color and sound. A clear, strong voice sounded in my head, "Alpha, alpha, go to alpha. We are in control of ourselves at all levels of mind. Go to alpha." I tried to relax, attempted to go to a deeper level of mind, attempted to reach the alpha state, tried to meditate. Nothing worked. Tossing and turning, with a melted head and impaired hearing while an eerie shakiness came from deep within my bones, I fell back into being an impotent victim.

I began getting psychedelic flashes in my head. In my mind's eye, more real than real, I began seeing shadowy figures disappearing down a corridor to the right of the reception desk, going down concealed steps deep into the bowels of the hospital.

The Master Controller resided there. Whoever was rattling my mind and body; whoever was playing with me as though I were some kind of toy; they must be met. God only knows what they wanted of me. Enough was enough. This must end. In the style of mighty Ulysses and the Avenger of Sunday's fantasies, I got out of bed. I was very shaky and physically weak. The hell with it. This must end.

The ward was darkened and deserted except for Danny sitting behind the reception desk. As I moved out into the corridor, he gave me an odd look and then went back to his reading. I began pacing back and forth in the darkened area between the reception desk and the ward entrance. The only light was at the reception desk. I kept to the shadows, hesitant to break into the small, lighted area in front of the desk. I began pacing faster and faster, still afraid to dart past the reception desk, afraid to enter that psychedelically seen corridor to the far side of the reception desk.

I would later find out that the corridor, rather than leading to a stairway that enabled one to get to the hospital basement, actually led to a padded, observation room. It would have been quite a joke if I would have raced past Danny and ran down that corridor, only to find myself in a padded room. Real funny. Sort of like dropped babies.

Danny distractedly glanced at me. He muttered to himself that it was going to be a long night. Under my breath, I said, "Yeah, a real long night." Determined to get to the bottom of this once and for all, I kept on pacing, building up anger and courage. I began having trouble walking. The magnetic pains of that morning returned. They stabbed my insides. Angry, confused and totally pissed, I struggled against the pain. Tired of being a weakling, buffeted by and helpless against all of the bullshit and paranoia of my days on the ward, I gritted my teeth in determination. Doubled up in agony, I continued to walk against the pain, turning in ever-tighter circles. I began getting external flashes of light, seeing energy doors. They would occur in front of and in back of me. They were fiery, neon outlines of doors, rectangular bands of fire and sparks that would go on and off.

Arggh. Oh no. Turning quickly to my left, I had run into one of them. My left hand was hit with electricity. Ohmigod, the pain. Clutching my left hand, doubled over in pain, I managed to get back to my room. Glancing over my shoulder, I caught Danny sneering at me. This was not going to be as easy as I had thought.

Sleep came, but not quickly. Thus ended my third day on the ward.

TUESDAY

A black nurse woke me up early in the morning. She was slim, competent and attractive. She must have been one of the night staff; this is the only time that I remember seeing her. She gave me my medication in a no-nonsense fashion and watched while I docilely took it. She remained waiting, making sure that I swallowed it. I felt good, almost normal. In retrospect, the medicine would tear me apart. Each day, however, I would become increasingly normal.

After breakfast, I found out that I could obtain and use a razor. Under Mr. Sam's watchful eye (don't let the crazy alone with that thing), I gave myself my first really close shave since coming to the ward. I scraped myself several times under the chin line. This has been a habitual problem with me; it usually happens every time that I use a fresh blade. The exciting thing about the shave is that when I looked in the mirror, I only saw me. It was a haggard, tired me with dark, sunken eyes, but a person that I recognized nonetheless. When borrowing Jack's electric shaver, I had not been able to use a mirror, but rather, shaved by touch. Even a bleeding me elicited no psychedelic flashes or mind terror. A couple of black nurses, standing in the hall, started clucking about my bleeding and urged me to use a wet compress in order to halt the flow of blood. I simply nodded in agreement as I was used to it, needing to use a wash cloth or tissue paper almost every time that I used a new blade.

Jack came into the room. He started to blanch at the blood and was ready to launch into one of his manic episodes. I paid him little attention. I just smiled and cut off his antics with a curt, "Hey man, I just cut myself, that's all, it's cool. It'll stop." Seeing that no one wanted to play his "freak out at the blood" game, he spaced out of it and went about his business. He was becoming irritating. His immaturity and constant willingness to act up were starting to get to me.

After shaving, I took another shower. Feeling relatively good, normal and together, the shower wasn't the bliss of Sunday's happening, but rather, a good, natural, ordinary act. Putting on clean clothes, I felt good. Things were looking up.

Returning to my room, I noticed that my bed still wasn't made. I asked Mrs. H., one of the day nurses, the one that looked like my prof's wife if it was okay if I made up my bed. She looked at me with some surprise and answered, "Of course. The patients are supposed to make their own beds." Too new to being normal to totally analyze the situation, I began noticing how slipshod things were. This was my fourth day on the ward. I had taken two showers at my own initiative. I had first borrowed Jack's shaver and then a razor from the desk. What was going on, here? If I had remained unshaven and reeking, would anyone have noticed? I let it go.

We had our first group therapy meeting that morning. It was held in the conference room next to Jack's and my room, the room where I had first met with Linda and Liam. Altogether, there was quite a crew of us: Dr. D., Mrs. S., the head floor nurse who was rarely seen, a black nurse, the one who shepherded Mrs. X around the ward, and about 8-10 patients. It was quite subdued, although it had a promising beginning.

We sat down with most of us wondering what to do. There were some new patients including myself. The other new patients seemed as spun out and disoriented as I was. Almost immediately, before we were all settled down, Mrs. X, the black patient who had rolled around on the floor yelling about the devil, made a request, something about clothes or visitors. Dr. D., who was preparing to get into the session, absent mindedly agreed to her request. He began giving out instructions to the group. The black woman, however, was on her feet, arms stretched out, and shouting "Oh thank you sir. Thank you!" She was quickly across the room, grabbing him in a bear hug, trying to kiss him. He froze, his face a momentary mask of disgust, not wanting her to touch him but also, not wanting to further freak her. He kept his aversion fairly well hidden, turning his face away from her. The black nurse, who had been sitting beside Mrs. X, was immediately on her feet and quickly next to her. She firmly, but tenderly, took the woman in her arms. Cooing to her, she was able to get the black patient to let go of Dr. D. Continuing to hold her firmly, but with compassion, she was able to get the woman back across the room and into her seat. Mrs. X was quieted almost immediately. Dr. D. sat red faced.

It had become ominously quiet. The black patient had spaced, staring off into nothingness. The nurse started to apologize for Mrs. X, but was cut off by Dr. D., who had regained his composure. "Well now," he began, "does anyone have anything to share with the group?"

Quiet. Stillness. This was my chance. After having blown it in two brief sessions with Dr. D., I could now get in one of my numerous requests. I could finally ask him a question. "Huh, sir, I was wondering if it would be okay if I could use the phone. I was..."

"Let's not bring up personal requests. Let's talk about things that we can share with the group." I had blown it once again. I was too late with my request. Mrs. X had beaten me to it.

Silence. Stillness. The patients sat like statues. A number of us started to fidget. Dr. D., after a long pause, said, "Well now, this certainly isn't like Friday. Doesn't anyone have any problems today?" Hmm, Friday, the day before I was on the ward. Sitting there, in this subdued, uncommunicative group, I began feeling that things would be quite different if I weren't there. Similar to the way that I had felt in the physical therapy room, I began thinking that something very strange was going on here. Everything would be different if I weren't there. I was the outsider. I didn't belong.

A few idle comments were made. Restless movement. The silence became uncomfortable. Mrs. X returned from wherever she had been. She launched into, "Ah just want to work, ah just want to go home, ah just want to do my work, ah want to work..." She went on and on, repeating herself. In a brief lull in her speech, while pausing for breath, Dr. D. jumped in and agreed that this was a worthy goal. With an "oooh", she was back on her feet, arms outstretched, moving toward him.

The black nurse was quicker this time and caught her before she reached him. This time, however, the nurse's cooing and tender restraint were not enough to quiet her. After several minutes of trying to quiet Mrs. X down, the black nurse was forced to leave with her. On her way out of the door, the nurse looked at Dr. D. with her face wrinkled into an "I'm sorry" gaze. She seemed very mollified by her ward's behavior. The nurse started to apologize for Mrs. X, but was cut off by Dr. D.

We were back where we started. Ominously quiet once again. I was too uncomfortable to just sit there. I had to say something. "I feel much better, ah, I think that I'm getting well. Anyway, uh, much better." No response. "I, ah, hear things though." There was still no interest. "Like I keep on hearing a Dr. Douglas being paged." With this comment, I shot a sidelong glance at Bertha. Did she know that I knew that it was her voice on the intercom that was continually paging me? Did she know that I knew that she was part of the power structure? Hah! I was learning to take chances. Let Quasimodo try and figure this out. Who did they think that they were messing around with, anyway? "Of course, ah, I, ah, know that there's no Dr. Douglas, so I, ah, must be hearing things." While verbalizing this, I flashed on the fact that I was working on a doctorate, although admittedly, not that of a medical doctor. I idly wondered if I was jumping time frames. Perhaps I would be the doctor that cured me. This new possibility so intrigued me that I only half listened while Dr. D. more or less repeated what I had said. I abstractly agreed with him that I, indeed, was hearing things.

My sojourn into verbalization started off several, "I'm getting better, but...," speeches. Dr. D. began looking disappointed. The head nurse kept on looking at her watch. It seemed as though they were waiting for some really good stories, something really intimate. It never happened. Occasionally, Dr. D. would look at Beth, so young and pretty. He even touched her once. At one point, his face even twisted into a psychedelic mask of lust. I was tempted to censor him, but was not able to move or say anything.

The session finally ended with little or no rapport ever reached. Both the patients and the staff seemed disappointed. Jack had sat in the corner, hunched over, asleep throughout the entire session. I had had a notion to do something really bizarre in order to liven things up. I had wanted to jump up, announce that I was a CIA agent and that everyone was under arrest for not complying with the Confession II Act. I was afraid, however, that the staff might take me seriously and that I wouldn't be able to pull it off as a joke. I was even more afraid that I, myself, would fall into it and then, I would be in real trouble. I simply bit my tongue and suffered through the drawn out session.

Later, wandering around the ward, I found myself watching Mrs. H. vigorously clean the kitchenette. She never paid me much attention, reminding me once again of my professor's wife. Muttering to herself, maybe to me, "Humph. I don't know why I'm cleaning this up when the patients are supposed to be doing it?" The thought flashed, "You're doing it because you're being controlled, you dummy." I let it pass, however. She seemed too together and just a little bitchy to be a total dupe. Actually, although I would have been more of a hindrance than a helper, I would have enjoyed helping her. She was young and attractive. A pat on the head and her thanks would have done wonders for my ego. I was a little surprised at her need to clean up. Bertha and Lillian, and to a lesser extent, Elaine, enjoyed making coffee and supervising our evening coffee clutches. They also took quiet pride in cleaning up afterwards, emptying the ashtrays, cleaning the cups and wiping off the tabletops. I guess they were only on night duty.

I continued wandering around the ward. For the first time since my room had been changed, I walked to the far end of the corridor. On my way, I passed an open door of a room that had no patients. It may have been my former room. Mrs. S., the head floor nurse, sat there, staring straight ahead, looking hypnotized. A tape recorder was going. An animated black nurse, the one that was always with Mrs. X, was walking back and forth, gesturing. I shivered in horror. We had used a tape recorder in Mind Control. Mrs. S. was obviously one of the controlled ones. Another white nurse looked on, slightly dazed. Would she be next? I managed to go by without them seeing me. I thought that I was okay. They wouldn't force me to sit in front of that circle of whirling lights, force feeding thoughts into my brain through their insidious taping machine. I wondered, almost aloud, "When would this end?"

Back in my room, any feelings that I had had about being together were quickly being dissipated. Bored, not having anything to do, left alone with my thoughts, trying to figure things out, was still a dangerous endeavor. Walking around, eating, shaving, taking a shower, talking, these were becoming commonplace. My attention span was still horribly short, however. Worse, in addition to my weakened depression, I was becoming very shaky, twitchy and nervous.

A social worker came to visit me. It was a welcome diversion. She was young and pretty with long, light brown hair and academic looking glasses. She had on a fuzzy, red sweater and a tight, black skirt. High heels set off her long, shapely legs. Somewhat nervously, she introduced herself and said that she would like to talk to me. I immediately liked her. We set off for the stereo sitting room. As we walked to the room, Jack saw us, giving her a leer while winking at me. I was having none of it and ignored him. My lust was reserved for Mrs. U. and my love for Linda. This was just a very pretty girl-woman.

We sat down in the stereo sitting room and began talking. She was trying very hard to be competent, objective, interested and best of all, helpful. She was very intent on doing everything right; I must have been one of her first cases. I began liking her even more.

At first, I was a little bit shaky. I had a difficult time talking. As I realized, however, that this wasn't going to be one of those five-minute quickies as with Dr. D., I became quite verbose. I felt superior to this young woman in an academic, professional sense. I began confidently talking about myself in analytical, schoolbook terms. I painted myself as an intellectual graduate student, succumbing to a variety of pressures, eventually experiencing several brief but intense psychotic episodes. I lightly touched on my paranoid schizophrenic tendencies. I enjoy talking about myself and really got into the whole thing. It was exciting. She was a good listener. She let me talk. She seemed concerned as well as interested in what I was saying. During my discourse, I mentioned that several of the patients seemed more normal than some of the help. To this day, for example, I would prefer Bertha and Lillian to Bojangles and Danny.

She interrupted me, "But you can tell the difference between the patients and the staff?" She was deeply concerned, probably recalling symptoms encountered in the classroom. Cynically flashing on all of the hidden conspiracies, I replied, "Yeah, I can tell them apart. The staff, it's easy to tell who they are. They're the ones who wear name tags."

Very serious and very worried, she countered, "But I don't wear a name tag and you know that I'm not a patient. Or do you?"

"Huh? Oh yeah, sure, you're too pretty to be a patient." Ah, Mr. Smooth may be making a comeback.

Laughter. How I liked this serious, trying-to-do-everything right, young woman. We talked and laughed for over an hour. She explained to me that she would act as my liaison with the outside world and that if I ever needed something that I should ask for her by name. I think that I impressed her and that she probably wondered why I was in there. We had a very good discussion. It had been a tremendous release for me, dredging up my symptoms and talking about them in graduate school jargon.

I had stayed normal, lucid, intelligent and perhaps even sophisticated throughout our entire meeting. I never let on. She never knew. Straight people are so very easy, so very unaware. A little over halfway through our meeting, I had felt the vibrations coming through the wall. They had been extremely strong. They encircled, caught up and drained the social worker. Talking, releasing some of my mind rot, I had become stronger, more sure of myself. The social worker, upon entering the room had stood tall and straight. Although new at the game and a little nervous, she had appeared sure of herself.

As we left the room, however, she was stooped and tired looking. On the other hand, I felt strong and really together. Our heights, or so it seemed, had changed in relationship to each other, with me having grown a foot or so. I actually bent over, hoping that she wouldn't notice the new difference in our heights. As we passed the television room immediately adjacent to the stereo sitting room, I saw that my guess had been correct. Cynthia lay there, curled up on a couch against the wall, some 10 feet directly behind where the social worker had been sitting. She was in a deep, heavy sleep or trance state. Cynthia had obviously caught the social worker in an energy drain.

Recalling the nurse in black, therapeutic shoes on the way back from getting an x-ray, remembering the easily duped staff, and rerunning the movie of Mrs. S. being mesmerized after the group therapy session, I had no real hope for this girl. I hoped that they wouldn't hurt her, as she was so very nice. She, of course, would be of no help to me.

The day passed very slowly with me popping into and out of a near normality. One moment, I would be relatively clear and lucid, the next, I would be back into confusion and disorientation. By this time, I was just plain tired. Having had a sickly childhood, I was used to the feeling. I was sick and tired of being sick and tired. I did not feel at all well physically.

I began feeling very sorry for myself. Having nothing better to do, I began trying to write once again. Even this did not hold together. I began repeating myself.

Those first couple of days I had been hallucinating so continually that I had been forced to live in the present. Now, however, I started to broaden my time frame. Not able to adequately verbalize it, it was as though I were on some kind of roller coaster that I couldn't get off.

Bored, troubled and in pain, unable to take the ups and downs any longer, unable to rationalize my ward experiences, I just wanted it over. After the brief hope of Liam's and Linda's visit of the night before and the near normalcy and strength of that morning, I simply could no longer handle it. The pain, the weakness, and the occasional tripping were just plain getting to me. It was as if my mind and body had declared, "Hurray! Ohmigod, I'm getting better!" and then here I was, getting worse.

The pain was unbelievable. It was totally out of any of my previous experience. The pain came from my very innards, from the depths of my being. My bones to the very marrow were alternately being crushed like nuts in a nutcracker and then, they would become all rubbery with an impossibly strong, sickly weakness emanating from within me. I couldn't stand it. Nothing that I did seemed to work or lessen the pain.

It was early afternoon. I lay in bed, tossing and turning in pain. Completely helpless, racked with a pain I didn't understand, I simply moaned, crying to myself. Already overly sensitive to pain, this weakness in the limbs and god-awful pain coming from the inside out was too much for me. My insides were like crunching teeth.

(Dear Medicos: Did it ever dawn on you that your medicine hurts? Did it ever dawn on you that humans could endure almost any pain if they know why and for how long? Can painkillers and tranquilizers be paired with your anti-psychotic medicine? You say that I never told you about my pain? Did it ever dawn on you that I was crazy? That I was locked up on a closed ward? That I was completely disoriented and scared shitless? I hope you never know my fear and terror.)

I began praying, to anyone or anything that would listen. I prayed to every god that I could think of, even to the Kid, the perfect master that had been the subject of the meeting that was held a few days before my commitment. I prayed for sleep, for rest, for a lull, for anything to make the pain go away. I began hallucinating.

With images floating through my head, I finally realized what was happening. I was being set up as the cosmic lure, the trap for masters. My mind twisted the old joke about the guy, who by continually baiting fish hooks, became the master baiter (masturbator). I was the bait, the lure. I was the worm on the hook. I had developed good karma through Mind Control, yoga, sending love and trying to be a nice guy. I was now serving as a lure for the bad guys to get the good guys. Or was it for the good guys to get the bad guys? I was cross-programmed at all levels of mind. I had used Mind Control to break the negative programming of my childhood and in turn, used drugs to get behind the Mind Control programming in order to see the real truth. I was and was not a mind control devotee, a Christian, a very newbie yogi, a nice guy, a carouser and more. I attempted to drift (the "flowing is" of my acidhead days) in order to allow the most powerful one to win, whether it was a force, idea, belief or entity. I kept on running into myself, however, with each version of me a microcosm of the macrocosm. In this war against myself, I realized that no one could win, as I was cross-programmed. I dimly realized that my real confrontation would be with myself, with my two polarized selves meeting in confrontation or merging back into the unity of the ONE. In this completely frazzled state, I really didn't care who would win. I didn't really care about me, as long as the pain would end.

Throughout this twisting and turning pain, this calling out to the gods that be, one thought held me together: Linda and Liam. Before I gave myself up to complete chaos and utter destruction, I would hold on and see them one last time. Linda my love, I will see you one more time. Liam, good buddy, I can last one more time. I had to see them one more time. I began chanting to myself, "Linda, oh Linda, my love, one more time. I'll wait. I'll hold on. One more time." I became obsessed with the desire to see Liam and Linda. I had to hold on. I just had to.

The pain changed. It grew more intense. I began crying. I couldn't stop the pain. Finally, I began shouting in my head, "Linda, oh my god, I'm so sorry. I'm so sorry. I just can't stand it any longer. Oh my god, I'm sorry." The pain changed again. It was as though I were being beat with a cat of nine tails. I could see and feel the welts opening up across my body. It was too much.

Giving in, giving up, twisted in aching unreason, on the edge of complete chaos, I staggered to the reception desk. Little Miss Glasses sat there. She was a new nurse's aide; it was her first day on the ward. She was white, very young, had blond hair and wore thick glasses. Her slightly crossed eyes appeared huge through her thick lenses. She was stocky with thick legs. I had briefly met her that morning. She seemed nice enough, although a little dumb. Thankfully, Bojangles was also there.

I addressed him. "Look, I can't stand it anymore. I can't wait any longer. I know what's happening and I can't stand it anymore. Please give me something to stop the pain. Please!"

I heard little Miss Glasses way off in the distance as if she were miles away. She was very precise, not having looked up or having noticed my condition. "The doctor says that you're not to receive any additional medication." Although new, she knew the rules.

Staring in horror at Bo, he just looked at me. He seemed to want to start laughing. Was this just another patient con, another joke? He was easily fooled at the evening coffee clutches.

I began shouting, "God damn it! I can't stand it. I can't stand the pain. I know what's happening. It's no use, I'm cross-programmed." He just continued looking at me. "Look, I'm the worm wiggling on the hook. I can't stand it. Give me something."

It almost seemed as if he understood what I was ranting and raving about. He seemed to be wavering, uncertain as to what to do. By this time, I was screaming, "I can't stand it! Do you want to see the wounds!?!" I started to rip my shirt off. I actually thought that my body was covered with huge, bleeding welts.

He just swallowed, looking down at the floor. He looked quite ill. He gestured for me to stop and then, with me waiting, doubled over in pain, he turned around and walked over to one of the large, metal cabinets. He came back with a little paper cup containing two large, brown pills.

I nodded a mute thanks, realizing that I had been defeated, that I hadn't been able to hold out against the pain, that I hadn't been able to wait for my loved ones. I gulped down the pills and made my way back to the room. I flopped face down on the bed and waited for the pain to go away.

I began to drift off. After a short while, the young nurse came in to see me. I abstractly looked up at her. She stood next to the bed, a worried look on her face. "How do you feel?"

I heard myself answer, dimly from a distance, "I don't feel anything inside of me."

Eyes squinting through her large glasses, pinkish face screwed up, she exclaimed, "Oh how terrible."

Terrible? Terrible! It was fantastic. The horrible, bone-crunching pain was gone. I felt unbelievably good. It was as though I were a thin shell with nothing inside or outside of me except for an incredible, golden lightness. I felt like an empty eggshell, similar to those eggs that are hollowed out, painted and used for decorations. Everything was so very beautiful. I was immersed in a gently, drifting sea of calm lightness. What was even better, I knew that I was on something and that I didn't have to worry about my perceptions. I was on a drug. I had no pain, no worry, no analysis, no braining. There was just a calm, peaceful floating.

Lying on my stomach, head to the side, watching the nurse, she seemed to dissolve from the hips down, with the energy floating up, over and into me like a genie's magic cloud. It happened. It was a drug happening, however. There was nothing to worry about. I'm reminded of a friend with whom I had tried to involve in a philosophical, head trip. A total womanizer, he had started shouting, "You know where my head is at? I'll tell you. It's up the ass of some chick and I'm digging it." I guess that he was talking about something else. The nurse's bottom covered me like a light shroud. I had a momentary, fleeting impulse to pull her into bed with me and merge energies. This quickly passed. At the same time, I also had a fleeting thought that this would be Bojangles' payment, the compromising of the nurse's aide and of myself. He would get a couple of extra points. They could have me as a crazy, then as an attempted escapee (although I did stop myself from running), and now as some kind of despoiler of young nurses or aides. These paranoid thoughts passed through my consciousness even more quickly than my momentary urge to merge with her. I felt too good and much too comfortable to move. Ignored, little Miss Glasses left.

I drifted. It was so good, so very peaceful and pleasant. The next several hours would be spent with me drifting in and out of a deep comfortable sleep while floating on magic clouds. In a dreamlike, dimly remembered awareness, everything was very good and beautiful, even fantastic.

I finally woke up. Getting up, wandering around, I was a little confused and disoriented. I then realized that I was on something. Yes! Wow! I was speeding my guts out. Hey! Hey! Yippee! A speeding and a zipping along life's merry way. It was soooo good. Energy just picked itself up and flowed into my bones. For once, I felt together and strong.

Everything had turned itself around. I was filled with joy, peace, and strength. I was on top of things, I knew what was going on. Happy and energetic, I greedily scanned my environment. Occasionally, colors would get brighter and sounds clearer. Hey man, right on! I was in control, bright and bouncy. Forget the bullshit, forget the braining, I was on something. No longer a crybaby weakling, I wanted to hug and shout. It was so very sensational. Hey, c'mon everybody, let's get it ON.

It was like walking out of a thick, soupy fog into brilliant sunshine and just enjoying it. I began to really see the ward, noting all of the observation mirrors and other paraphernalia that had so freaked me. It was as if I were awake for the first time since I had been on the ward. I began enjoying the other patients and the staff, wishing only that they weren't such mopes and so very down. Supper was an experience, with the food tasted and savored. Filled with a new awareness and appreciation of my surroundings, I just let it all hang out, enjoying myself immensely. I felt clear, crisp and strong.

By the time that Liam and Linda got there, I was zippy to be sure. What a relief. I would have someone to play with, someone that could understand and enjoy the experience with me. They, however, straggled in, all drawn and tired looking, with circles around their eyes. Boy, what mopes.

I ran up to them like a whirlwind. "Hey, wow, come on you two, stand up straight for goodness sakes. You both look worse than I do." They just kind of looked at me, too slow to react to this new version of me.

Undaunted, I pulled Liam aside, hugging him, moving quickly, not allowing him to catch up to where I was at. In mock seriousness, "Hey man, look, you need a rest. Look, this hospital deal isn't so bad. Look, you don't have to do any work, you have a nice clean bed, fantastic meals, all kinds of games and magazines and television to keep you amused and drugs, hey man, there's all kinds of drugs that you can get. I mean, screw this driving a cab nonsense."

I started putting the two of them on, surprising and shocking them. They began looking at me a little strangely. Could this be the weak shit of the previous night? Not waiting for them to figure it out, I told them about what had happened that afternoon, about the pain and the magic pills. They quickly began to understand. I got them laughing. Their energy level started to do a thing, climbing and almost catching mine. Whew. They were going to be okay. It was going to be a fun visit. Thank goodness, they were together enough, not to be caught in their dead-head moods.

Linda finally realized that this was, indeed, her man, all happy and manic. It was someone that she could remember, someone with whom she had fallen completely in love. She just burst open, flowering into joy. She became irresistibly happy with her eyes crinkling, her mouth and lips only able to form big smiles and her arms and hands continually hugging and squeezing me. She looked like she wanted to run and shout, crying out to the world that her man was back and that everything, come hell or high water, was going to be just fine. Everything was going to be okay.

Liam just dug the happening. Suddenly serious, he leaned over to me and said, "But really, how do you feel?"

"Hey, look man, I'm speeding my guts out. I feel so good, so strong, so together. The only bad thing is that I have nothing to do. Shit, I could scrub down all of the floors, wash the walls, and do a whole number on this place. I feel great."

"Hey, great. Wow." He looked at me, beaming. Then, getting worried, "Hey, what happened to your hand?"

I looked down at my left hand. The top two knuckles were all bruised and swollen. Huh? I began getting psychedelic flashes of the previous night. What the? Had the energy door been for real? Had I really run into it? I started to get into mind terror. Huh-uh. Nope. Not when I was so ON.

"Huh, nothing. I just ran into a door." I laughed to myself at my pun. Yeah, I had just run into a door. I felt too good to be bothered about it. I straightened my arm, holding my hand out, flexing my fingers. The bruised knuckles went slightly psychedelic with the colors swirling and deepening. They seemed to get better before my eyes. "See, look, they're okay. There's nothing the matter with them."

We continued talking with the three of us all happy and excited. Linda and Liam were overjoyed that I was so ON and obviously so much better than I had been on their two previous visits. We were sitting in my hospital room. Mrs. U. came and chased us out. Visitors were not allowed in the rooms of patients. I started to protest, but Liam and Linda were on their feet and moving as soon as she asked us to move. I went along with them.

We sat down in the television room. It was crowded with patients and visitors. We sat at a table almost directly under the television. Liam sat facing me with his back to the television. Linda sat on my right, holding my hand, hugging and squeezing me.

I began painting an intricate mind fantasy for Liam. The night before I had tried to tell them about my paranoia. I had not been very coherent. I had only been able to bring up bits and pieces, such as my brief interaction with Dr. D. when he had spoken Russian to me. Indeed, although I had rehearsed and tried to keep my perceptions somewhat logical, I hadn't really had any full-blown Change or Prisoner theory. Rather, it was something that I popped into and out of. The only thing that had really made any sense to Liam was when I was able to explain to him about being so scattered.

Now, however, I had more strength and was more coherent. I began detailing a prisoner fantasy. "Look, just suppose, that this and this were true. Now then..." As before, he listened and concentrated on what I was saying. The night before, however, he had remained open and non-judgmental, playing the role of a passive listener. With the new me, he was taking my word patterns, making extrapolations, forming his own concepts. We had done this many times together, talking on into the night.

The sitting room was crowded. The group at the next table began listening to me. I felt them, before I observed them listening in. I lowered my voice. They could still hear me. Liam and Linda seemed unaware. I began falling back into my scattered fear and hopelessness. Nope, not tonight; tonight I was going to stay on. I felt too good. Time to lighten up.

Liam and I had been in deep conversation, both hunched over the table, looking into each other's eyes. I straightened up and began scanning the other people in the room, the room itself, and the television. The television. Oh shit. Idly watching it, while still talking to Liam, I realized that the intricate mind fantasy that I had been painting was patterned after the television program. When would my thoughts be my own?

We all mimic our environment. It has always irritated me, especially when I would find myself blindly repeating something that I had just heard. That night, more in sync with my immediate environment, together with the heightened awareness of those magic pills, I realized that my well thought out, serious head rap both paralleled and imitated the current television program. I may be easy, but not that easy. I cut the rap.

Liam, who had been drawn in and was attentively following my train of thought, was disappointed. "Hey, man, I was just getting into that."

"Yeah, I know, but it's all nonsense. Forget it."

Even though I realized that my earth shaking head trip was no more than a once removed interpretation of an ongoing television program, I didn't flip out. The hell with it was my only reaction. I was still too ON. I was together, a zipping and a spacing down life's merry way. Flow on, my boy. There's new action up ahead. Hang on but don't get hung up.

We all lightened up. They shared their news with me. I could even be interested in something other than my own situation. We talked and laughed. It was over, all too quickly; visiting hours were drawing to a close.

We walked back to my room in order to get their things. Away from the television room and its listeners, I quickly spaced back into my "something strange is going on here" routine. I began trying to verbalize my fears of being a prisoner.

I had been too up and had appeared too normal for either Liam or Linda to worry or take me seriously. Liam, in mock seriousness, quickly came back with, "Hey man, don't you worry, if it comes to that, I'll come back with every head that's fit to walk. We'll bust this place wide open. We'll blow this place apart and get you the hell out of here." This was said with a conspiratorial wink.

What a pair. What good friends. They could even joke with me. Linda got into it. I also did. On the way to the door, the three of us elaborated on how Liam would rescue me. We all made light of it, with them getting me to laugh at my paranoia. Seeing them out the door, I felt very good. They were so much fun and such reality inducers. They allowed me to recall a reality that was so much fun that I just had to get myself together. Life was too good to spend on a closed ward.

I felt so good that I didn't even mind the voice. For you see, while Liam and I were joking about my rescue, there was a voice screaming inside of my head, "The programming… the programming, what happened to the programming?" I guess that a portion of me wanted to take the whole thing seriously. The television program had been about a desperate, trapped person, who was trying to escape from some devious scheme. He had been trying to convince others of his plight. Oh yeah. Sure. In my peace, love and happiness days, the word had been, "Some people have dreams; we live ours." This had been great when the dreams and living had been of peace, love, happiness, nature, bliss, nirvana, and God. How had I fallen into being the goat of science fiction, spy thrillers, disintegration, and masochism?

I was still zippy after Liam and Linda left. The coffee clutch gathered. Similar to sitting around and getting stoned, I really enjoyed this one, as I was still higher than a kite. For the first time, I was an active participant. We talked about drugs, past experiences and more. For the most part, I was on top of things. I had taken my regular medication, however, and was starting to feel nervous and hyper. I would occasionally drift out of the conversation, with my attention centered on my body. What was happening to me?

Instinctively, I was drinking grape juice after grape juice. Drinking it out of a small paper cup, I was constantly getting up, going to the refrigerator and getting refills. I was even together enough to pour coffee for the others. The excess fluid and vitamin C would flush out my system and help counteract the drugs. It had been gospel in my trip days. Alcoholics need vitamin B. Other than actual physical damage such as to the liver, some of the side effects of excessive drinking such as Korsakoff's syndrome and delirium tremors can be avoided by taking vitamin B. Big drinkers going on benders do not eat well. Their mind-bending pink elephants are due to a vitamin deficiency. Druggies need vitamin C. A number of acidheads that I had known had taken huge quantities of vitamin C in order to counteract some of the disturbances that drugs had made to their physical equilibrium.

Talking with Lillian, I found out that she was a registered nurse. She was self-committed because of severe migraines. Due to extreme nervousness, painful headaches and a tense life style, she had sought professional help several times. She could return to the outside world any time that she thought that she was ready for another go-around. I told her about that afternoon. She asked me to describe the pills that I had taken.

"Why, I know what those are. They're…, a very strong tranquilizer."

Oh boy. Downers. I had never made the uppers and downers circuit. I distrusted drugs. I had rationalized taking psychoactive substances as a search for awareness, although they did become recreational. Some of our solid citizens, outraged by marijuana, seem to do okay when it comes to pep pills, caffeine, nicotine, sleeping pills, tranquilizers and alcohol. The only time that I had felt like this was on the speed found in most psychedelics. I had thought that I had been given some kind of amphetamine. I was speeding, felt strong, alert and energetic. And yet, I was on downers. The tranquilizers had woken me up, filling me with energy. This new information, combined with my regular medication, made me very jumpy. How would I get my system to stabilize?

Interacting with the patients and staff that night, I saw everything from a different perspective. It was actually fun. Everyone seemed increasingly normal, although it should be noted that Cynthia, Mrs. X, and other severely disturbed patients were not there. Observing the conversation, for once in on the jokes, I expanded on my musings of the previous night.

We can tell about people by what they are able to laugh at. Thoughts and ideas cascaded through my head. Per a remembered psychology book, laughter can be used to express latent hostility, such as our laughing at someone slipping on a banana peel or to identify incongruity such as the unexpected punch line of most jokes. My favorite joke: A drunk is leaning against a lamppost, walking around it. He turns to his equally drunk buddy and exclaims, "Oh my god, we're walled in."

The caretaker staff didn't seem to know when or where to laugh at the jokes that the patients made. On the other hand, certain jokes about being crazy or human frailty hit too close to home and would bring fear to the eyes of someone like Elaine. Jack would laugh at anything as long as he could release energy. Little kids many times don't know why their parents and other adults are laughing. The jokes are over their head. Teens, getting into off-color jokes, may be the brunt of ridicule if they don't understand a certain joke.

There, at that coffee clutch, my mind roamed over a whole series of insights into laughter and its significance. I was reminded of "laughing ourselves to death," "laughing our heads off," "he who laughs last, laughs best," and "the devil's laughter." I got into a whole mind game and began developing experimental approaches on how to measure the significance of laughter. It was a normal experience for me. Some call it thinking. I was getting better.

Zipping around, developing innocuous head trips, interacting first with Liam and Linda, and then with the other patients and staff, I felt good. Except for the ever-growing shakiness, I felt on top of things. There were still some strange things happening, however. I was still hearing voices, although now, the voice inside of my head was usually my own. While still having certain bizarre experiences, it was as though I could stand back from them. I was no longer a total victim of my surroundings and perceptions.

It's a shame that all of these new feelings and heightened awareness only lasted those few hours. It was, however, a welcome change. By the time that I was ready for bed, I was nervous, jumpy and hyper. I was not tripping into any new mind or body horrors, however. Even though I was shaky, I was able to burrow into my sheets and blankets, feeling good, remembering Liam's and Linda's visit, amused at some of our jokes. I fell asleep, feeling optimistic.

Thus ended my fourth day on the ward.

WEDNESDAY

WEDNESDAY

I surfaced Wednesday. Still sick and horribly weak, I surfaced. Fragile and childlike, I was now walking ever so gingerly on solid turf.

Those first four days were and are a blur. Although a number of incidents from those first few days are bright and clear, still existing in small pockets of my memory, they are trip memories. The first two days are especially blurred. Saturday and Sunday had existed forever. While Monday and Tuesday seem more real, my memories were still those of an unreal, kaleidoscope-like experience. Those first four days had been spent underwater. Even the gusto and strength of my Tuesday tranquilizing had been spent buried. The air had been thick, with me covered by heavy layers of a limited, restricting environment.

If our journey through life is thought of as a ship sailing the seas or a boat making its way down a river, it can be seen that we are subject to both calm lulls and tempestuous storms, quick and slow currents, large and small waves. We stop at this and that shore, occasionally adrift in muddy reeds, sometimes racing across the water. At times, we have a strong and sure handling of our craft, while at other times there is an improper fudging of the controls. I had been shipwrecked.

First, I had been immersed in a watery energy that reached to my chin. Then I was underwater, reaching for that anchor of a hospital sign. With that shot of Thorazine acting as a catalyst, I had blacked out, waking to a world similar to that of a drowning swimmer attempting to move his mass through a thick, heavy, constricting liquid. Gulping for air, still able to cope after a fashion, I had eventually passed out. Somehow, I had miraculously reached shore. Now, still horribly weak, I had finally awakened. Not quite remembering how I had gotten so deep or why I had come so close to complete destruction, I was finally on solid ground.

I timidly approached the desk, asking the nurse on duty if I could borrow a razor. She looked at me quizzically, cocking her head. Finally, "Wait a minute. Come with me." I walked along with her, going to a part of the ward that I didn't know existed. There were some lockers, probably off of the shower room. She opened one of the lockers. There, on a shelf, were all of my toilet articles. My razor, shaving cream, toothbrush (I had been using a ward issue one) and more were sitting there. Linda had brought them for me when I had first been admitted. I would no longer have to rely on Jack's supplies.

There was some bedding there. I found out that I could take some clean sheets and change my bed. Welcome news as most of my ward experience was spent in a sweating desperation.

My arms full, I made my way back to my room. I felt like a conquering hero with all kinds of booty or a child that had done well at Christmas. Making my bed was somewhat of an effort as my physical coordination was still not what it should be. It was good to feel useful, although it took me twice as long to make my bed, as it would usually take.

With my new haul of stuff, I was starting to accumulate quite a few things. Linda, on each of her visits, had brought me some more of my clothes as well as a number of surprises. Looking around the room, seeing it as if for the first time, I noticed that Jack's area was severely depleted. He had had stacks of all kinds of things, including his guitar and sheet music. Although it had not been obvious to me, each day he had taken more of his stuff to another room, probably the stereo room. His guitar had disappeared almost immediately after I had briefly used it. Although he had said that he didn't mind my using it, it had been quickly gone. Gaining in strength, seeing my supplies grow in relationship to his, it was as though I were replacing him, pushing him off to somewhere else. I was becoming dominant. I felt a twinge of regret, perhaps even guilt.

I met Bill that morning. He was slow moving and slow talking. A severe hip injury greatly retarded his movements. Recently admitted, he appeared to be quite normal. He had a clear, good-looking face, black wavy hair and a construction worker's body. He was on the ward because he had attempted suicide. In order to quiet the pain of his injured hip, he had gulped a bottle of sleeping pills. In pain, he had sought the nearest relief. He did not appear, however, to be either psychotic or suicide prone. I guessed him to be in his thirties. I would find out that he was 28, about my age. His restricted mobility, together with the fatigue and pain lines in his face, made him look older.

We played gin. A carpenter, drinker, and card player, Bill was fun to be around. He was someone to whom I could talk. When we first sat down to play cards, I knew that I loved playing cards and that I was good at a variety of games, including gin. I had trouble, however, holding and dealing the cards. Something new was happening. My physical coordination was getting worse. My strength and dexterity were on the wane. Confused, things became fuzzy. I had trouble concentrating, while Bill slowly explained the game. He seemed unconcerned with my bumbling.

Pop. I was back, knowing the game well. I had taken his slowness for stupidity and began holding back, as in that long ago game with Bertha. I was wrong. Bill was good. I was forced to play as well as I could. Although I had a tendency to win more hands, Bill had a tendency to win the game, as he would get bigger scores when he went out. As with any good card player, he didn't worry about losing a hand; he just concentrated on winning the next one. With him, I didn't have to walk on eggshells, or worry about being too good or too sane. About my age, he was an equal in many ways. Spending time with him helped to pass the interminable day.

Now that I had surfaced and was no longer tripping my guts out, the scene had shifted. It was boring. Little was happening. Increasingly, the ward was becoming what it really was: a closed hospital corridor with a paucity of stimuli and a restricted mobility.

Something strange was continuing to happen, however. I was losing my physical coordination. My bones were filling with bubble gum. I was becoming spastic. I retreated to my room. My thoughts wandered to Barbara's husband.

Mrs. B., the white day nurse who had helped me get my things that morning, looked incredibly like Barbara, a girl with whom I had grown up. Although Barbara and I had not been related except by the closeness of our two families, Barbara and I had been treated as cousins.

The nurse and Barbara had the same first name. I had told Mrs. B. all about Barbara. She listened, all sweet and attentive. She was very kind and understanding, just like Barbara would have been. As I told her the Barbara story, I was kind of hoping that finally, after I had given her enough clues, that she would break out laughing, giving away the joke, and tell me what was going on. She didn't, however. After several days of observation, I would finally know that, indeed, she wasn't Barbara, just as I would realize that Mrs. H. wasn't my prof's wife. For a while, though, even after I realized that they weren't physically people out of my past, I would hold to a type of reincarnation theory or an astral cloning hypothesis.

Barbara was the daughter of one of my mother's closest friends. She was sweet and very religious, having almost become a nun. The two families had always hinted that it would be nice if the two of us would get together, although the differences in our religions prohibited it. After various pitfalls, looking like she would become an old maid, Barbara had married a paraplegic, who was confined to a wheelchair.

He was one of the last Mind Control cases that I had worked. I had sent so very much love and energy, fighting in my mind to picture him able to stand up and function. I had thought that I had been able to get through to him and may have been able to help him. He had, however, become worse. The marriage had eventually been annulled.

Now, lying in my room, I became increasingly debilitated. Although I didn't have the pain of the previous day, it was almost worse, as I became all rubbery, first losing my fine motor skills and then almost total control of my body. I fell into a feverish half sleep.

Tossing and turning, I received strong mental pictures of Barbara's husband. It was as though I were merging with him, becoming him. That was it, then. I was to take his place as a hopeless cripple. Total fear. Total frustration. I could no longer control my body. I fell into a deep sleep.

Later, when I woke up, the head terror had passed. The rubbery weakness had not. I did, however, have more control over my body. Depressed, feeling sorry for myself, unable to handle these relapses very well, I was able to finish my major piece of writing that I did while on the ward. By this time, I realized that I must have done something very wrong to be suffering so much. It started out as a true confession to purge myself of sin.

True Confession
- *spent a year in bed with tuberculosis*
- *have been arrested twice*
- *have had almost all childhood diseases*
- *have done many bad things*
- *have been beaten, scared, tired, …*
- *pushed my way through school studying into the night*
- *have sat spun out for months at a time--summer of xxxx*
- *have had zillions of shots and x-rays*
- *have watched people disintegrate before my eyes-- stepfather, grandfather, …*
- *tried to be a saint*
- *tried to find the truth*
- *did/tried many things*
- *have been throughout the states, Mexico & Europe*

The last year or so have sent love to everything I came into contact with until the last 4 1/2 days I was at a place where I loved and appreciated everything and everyone I came into contact with I faked insanity and allowed myself to be committed
- *I die every time I go to sleep & am reborn each time I have an "aha!" insight or, in other words, wake up*
- *I have always felt compassion until*
- *I allowed myself to be put in here*
- *Everyone talks in riddles & sees & does things that I don't understand*
- *I am drained of love and can only try to do what I am told*
- *I have nothing against any minority or majority group since we all are in essence GOD*
- *People seem to think & do things of which I know not*
- *I want no visitors & if you're going to do it--do it quickly & cleanly*
- *I have no real desires except freedom*
- *If my ego-death can help someone please let me go quickly & cleanly*

Exhausted and starting to repeat myself, I stopped writing. On this level, I was just tired, confused and in serious pain. Dropping back into thinking that I was lost forever, a swift, clean death was preferable to the slow torture. The above starts out with a, "Haven't I suffered enough?" introduction. Mentioning my travels was important, as the **enemy** would have a difficult time duplicating me. It was important to me to put down the bit about minority groups as I usually thought of the Master Controller as Japanese. I may have surfaced. I certainly wasn't well.

We had arts and crafts that afternoon. A nurse came and got me. Not feeling especially well, I had spent most of the day in my room. She led me to the kitchenette. A number of tables had been pushed together, covered with rolls of paper. Jack, Beth, Bill and a couple of others were doing watercolors. Each of us was given a wooden plaque with a figure on it. The plaques were around 4" by 8". We could color them in. Everyone seemed intent on his or her painting. Even Jack was getting into it, and he was neither manic nor acting up.

I immediately experienced a testy moment. I couldn't open the paint bottles. Bill did it for me. My fingers were like large twigs. I had little strength and next to no dexterity. Bill took my plaque and showed me that there were five or six different ones that we could color in. I chose a picture of a revolutionary soldier. I needed to hold the paintbrush in two hands. It took complete concentration. I worked for over an hour, losing myself in my task, trying to color within the lines, while I chain-smoked several cigarettes. I crudely colored in the soldier, leaving the background blank. In better days, I could have done a better job in some 5 or 10 minutes.

The nurses were sympathetic to my condition. Their only advice, however, was to keep moving and to continue to try and do things. Western medicine, with its getting sick in order to get better, can be a trying thing for its patients. I still did not connect these various physical maladies with my medication, however. Oh well, the medication did clear up my head.

I was quite proud of my unfinished painting. For the first time while on the ward, I thought of someone else. Linda. I would make her happy. I would give her a present. I scrawled, "To Linda, with all my LOVE", on the small plaque, signing and dating it. I found some thick, shocking pink, near fluorescent, corduroy-like yarn. I tied this cord around the plaque as if I were wrapping a package, finishing it off with a large bow. I have always loved giving people gifts, surprising them with small sentimental doodads. Taking my little plaque, I carefully put it aside. I was so excited by the prospect of giving it to her. To me, it was more important than the crown jewels. It had been a labor of love. Her man, slowly but surely, against impossible odds, was working his way back.

I saw Dr. D. that day. Briefly. We met in the hall. His, "How are you feeling?" was answered only by my, "okay." I made no attempt to tell him about my pain of the previous day or the rubbery weakness or the lack of coordination in my fingers today. He told me that my mother and sister would be coming to see me that Saturday. He even hinted that if I were okay that I could be released in their custody. I took the news in a "matter of fact" manner, even lightly. It simply didn't register. It was too good to be true, too unreal, too much out of my sphere of comprehension. It hardly dented my awareness. I simply stood there, a subservient patient, shuffling my feet. I thanked him and mumbled something about how I was glad that I was getting better. There were no cartwheels, no shouts of joy.

As I started walking back to my room, a thought crossed my consciousness. I stopped, turned and was able to catch him before he went into the sitting room to meet with another patient. "Sir, is it okay if I call one of my professors at the university?" His face tightened in a grimace. He didn't seem pleased.

When I mentioned Dr. Dwayne, however, he immediately lightened up. "Oh, yes. Of course you can. I know him." I had finally remembered to ask for phone privileges. I had even gotten them.

He disappeared into the stereo sitting room. I wandered around in a daze. My family was coming. I could make a phone call to the outside world. This was too much. I couldn't lose it now. I began tightening myself against any head terror.

I slowly walked to the reception desk, timidly approaching the nurse stationed there. Addressing her, "The doctor says that I can make a phone call. He said that I can call one of my professors at the university."

No drum rolls. No excitement. No medal of achievement. She simply nodded toward the phone used for making outside phone calls. "Okay, there it is. Make your call." She went back to her work.

Small tears had started in my eyes. "I can't dial the phone." Her head jerked up with a sharp look of surprise on her face. In response to her glare, I said, "I have no strength in my fingers."

Without questioning me about my disability, she looked the number up. Dialing it, getting an answer, she handed me the phone. She returned to her paperwork.

Talking to an outsider was exciting. Dr. Dwayne was surprised, but glad to hear from me. He had wondered what had happened to me. He stated that he knew that I wasn't irresponsible and that when I didn't show up for classes, he had wondered if I were ill. For the first time, I would tell another human being that I had had a nervous breakdown. He showed sympathy and told me that he would visit me the next day. It was a short, but rewarding phone call.

I went back to my room, assured in the knowledge that people still remembered and liked me. My years of confinement and terror were, after all, less than a week and two missed classes for Dr. Dwayne. It was difficult for me to grasp. Less than a week?

With little or no control over my digital movements, together with an all-pervading elastic weakness, I realized what happiness is all about. Simply, it's being able to walk and talk at the same time. Going back to my room, I promised myself that if I ever became normal again, if I ever regained my physical strength and coordination, if I ever recovered my memory and intellectual skills, why then, I would never, ever, be unhappy again. Hah! What amazing, strange creatures we are.

Back in my room, I thought about it. They're coming, does that mean, is it possible, could it be, I mean... Caught up in my own life, I hadn't thought very much about either my mother or my sister. Certainly not at all, while I was on the ward. I had first been totally caught up in myself and had then been able to focus somewhat on Liam and Linda. Now, however, I was filled with how much they both meant to me. My sister had married early and had moved to California. She and her family had moved back to Chicago when my stepfather and grandmother had died. She and her husband were busy raising five children. They lived in the house in which I had grown up. My widowed mother, in her sixties, lived alone in what was formerly my grandparents' house. They were coming to see me. They really were. It was hard to believe, virtually impossible, but maybe, just maybe they were really coming.

Over the next several hours, I was able to write several letters to them. With use, my fingers were improving. The letters, although written in a babyish scrawl, were still legible. I was still a little off in my time orientation and carefully dated them.

Date

Dear Mom & Sis

The doctor tells me that you are visiting me Saturday, x/xx/xx. Thank you very much. I love you both very much & don't want you to see me like this. However I love you both so much that I do want to see both of you. If you think that it's okay and you both want to I would really appreciate it.

I lived a lot of different ways & I guess you'll find out how deceiving I was. I'm sorry but I have lied a lot.

When I got here I thought I was dead (again) & tried to play everyone's games but I didn't know the rules & have brought unhappiness to some people.

Like when I was a little boy I was always shy. I'm still shy and now some people are trying to play my game but my only game is to try and be myself.

Please forgive me but I want to be a big guy and play cards, mow lawns, fix houses & that kind of thing.

Don't let my troubles hurt you. I would like to come home and help things keep going again.

Love, ----

I love you so much that I will try to be okay when you get here. Maybe the doctor will release me in your custody

Love, ----

As you can see by these letters I'm still a little disoriented. However I am still a fast learner (memory & vocabulary). I have miraculously returned to my old self & I think people think that I was only fooling & that I am some kind of spy. You know I'm not. Sorry to cause you all of this grief. God bless us.

Thanks
I'm sorry I'm crazy See you soon (maybe)

I was still fuzzy and weak. Going home to live with my widowed mother or with my sister and her five kids was so fantastic that I couldn't even come right out and believe that it could possibly be true. Turning 30, a former teacher, systems analyst and project manager, working on a doctorate with a bachelor's and a master's degree, basically out of the nest since I went away to college at age 17, going home to momma was good beyond my most fantastic dreams. Sure. Why not?

By Wednesday, I was increasingly aware of my changing status. I had quickly gone from one of the most blown out, disabled patients to one of the most subservient and rational of those confined to the ward. Increasingly, I would take every opportunity to talk to the various authority figures, all those nurses that seemed together. Several of the patients, especially Jack, and some of the caretaker staff would eye me suspiciously. Why was I always writing? What was I writing? What was I doing, always talking to those in charge? I became very sensitive to their stares and whispers.

Liam and Linda were late that night. My jumpiness had abated to some extent. Still weak, without complete control of my fine finger movements, the frustration of that afternoon had passed. I nervously waited for them. With the other visitors filing in, I began becoming quite despondent. Liam and Linda were my reality base, my contact with the outside world. To a certain extent, they were the carrot leading me off of the ward. I needed them. I began to worry that they were not going to make it at all. I would start to shake, breaking out in perspiration. They had to make it. Oh please God, let them be okay, let them be able to make it.

Unable to handle the television room, crowded with visitors, I attempted to stay in my room. It didn't work. I constantly walked to the reception desk in order to see what time it was. Ages spent waiting, but only minutes by that big, old clock on the wall. I began feeling fear. Maybe they weren't going to make it. Maybe they weren't okay. Maybe, just maybe, the hope of that afternoon was just a joke, just another way to break me. Maybe, Liam and Linda were...

And then they were there. They were only a half hour or so late. They came in with a rush, both talking at once, both filled with energy. They apologized for being late. Liam, who was the town's first freak taxi cab driver, had had a last minute call. Relief. They were here. They had made it. I was so very glad to see them.

As per usual, Linda brought me a bag of surprises. Cigarettes, candy and some more clothes. What a wonder she was. While I went through the bags of gifts, we all tried to talk at once. They were at a much higher energy level than the night before. Perhaps due to the two of them racing to the hospital, knowing that they were late. I, however, was in much worse shape than the previous night. To their consternation, I began telling them about that afternoon, about my physical maladies. It must have been confusing for them. They remained basically the same while I changed so radically each time that they saw me.

Opening their packages, telling them about that afternoon, I remembered Linda's gift. I jumped up, told them that I would be right back, and went to my room to get it. Returning with it, I felt a glow in my chest. Shyly, smiling to myself, I gave it to her, "Look honey, I know it's not much, but wow, if you knew how long it took for me to make this. Here." I gave it to her, waiting for the explosion of mirth and love.

It never happened. She took it, looked at it, didn't know what to say, put it in her purse and forgot about it. Liam had started telling me about something. Linda just listened attentively to what he was saying, ignoring my gift. There may have been a brief, forced smile or a thank you that I did not hear. I was the little kid, who had worked all afternoon on a butchered mother's day card. Coming home from school, presenting the scrawled atrocity to mom, knowing how pleased, even proud that she would be, and I had been dismissed with a, "Thanks. Now go wash your hands and get ready for dinner." Oh Linda. It was the first time that she had ever hurt me. It was a sin of omission rather than one of intent.

As always, the visit with Linda and Liam was enjoyable and good for me. I hardly remember it, however. They were filled with telling me about their lives. Perhaps my high energy level of the previous night had inspired them to be up for me, to remember and rehearse anecdotes about what had been happening to them. Liam, for example, began telling cab stories, going on about his passengers and their idiosyncrasies. I listened with half an ear, smiling now and then. Linda really got into it, amplifying stories that Liam started.

I wasn't quite ready for it. My world still began and ended with me. My thoughts could not go beyond my situation on the ward. They either didn't notice my weakness and fragile, self-centeredness, or else, they weren't able to switch gears. More importantly, I was still stunned. My love hadn't done cartwheels, hadn't exploded in joy over my gift of love and effort. Once again, I had failed.

For some time before my commitment, I had not known what failure was. It was not that I was a success; it was just that success and failure were out of my context. Sure, I failed. That had nothing to do with my being a failure. Each of us does what each of us does. I was concerned with out there, building search and psychic skills. I had a dream about more fully developing all of man's potential, of reaching the stars, of cutting through all of the self-deprecating bullshit, of actualizing myself and all of mankind into a rebirth of mutual love, respect and understanding. My god was AWARENESS. I had perpetuated numerous atrocities on my body and soul, indulging in numerous perversions, getting lost in innumerable side trips of fear, depression and horror. But it was all a game. All of my inadequacies and hang-ups, together with the crap that I went through, were just part of the game. The bad things were just transitory, side trips and false trails. Eventually, everything would be okay. It had to be.

The dream of being part of growing awareness and helping to develop human potential had been a good one. On the one hand, I fancied myself an explorer of inner space, delving into my mind, seeing how far I could go. What am I capable of? What are we capable of? With a background in psychology, education and systems, I would first work on me, building as much knowledge and as many skills as I could. I would then work on us. I had a dream of helping to build optimal learning environments. What variables and structure are needed to more fully actualize each of us to our full potential?

If I lay torn and shriveled in my Chicago apartment, beset by horrible monsters and visions of a world gone mad, that was fine. I had screwed up. My mind was misinterpreting the wonder of it all. The wrong combination of chemicals had brought on a bad trip. It was okay. That's it, ride with it, cry a little, go into yoga position 42B, that's it, it'll be okay. This too will pass. We'll get back on track.

Somehow, I had lost it. First I had lost the dream and then the ability to do anything about it. The true horror of my ward experience may have begun that Wednesday evening. I was back, functioning in this world. For me, it was the second time around. In order to survive, I had been forced to bring back the old me, dredging the memories out of a buried-in-the-catastrophe, but still intact vaults of my mind. So many of the things that I had learned as a child, as a teen, and as an adult, would have to be relearned. No longer, a brave, fearless seeker of the unknown, no longer concerned with TRUTH, I was just a frightened weakling on a psychiatric ward, attempting to get well enough to escape a closed ward. Sure, I was back. But who or what was I? Needing to hold a paintbrush with two hands and not being able to make my love happy. My feelings of failure would only get worse.

After a scattered visit, filled mostly with small talk, Liam and Linda left. Surprisingly, we hadn't talked much about the impending visit of my relatives. Linda did mention that she had called my sister. I was still in no position to be able to believe that my family was actually coming and that I would be able to leave the ward. It was still beyond my comprehension.

At the now habitual coffee clutch, although shaky and lethargic, I was able to enter into the group discussions with considerable gusto. I was talking to Lillian when someone mentioned Bill. Lillian said that it was nice that I had someone to play cards with. I replied, "Yeah, but he would much rather talk to you than play cards with me." At her surprise and pleasure, I continued, expanding on how he had kept on looking at her, liking what he saw. She took to shushing me with a, "Don't say that." I kept on. It was fun.

Lillian, only a little embarrassed and obviously pleased, began preening. In truth, Bill had been impressed by her and had asked about her. Later, whenever Bill was around, Lillian would always shoot me glances as if to say, "If you say anything, I'll brain you." I almost got into it. I almost pulled a, "Ah Bill, come sit over here, I want you to meet this friend of mine." I almost was able to do it, but not quite. With practice, I could have been the ward matchmaker.

Bertha was at the coffee clutch. She kept on asking me questions about myself and about the two friends that always visited me. I began telling her about a day that Linda and I had spent together while in Chicago. It started out as a horror story, with me attempting to explain how I had begun completely spinning out. She became so engrossed, however, centering on the activities and antics of Linda and myself, that it became an adventure story. To a certain extent, both of our attention spans were too short to tell her an involved story with a punch line of growing dissolution.

I told her about how I had picked up Linda in mid-afternoon in Chicago's downtown section on the day before Christmas. She was able to get out of work early. We did some last minute Christmas shopping. Linda was dressed to kill, as she worked in a somewhat fashionable Loop clothing store. I, on the other hand, several weeks into my goodbye acid trip that didn't seem to want to end, had on my parka and grubbies. Everything looked bright and different. I was stoned, manic and happy. We had wandered through several State Street stores in downtown Chicago. Running in and out of these stores, I had pulled several bits, such as dancing with a floor mannequin until a security guard moved us along. At my bank, I had pretended to have a shoulder holster, fast drawing my trusty 45, not in order to get any money, but rather, to get some of the people out of line. At a very large, classy retail store, we had run up to three different salespeople, with me literally shouting, "Where are the toys for two year olds?" We had received three different answers from the surprised, foreign sounding, temporary Christmas help. As I ran around doing these various bits, Linda had constantly broken up, muffling her laughter. Nothing spectacular happened, but it was fun.

As I related these homely events, Bertha really got into it. She kept on telling me, "What a dynamite feller you must be." She began asking me if she could touch me. She asked in a way that indicated that I would flip out if she did. A portion of me wanted to kid with her, grab her and say, "What's a little physical contact between consenting adults?" Another part of me cringed; I almost began screaming, "Don't touch me. Don't touch me." Lillian saved the day by saying, "Come on Bertha, leave him alone, you're embarrassing him." Thankfully, Bertha did leave me alone, although she continued to eye me as though I were fresh meat.

I never did get to any of the head horror that had started me telling Bertha about meeting Linda in Chicago's downtown section. Probably a good thing as I don't think she would have understood. I certainly wouldn't have been able to handle it. There had been a reason for my being so happy and manic with Linda. She was my balance, my other. With her, I could laugh and joke. The world was real. I could dance with a statue; pretend to have a gun, put other people on. The world didn't go mad and if it did, she was there to bring me to a reality that I could understand.

On the way to see her, I had been alone. I trudged along Chicago's State Street, lost in my own thoughts. It was lightly snowing. Although the sidewalks were filled with last minute shoppers, everything seemed unreal with the people closed machines. There were no smiles or laughter. Although I was surrounded by hustle, bustle and commotion, I suddenly realized that I couldn't hear anything. Startled, my head jerked up in surprise.

Looking around, I became terrified. My world was literally becoming gray and unreal. The only person that looked real to me was a burnt out hippie standing across the street, selling underground newspapers. I knew him by sight as he was always selling papers around the Old Town area where I lived. Here, just south of the Loop, on State Street, he was the only thing that appeared to be substantial.

Disoriented, seeing my world literally becoming a gray void, I turned around, and began walking away from where Linda worked. Everything began fading. It was as though my world was being erased. First sound, then color, then it was as though people, places and things were beginning to disappear before my very eyes. Frightened, I began crying out, not aloud, but to myself, "I need to talk to a head. I must see a head, someone real." Although things became real again, I knew that I was in trouble. I needed to talk to a trip head, someone else into the psychedelics, someone that could talk me down.

I ran into a robed member of the Process. Although I never got into their shtick, the Process was common in Chicago in the early 1970's. They stood around on street corners, dressed in robes, peddling their brochures. As I understood it, they were devil worshipers, with Satan being a good guy, the executioner destroying the chaff, a necessary complement to the wheat of Christ's kingdom.

"Would you care to read about Death?" With this, she thrust an ominous looking glossy in front of me. The front cover was a picture of a large skull. Sure. It was just what I needed. A head.

"Uh, death's kind of boring."

"What could be more interesting than death?"

"Why, the whole life and death _____." Insane laughter. Mine.

"We're having a meeting down by the lake in an hour. Be there." Serene calm and nodding approval. Hers. And then she was gone.

Shivering, I shook my head, cursed a few times and set off to see Linda. I had had enough of this fading world, skulls and bullshit. My Love was waiting.

139

Oh well. Ghost stories may be fun around a campfire. A closed psychiatric ward with me recently shattered was not really the right time or place to try and tell them.

I was beginning to like both Lillian and Bertha more and more. No longer, the chief perpetuators of a sinister plot to change me, they were simply two nice women in their thirties or forties, who had adjusted well to ward life.

That night, the three of us laughed well and long. I enjoyed being the center of attention, recounting my past adventures. Prodded, I even began telling them about some of my first impressions of the ward. Before I got very far, Lillian remarked about how cute I had been, throwing all of my clothes into the garbage that first day on the ward. I weakly smiled and let it pass, as I had no idea what she was talking about, although a brief movie of my Mr. Clean routine traveled through my head. Before I was able to go on or get into any of my paranoia, Bertha asked me if I could remember that first night on the ward when we had played cards. I said, "Sure," but involuntarily shuddered. Although I could dimly recall playing cards with her, the episode had been too close and too psychedelic to remember well. I wasn't ready for another similar experience. She just got shy and remarked that I had been pretty well gone that night. We were even able to laugh about it.

It was getting late. The excitement of talking and laughing about the past was dwindling down. The conversation was getting too close for comfort. Time to go to bed. I excused myself and left them there.

On the way to my room, I had a brief moment of horror. They wheeled in a stretcher with a girl in her late teens on it. She appeared weak, helpless, crippled and in pain. She wore glasses. Ah yes, of course. It was poor, little Miss Glasses. They had gotten her. It was a shame, as she had seemed nice enough. I wasn't able to dwell on it, however. The nurse quickly wheeled her by me with the two of them disappearing into one of the rooms. Just as quickly, any thought of her passed through my consciousness. I would find out the next day that except for the glasses, the new patient did not look at all like the nurse that I had dubbed Miss Glasses. There was that microsecond of horror, however. I may be getting better but I certainly wasn't well.

The end of my conversation with Bertha and Lillian as well as seeing the new patient rolled by me had been psychological shocks to my system.

They were slight, brief shocks, however. Physically, I was experiencing a growing shakiness. Despite this, I was able to sleep well that night. My paranoia about the secret doings on the ward was slowly dissipating. My fantasy of being a helpless victim, subject to the dissolution and destruction of my identity by some hidden master or secret power was abating. Relapses aside, I was getting better.

Thus ended my fifth day on the ward.

THURSDAY

After breakfast and morning clean up, I found several sports magazines and took them to my room. Lying in bed, I began reading them. Although a way to pass the time, it was more than that. I was actually reading them. No longer a helpless scanner of the written word, I was attempting to assimilate the new information. I was able to recall memories of teams and players, comparing my memories to the new information. Oh, so and so is really on a hot streak. Rather than flipping out, I was able to accept that a given team or player was actually doing significantly better or worse than they had in the past. I went so far as to read the standings, go on to an article, and then, magazine closed, try to recall which teams were in what place in the standings. I would then check my memory. I was slowly working myself back, regaining my lost recall and retention skills. I became totally absorbed in my reading.

She was a surprise, popping in on me. The social worker was back. During our first meeting, we had talked about insurance. I had told her that I had an old hospitalization policy with a very limited daily benefit. It was to be even worse, as the benefit was about a third of what I thought it was. Having quit work to return to school, I did not have any regular health insurance. As I was getting better, the real world would begin to impinge upon my consciousness. Rather than paranoid fear, there would be realistic worry. Paying for the hospital and doctor would put a serious dent in my savings.

She greeted me with a cheerful, "Hi. How are you?" She seemed to be glad to see me. I was certainly glad to see her. She had some forms and release papers for me to sign. She had caught me by surprise, while I was in deep concentration. It was a little difficult for me to switch gears. I half-heartedly attempted to scan the forms, while she explained to me what they were about. She indicated where I was supposed to sign the form. Dubious, unsure of myself, yet trusting her, I signed it in the indicated place.

"Okay. Good. Now then, you also have to sign it here."

Oooops. Oh no. I knew what was happening. I was signing away my identity. First, I had to sign the form for the old me. Now, I had to sign it for the new, still shaky me. I stopped. I began shouting, "I know what you're doing; I know what you're trying to do."

My sudden anger and shouting surprised her. Startled, she just looked at me, not knowing what to make of my angry resistance. She tried to reassure me. I was having nothing to do with it. On the one hand, I knew that I was being squeezed. On the other hand, I also knew that she didn't know anything about it. It was ***them***. I began fighting with myself, trying to bring myself under control. She was so very nice. Our first meeting had been so very good. It had been a sane and rational rock in a sea of horror and disorientation. Now, I was frightening her.

She mentioned my mother. It was either that they would notify her or that my mother had agreed to something. My mother? Ah, here was something. They had slipped up. "The hospital has no way of knowing who my mother is. None of my identification has her name on it. Her last name's different than mine." Hah. Let them try to cover this error up.

I give her credit. Although new at the game, she did well. "Look, I'll get your mother's name from the reception desk." Huh? They've gone this far? At the fear in my eyes, the social worker continued with, "Look, they probably got her name and address from your admittance forms. You have to put down your closest relative." I became uncertain, as I didn't remember doing anything like that. It didn't dawn on me that Linda had filled out my admittance forms or that Dr. D. and the hospital must have known who my mother was, if she was coming to visit me in a couple of days. I mutely nodded acceptance of the social worker's proposal.

She nervously hurried off to the reception desk, high heels clicking across the linoleum. Gawd, she had beautiful legs. More importantly, I noticed that she was not yet wearing those special, restrictive shoes. Good for her. Maybe there was hope for her, after all. I felt sorry that I had upset her. I hadn't meant to let her know that I was not as normal as I had seemed at our first meeting.

She was back almost immediately. She had a small slip of white paper with my mother's name written on it in a fine hand. I reluctantly signed the necessary forms. "It's okay. I know what's happening. It's okay, though." She left, probably a little shaken and confused by my behavior. I simply dismissed the whole thing. They had done it again. I returned to my sports magazines.

Later, although still weak, I felt normal. A nurse came up to me and said that I would have to have my chest x-ray retaken. The first one had not come out. Sure. Of course it hadn't come out. I had purposely moved at the last moment in order to confuse the Master Controller. This time, however, I was able to wear my own clothes and walk, not ride in a wheelchair. What was that all about?

On the elevator, I was silent as was the nurse. I waited for the horror to start, but it didn't. Once on the first floor, she led me to a new, more interior, x-ray room. We didn't go by the hospital's main entrance with its crowded waiting rooms. There was no motion or commotion. Once at the x-ray room, a slim, white nurse took my x-ray in a very matter of fact manner. It was over in a couple of minutes.

On the way back to the ward, still silent, I wondered what had really happened that first time that I had been taken for an x-ray. I had no idea then, nor do I now. The glue holding my rational, cognitive self together was still too fresh to handle the pressure of dwelling on any of my ward experiences. Enough was enough. I let any musings about that first x-ray slip through my mind. It was time to think about other things.

Later that day, I had another bout with physical therapy. Jack refused to go, throwing a temper tantrum. It was a bad morning for him. He was completely hyper and especially manic. He would spend some time in the padded observation room that I had never seen. Someone mentioned that it was at his own request. He needed to let off some steam; the isolated room was a good place to yell and shout and pound walls without disturbing anyone.

I ended up going to the exercises with Beth, Cynthia and Jane. Jane was the new person admitted the previous night. The one with glasses. She had made a remarkable recovery. She seemed very together and normal.

She had had a bad drug reaction. Attempting to go to sleep, trying to come down from the speed of diet pills, she had either taken too many sleeping pills or else, the synergistic effect of taking both the barbiturates and diet pills had flipped her into a very bad state. She was young, maybe 19 or so, wore glasses and although plump, she didn't seem fat enough to have to worry about diet pills. She spent her time on the ward reading paperback books. I had seen her earlier in the television room. It was only while on the elevator that I connected her with the weak, groggy, helpless, new patient of the previous night. She only slightly resembled Miss Glasses of my Tuesday episode.

Going to the therapy room, Jane was in an animated mood. She kept on asking us what it would be like. Beth, buoyed by Jane's amicable energy, did not seem as upset by the impending workout as she had been previously. Cynthia simply stared into space, although she did not seem to be as withdrawn as usual. She even seemed to be able to attend to some of what Jane was saying. She was still not able to speak, however. When Jane asked her a direct question, she simply switched her gaze to the floor. I mumbled a few things, letting Jane engage Beth in a question and answer period. I continued to regard her a little strangely, but no, this wasn't Miss Glasses. Hmm. My Change theory was not necessarily so.

Entering the physical therapy room, I made sure to take a look into that side room. Now, it only contained an empty bed. As the physical therapist began leading us in our exercises, I was struck by the irony of the situation. Here I was, male, near thirty, lying on the linoleum floor of the physical therapy room, doing exercises with three teenage girls. Rather than experiencing psychedelic horror, I felt kind of silly. The therapist would say things like, "Now girls, this is a good one for slimming down your hips." Remembering me, she would stop, look at me sheepishly and say, "Well, it's good for everyone." She took to saying things like, "Now girls, and let's not forget the gentleman, this next exercise..."

I was still hypersensitive to my environment. On my back on the floor, doing leg spreads, I could feel the girls around me. Their energy seemed to reach across to me. Was this, indeed, some kind of scheme to feminize me? The thought quickly passed as I concentrated on the exercises. I enjoyed them. It was good to stretch my stiff, unused muscles. Girl Scout atmosphere aside, it was fun.

The session was over all too soon. On the elevator, as we returned to the ward, Jane and Beth were all bubbly, going back and forth in bright, alive chatter, talking about this and that. Cynthia's eyes tried to follow their conversation; she even smiled occasionally. I felt like I was with a group of girls after gym class. I held my peace, not attempting to join their discussion.

That afternoon, I was once again in severe pain. I had a truss with the devil, fighting some invisible entity that seemed to be trying to break up my body and mind. The pain was a thick, pervading crunchiness that came from deep inside of me. In some ways, it was a combination of the pain of Tuesday and the rubbery weakness of the day before. Both aspects were less intense, however. I tossed and turned, struggling with both this deep, inner wrenching and myself. The pain came at me in waves from within, rising and falling in both strength and sharpness. At its ebb, it was like having a dull toothache that came from my very innards.

First, I would be totally at its mercy. Then, I would be on top, almost in control. But no, the pain was too strong, too severe. I bit my pillow, dug my fingernails into the palms of my hands, and tried to talk myself through it, anything to shut off this god-awful pain. I cursed and struggled against the pain, thinking of it as something tangible, something other than myself. Nearly delirious, I tossed and turned, praying for peace, for rest, for sleep. For over half an hour, I muttered and cursed, tossing and turning, not willing to give in. I was determined. There would be no magic pills this time. Finally, without really knowing when, I collapsed into a deep sleep, still fighting the demon within.

They woke me up. I had a visitor. Dr. Dwayne, one of my professors and a major reason for my returning to graduate school, was here to see me. I felt different, somehow. The screaming crunchiness was gone. It was as though I had won the battle with myself. Having had a number of serious illnesses throughout my life, I recognized the feeling. It was as though my fever had finally been broken. Looking back, I feel that this was my major turning point during my ward experience. Although I had surfaced the previous day, this was the first time that I would really seem myself. After that restless struggle against the pain within, it would now be a downward slide into the real world.

I was still a little weak and groggy from having been awakened. They let Dr. Dwayne meet with me in my room. He sat on a chair at the foot of my bed. Other than Linda and Liam, this was my first interaction with someone that I knew from the outside world. He appeared to have his clinical hat on. Could he be one of them? No. This was Dwayne. He was too together, too himself.

Dwayne is one of the nicest human beings that I have ever known. Both he and his wife are just plain, good people. He was in his fifties, with a muscular, stocky build going to a softer pudginess. He wore glasses and was completely bald with any fringe shaved off. He is a quiet, attentive man, passive and gentle almost to a fault. He sat there, studying me. He seemed accepting of my situation. I was still his student, friend and near peer.

How I liked this man. Although I had just returned to school the previous month, after a five-quarter absence, he had treated me as if I had just left the previous day. When I had expressed some problems and doubts about having returned, he showed me some things that I had written that first time around. I had been asked to assess the psychology program. I had made a number of recommendations. He had been very impressed. I was impressed that over a year later, he still had my paper and used it as a reference.

Talking to me in his typically soft-spoken manner, he asked me how I was doing. He told me that Dr. D. was a good friend of his and an excellent doctor. Although I didn't agree with this assessment, I had never really given Dr. D. a chance after that first, muddled interaction. Also, Dwayne tended to think highly of almost everybody. He mentioned his surprise at my missing those classes and also, my not showing up to administer some intelligence tests that I had been scheduled to give. As in our brief phone conversation, he reiterated that he knew how responsible I was, that I was not the sort of person that didn't fulfill my obligations.

I explained to him how I had just finished fighting the devil and how I thought that I was going to be okay from here on out. He was very sympathetic to my condition. He urged me to write about my experiences, especially in light of my training and professional inclinations. We had a good talk. He mentioned that he would be out of town that weekend for a Reserve meeting, but that if I ever needed him for anything that I should be sure to look him up and feel free to ask for his assistance. He told me not to worry about trying to finish that quarter of school or about any other problems. I should spend my time and energy on getting well.

Jack, together with some of the other patients and some of the staff, continually eyeballed us. Who was this new visitor, allowed to meet with me in my room during non-visiting hours?

On the ward, this was an event. After wandering back and forth a couple of times in the hall, Jack barged in on us. Dwayne was polite and attentive to Jack's need for attention. Jack asked a few questions, and then started to dominate Dwayne's time, centering the attention on Jack. Dwayne was very good. Politely and without rancor, he was able to get Jack first out of the conversation and then, out of the room.

Dwayne did not seem at all concerned about my present circumstances or future competence. When I was ready to resume my academic training, there would be someone in my corner. He stayed for some 30 to 45 minutes. We ended up talking about the trivia of graduate school and daily life. By the time that he left, I was feeling quite well and for the first time while on the ward, even sure of myself. That far away spark of hope was beginning to flicker too brightly for me to ignore. Maybe, just maybe, I was going to make it.

The rest of the day passed, as all must. For the most part, it was unremarkable. Time was spent in boredom and weakness. I played some cards with Bill. This brief interlude of activity was ended prematurely as we had to quit in the middle of a game due to his hip beginning to hurt him too much. I watched some television, read a little, and talked to this patient and that nurse. I wandered around, thought a little (but not too much), and waited. There was always the waiting. Except for meals, the major ward activity was waiting.

In short, my time on the ward was degenerating into bored waiting. No longer tripping into mind-blowing terror, I was now able to put up with my diminishing physical pain, while slowly regaining my strength and memory. I was also learning some new things, namely, boredom and patience. The only real times, the only time of being completely in the here and now, was when Linda and Liam came to visit me.

Visiting hours finally approached. As always, the waiting increased in intensity. Linda and Liam were coming: my love and my compatriot. I would get to see them once again. Nervous anticipation. Uneven waiting.

As the visitors flooded in, I anxiously looked for my two loved ones. Would they be late once again?

Bojangles interrupted my anxious waiting. It was time for my medication. I had just finished taking it when they were there. It was so good to see them. Hugs and greetings done, we looked for a place to sit down.

Feeling better, I wanted to share my loved ones with the other patients. This was a familiar, even habitual pattern of behavior of mine. I have always prided myself on having a large number of really interesting, diversified friends. I have always tried to get these quite different people together, hoping that they would enjoy each other as much as I enjoyed each of them. It usually didn't work. This would prove to be especially true on the ward.

Come on. I'd like the two of you to meet some of the people that I've met on the ward. We first went into the kitchenette. Elaine and her husband were there. There was a try at small talk. When I went to introduce Liam and Linda, I realized that I didn't know Elaine's name. I don't think that she knew my name. Patients didn't wear nametags. It was kind of sticky. Social amenities aside, we finally got all of the names straight. Liam, Linda and I sat down with them. It was difficult making conversation, as we didn't really have anything in common. I realized that my real period, the two hours of animated conversation with Linda and Liam, was being wasted.

We quickly excused ourselves and got out of there. The adjoining television sitting room was crowded with patients and visitors. We sat down at the one empty table. Beth was at a nearby table, playing scrabble with Jerry. She had not been getting any visitors lately. The previous night, at the coffee clutch, when Bertha had asked me about my two visitors, I had gone on and on about how great they were. Beth had been very downcast, saying that she wished that she had friends like that. I had told her that I would have her meet my two friends. She had quickly cut off the conversation, "Oh no. That's okay. They're your friends." Now, seeing her, I tried to get her attention. When I finally caught her eye, she quickly looked away. She was too shy to meet them. I felt so bad for Beth, as she was so cute and fragile. I really felt a need to somehow help her.

I was still trying to get Beth's attention, when I found out from Linda that the incredible rumor was true. My mother and sister were indeed coming. She had talked to them. Depending on travel arrangements, they would either be there the next night or on Saturday. If everything went well, they would be able to visit me the next night. Although neither of us was able to come right out and definitely say that I was going to be released into their custody, it did look as if I would be able to go home with them. The full importance and excitement of escaping the ward still didn't completely register on me. I was excited, however, by the thought of my family's imminent arrival.

Our visit was a little scattered. I was still distracted by not having them be able to meet Beth and by the aborted interaction with Elaine and her husband. Also, I was having a difficult time in really listening to Linda, in absorbing the details of the impending visit. Who would pick them up at the airport, where they would stay, all of this was beyond me. It was difficult enough to really understand that they were coming. My attempt at trying to follow all of this information was quickly put aside. Our meeting became centered in the immediate.

Simply, my face began pulling to the side. No longer attending to what Linda was saying, I tried to tell them about it. My face was bunching up on the left side in a spasm of muscle and nerve contraction. I could only speak, barely and with effort, through the right side of my mouth.

I didn't have to tell them about it. They could see it. They looked at me with shocked dismay.

"Oh my god, are you okay? Has this happened before? What can we do for you?"

Liam was the first to get himself together. He told me to hold on. He ran and got Bojangles. Trying to tell Bo about it, Liam and Linda were both talking at once, babbling, "Look at this. Something's the matter with him. Look how his face is bunching to the side. What can we do about it?"

Bo just looked at me, not knowing what to do. "Has this happened before? Does it hurt? How does it feel?"

Speaking out of the right side of the mouth, I was able to tell him that this was the first time that it happened, that it hurt and I didn't know what to do. It must be the medication.

He just continued to look at me, his mouth slightly open. With effort, using both my hands and my facial muscles, I was able to pull the bunching slightly back. It didn't get worse. With effort, I was able to hold it back somewhat.

Bo just kept on looking at me. Finally, he came up with, "It should be okay. It should pass. Just keep trying to talk. It'll be okay." With this monumental advice, he left us sitting there.

The rest of my visit with Liam and Linda was spent in putting down Bojangles and the rest of the staff as well as ongoing concern about my frozen face. Liam was the most vocal. He flat out stated that there was something wrong with some of the staff. They just seemed to act strange. Bojangles gave him the willies; Liam just plain didn't like him. He mentioned how some of the staff would watch the three of us, looking at us rather oddly. It was as though they were paranoid or hiding something. They were just strange, plain and simple. Right on, brother.

My reality base was Liam; although not able to put his finger on it exactly, he also sensed that there was something that was not exactly kosher, up to snuff, or on par with the staff. Although subtle, there was something in the actions of some of the staff, something in their behavior that was not quite right. Liam only reinforced my earlier impressions. Perhaps there had been more of a basis for my apart, scattered self to indulge in all of those paranoid delusions than just my own projected fears.

Liam wouldn't let it go. He began putting Dr. D. down. "Ya know, your doctor is kind of strange too. Dr. D., the few times that I've been able to talk to him, just insists that you've been on drugs for a long time. I keep telling him that that's not true, but he won't listen to me."

To my surprise, I found myself defending Dr. D. "Yeah, I know, Liam, but I did tell him that I was on drugs. It seemed easier to explain my behavior. I guess that I really was into some kind of acid residual or something."

"Yeah, I know, you mentioned that. He still acts kind of strange. I don't know about the staff here."

It's kind of funny, but Liam, during my ward stay, always seemed to have the right kind of words for me. Earlier, when I was so scattered, he had been able to really listen to me. Then, he had been able to recast my paranoia and hallucinations into a world that I could relate to, that is, the occasional bad trips and scattered vibes of my acid days. He had been able to join me and laugh with and at me when I had been high on those tranquillizers. Now, he was able to reinforce some of my suspicions about the staff.

Although I agreed with what he was saying, I also found myself defending some of the other staff, pointing out that they were only human. After all, they were my staff.

By the time that Liam and Linda left, I was doing much better, although the left side of my face was still stiff and numb. As per usual, I would forget to mention it to Dr. D. the next day. I guess that Bojangles just forgot about the incident, as it was never mentioned again. I was becoming increasingly suspicious of my medication, however.

The staff. I just don't know, anymore. There were so many of them. Other than Dr. D., Liam only interacted with the after hours, night staff. I had originally thought them to be interns. I believe, however, that they were aides. Perhaps they had little or no training. Maybe they were just slow people attempting to interact with us crazies.

The aides that I remember include Bojangles, Danny, Mr. Sam, Jerry, and Miss Glasses (seen only on Tuesday). Bojangles and Danny were definitely a little strange. Perhaps they were dipping into the medical supplies. In a way, they were ward bosses during their shifts and had more interaction with the patients than any of the professional staff. I had had a dimly remembered interaction with Danny while almost totally spun out on one of those first days that I spent on the ward. There were three of us standing at the reception desk. The third person wore glasses. Danny was playing with our heads. He had said something to the effect that we could probably all get off of that ward and could get that big, old ward door to just open, if we just had five eyes or was it, "ayes." I snapped to attention, as the number five was so important to me. I tried to figure out his riddle as there were three "ayes" and six or eight eyes depending on whether or not you counted the glasses. He caught me counting and started in on me, "My, my, aren't we literal. Yes sir, we're so literal that I just guess that we can't do it." Innocuous enough, perhaps. Except for the simple fact that I remember horror and disorientation and had to get away from the desk as quickly as I could.

Mr. Sam was affable enough, with his constant, "Mr. Douglas, sir." I always pictured him as slipping off to have a beer, although it was probably coffee. He loved to run errands and was always disappearing off of the ward. Jerry appeared deeply sensitive with intelligent eyes. Other than my catching him watching me, even staring at me in an odd manner, he seemed okay. My only remembered interaction with him was that first day that I was on the ward.

Mrs. H. and Mrs. B. were two competent, white, day nurses. They were only there from 9 to 5 on Monday through Friday. They seemed to be more wrapped up in the administrivia of ward life than any kind of patient interaction. Mrs. U. seemed nice enough, although other than her nicely rounded body and a couple of meaningful episodes, I only remember her with her head cocked in quizzical amazement. Mrs. S. had "head nurse" on her nametag. I would see her the next day. Other than that, I only remember her from the group therapy meeting earlier in the week. I never spoke to her or interacted with her.

There were a plethora of black nurses. They seemed to come and go, with most of them weekend or odd-shift staff. Except for the very nice one who was always with Mrs. X and the heavy set one who had helped me by finding the Bible for me, I don't really remember them.

The only doctor that I remember seeing was Dr. D. While I don't think that he could possibly have been the doctor for all of the patients on the ward, I don't really remember seeing any other doctors on the floor. Since, however, they would probably meet with their patients in the stereo sitting room or in the conference room across the hall from it, both of which were right by the ward entrance, it would have been easy for me to miss them.

On that first weekend, probably Sunday, there had been a group of important looking men in suits and ties that visited the ward. I took them to be hospital administrators. They could have been doctors. Whatever the case, they had been given the grand tour with the staff deferring to them. One of them turned to me and asked me how I was being treated. In my most weakened, paranoid state, I had almost told him what an evil place it was and how he should run for his life. I fell, however, into a movie I had seen about women in prison. They had been horribly mistreated. A well-dressed visitor had approached a new prisoner. He had asked her how she was being treated. She had told him the truth about her terrible mistreatment. It turned out that he was one of the chief perpetuators of the prisoners' mistreatment. Her situation became much worse after she tried to tell him about her predicament. In the moment that it took for me to answer him, I had raced through the entire movie and had ended up mumbling, "Okay, sir." Satisfied, he had gone on with the tour.

Actually, after that first weekend, I hadn't really had all that much interaction with any of the staff. I was lucky. No one was cruel. The constant shift changes, together with the number of staff needed to cover the ward for 24 hours a day, resulted in a large number of dimly remembered people who always seemed to be coming and going. One sadist could have caused a considerable amount of damage to me and the other patients.

That night, I was a passive participant for only part of the coffee clutch. I sat around for a while. The stiffness in my face remained so I was not up to talking very much. Thankfully, the bunching of tissue had abated. Also, I was preoccupied by thoughts that I was really going to go home. I listened to everyone for a while and then excused myself and went to bed early.

I was shaky and nervous. My body became incredibly tense. However, no new horrors or head games surfaced. I was simply intent on getting well, returning to the outside world and to society. The stiffness in my face slowly dissipated.

Thus ended my sixth day on the ward.

FRIDAY

I woke up Friday morning feeling fine, feeling good, and feeling better than ever. Each day, I was becoming increasingly together. Although still shaky, with diminished faculties, I was now a person that I could remember, no longer living in a completely strange and alien world. In celebration, I wrote the following. It was the last piece of writing that I did while confined to the ward.

> *Well, I'm back--just a little shaky. Thank you Lord for making me whole! Thank you forever & ever. God is good to those with the will to live. May I be okay & not continually screw up.*
> *May life be good to my friends. God bless you Linda & Liam. God bless mom & family. May I get better & better & may I be able to repay the good karma laid on me. Thank you.*
> *Friday x/xx/xx*

After breakfast, I sat chatting with Bertha. We filled out our menus. Each day, we would receive a small menu, making our food choices for dinner, supper and the next day's breakfast. On my first day on the ward, the staff must have filled it out for me. On Sunday, I had simply stared at it. Bertha had filled it out for me. On the following days, I had filled it out with some difficulty. At first, I had had a fogged in head, unable to concentrate on my choices. Choosing my meals had been a major, decision-making process. Then, beset by physical difficulties, with little fine finger dexterity, I had some trouble making the correct entries. I remember the pain-staking slowness of trying to move the pencil to the correct boxes.

On Friday, however, I quickly filled the menu out. It was no problem, whatsoever.

I joked with Bertha. "You know, up north, we call it lunch. Dinner is another word for supper. The only time that you have dinner during the day is on Sunday." I crossed out the word, "dinner," and wrote in "lunch." At the bottom of the menu, I wrote, "(us Northerners)". Bertha got a big kick out of it. She took our menus and gave them to one of the staff.

We continued to chat, waiting to go to another group therapy meeting. I told her about my reactions to the first one, about how, in order to liven things up, I had had an urge to jump up and shout, "I'm a CIA agent and you're all under arrest for not complying with the Confession II Act." She got an even bigger kick out of that, going on about what a "dynamite feller" I was.

We walked to the group therapy meeting together, continuing to talk and joke. We were both in good moods. She would go home that night; if the incredible rumors were true, I would go home the next day.

Sitting down in the conference room, I found myself watching the other patients. Jane was a new group member. Bill, with his aching hip, was not there. Neither Lillian nor Elaine was there. Lillian and Elaine had also missed the first session. Either participation was voluntary, or else, the meeting was only for Dr. D's patients.

We just sat around. Once again, not much was happening and there were no great revelations. Bertha began talking. As she talked, she shot me sidelong glances, watching me out of the side of her face, eyeing me both shyly and slyly. She recounted my preparation of the day's menu, going into detail about how I had crossed out "dinner" and wrote in "lunch." This started both Dr. D. and Mrs. S., the chief nurse, talking. They brought up other north-south differences. Dr. D. watched me closely as he drawled out a couple of examples of regional differences, almost as if to say that he could also follow this line of reasoning.

I squirmed in my seat, nodding politely as he and Mrs. S. talked. For the most part, the other patients sat passive and unimpressed. Although I usually liked being the center of attention, I always felt uncomfortable around Dr. D. My only hope was that I would appear sane and normal. He had my life in his hands.

North-south differences dismissed, everyone continued to sit around, waiting for someone to say something. Bertha had been a momentary hit. She once again assumed center stage. Having found her tongue, she began telling everyone about how I had wanted to play secret agent at the last group therapy session. She went into detail, repeating everything that I had told her, going on and on, even embellishing the whole thing. I cringed.

I wanted to jump in and tell everyone that it had only been a bit, a joke, something to break up the monotony. Look, Dr. D., I'm okay, I'm not really a paranoid schizophrenic. I just kept swallowing, looking at my feet, hoping that she would run out of words and that everything would be okay.

Dr. D. went professional, drawing himself up, saying, "I'm sure that I've done nothing in which the CIA would take an interest." Ignoring Bertha, he kept staring at me. I just sat there, smiling weakly. Bertha, you're a dead woman. Please be quiet. Please shut up.

Although Dr. D. didn't seem at all amused, he thankfully didn't take it seriously enough to enter into some kind of discussion with me about paranoia. He still seemed bored in his matter of fact manner. I was starting to sweat and only hoped for all of this to be over. Soon.

Thank goodness for Jane. She started to talk. She was quite verbal, going into detail about how she hadn't been able to sleep and hadn't been eating well. This, combined with the sleeping pills she took, had caused her to flip out. She took over the session, with both Dr. D. and Mrs. S. appearing to be interested and supportive.

Relieved to no longer be the focus of the meeting, I missed most of it. I was thinking about other things, mostly humor. I had gone full circle so very quickly. As small children, learning so many new things, we are forced to focus on the immediate. As adults, many of us are distracted by the past or future, thinking about other things while going through the motions of living. I had realized that the greater part of my adult life was spent in thinking, while I did other things. Dwelling on my thoughts, I would put up with my environment, not particularly noticing what I was eating or otherwise doing. Drugs had changed that. The new perceptions had forced me to center my attention on the present. While living in the present is a desirable goal for many of us, my method of doing it had proven to be counterproductive.

While most of us are multi-channeled, that is, able to hold more than one train of thought at a time, it's amazing what barren lives so many of us trick ourselves into living. During conversations, we rehearse what we're going to say rather than really attending to and listening to what others are saying. And then, there is waiting. At work, we wait for lunch or quitting time. On weekdays, we wait for weekends. During our normal, day-to-day lives, we wait for vacations or special events. Finally, some of us realize that we have spent a major portion of our lives not attending to what was really going on. We have spent our lives anticipating the future or worrying about both the past and future, without remembering to enjoy and live the present.

While I can no longer recommend drugs of any kind (I still distrust aspirin), I have also spent a considerable amount of time learning meditation techniques and other disciplines in order to allow myself to center in the present. "If you live in the present, you live forever." In order to see the kingdom of heaven, each of us must become as a small child, absorbed in the moment with each experience a new source of wonder. If we totally attend to the moments of our lives, centered in the present, time becomes a myth.

Waking up on the ward, shattered, with no memory, I had been forced to live in a present that I didn't understand. It had been a fearful hell, filled with sensory aberrations, physical pain, weakness and disorientation. In self-defense, I had been forced to delve deep inside of myself, resurrecting a former, more capable me. Gaining strength, I had been forced to continue to live in the present, as I did not have complete control of my thoughts or of my body. Simple things required my complete attention. Now, in less than a week, I was able to go multi-channel, sitting in a group therapy session, half listening, while attending to other things.

The pain of the ward experience had taught me what so many of us exposed to pain and tragedy have learned: we may need screens to protect us from the present. The ego defense mechanisms of Psychology 101 are valid and necessary. I had already gone a step further, however, falling into habitual modes of behavior, putting up with my environment while thinking about other things. Friday would be taken up in waiting for release. My eventual freedom would be a diminished one, however, restricted by haunting memories of the past. It would be quite some time before I would be able to center in a present filled with wonder.

I'm sure that Jane's story was an interesting one, deserving of my attention. My head was filled with thoughts about humor, however. Expanding on my earlier insights, I began trying to develop a theory about humor and its role in helping psychotics and severe neurotics to cope with their worlds. I was reminded about how the aides never seemed to know when to laugh during the coffee clutches. I was tired of the overly serious professionals. A good joke would do wonders for all concerned. My thoughts and ideas about humor are somewhat inconsequential. They were never fully developed. The process or the way I began thinking, however, cannot be dismissed so easily. In less than a week, I was already becoming immersed in a familiar mode of behavior. A way of thinking, developing theories, hypotheses, whatever. I was, indeed, getting better.

Dr. D. met with me after the group session. It was true. I was going to go home. My family would be there the next day. I agreed with Dr. D., that having experienced a brief but severe, disabling episode, that it would be best for me to be released in their custody, return to Chicago and live in familiar surroundings. Although I would have agreed to anything in order to be released (yes, of course I can walk on water), it did seem like a sensible solution.

I remained tight but calm with Dr. D., concentrating on his every word, nodding and agreeing with everything that he said. I said, "thank you," several times. Although a small portion of me started to bubble into manic joy, I just sat there, nodding, trying to absorb the wonder of it all. I was going home.

After meeting with him, I walked around in a daze. I was actually going to go home. For the most part, the rest of the day was spent in waiting. The day was long. It went on forever. It was a nervous, hyper, anticipatory, and sweating like a pig, endless day of waiting. I was in a real time frame, however. It was not the psychedelic infinity of the previous weekend.

Restless, I roamed the ward, talking to the nurses, to the patients, to anyone that could help pass the time. I ran into Lillian. She was able to share my excitement at going home. "See, and you kept on saying that you were never going to leave, that you were never able to go home. Bertha is going home tonight. She's getting her hair done now. She'll be so excited that you're going to go home." I had a passing thought of regret. The ward would be a different place for Lillian with both Bertha and myself gone. It was a very passing thought that I never verbalized. I was too excited. I was going home.

Lillian, and later, Bertha, were the only two patients that I talked to about my being able to go home. I wanted to go around and shake hands with some of the others, especially Jack and Beth, say something witty, something that had some closure to it. But what was there to say? I was going to go home; they weren't. Lillian and Bertha would mention it, however. "See, he's going home." The other patients would just space. There really wasn't anything to say. I remember Jack's, "I wish I could go home" and Beth's forlorn, "I'm just not ready to leave."

The anticipatory excitement of going home was almost too much for me, draining me of what little energy I had. It was difficult sitting around the television room. On the one hand, I couldn't sit still. On the other hand, I was filled with empathy for the other patients. I didn't know what to do for them, as they really couldn't share my joy. Growing weaker, I retreated to my room. I tried to read. I would do anything to pass the time. When would they be here? When could I actually leave?

I had a surprise visitor. Dr. Brian, another one of my professors, came to visit me. He was a welcome diversion. Brian was Sonia's husband. If I had been more together, I would have told him about Mrs. H., even introduced him to her. Maybe we could have compared a picture of his wife to how she looked, in order to see if there really was a resemblance. I was better, but still not well enough for those kinds of mental gymnastics.

Dr. Brian was nervous. Very. We met in my room with him sitting on a chair at the foot of my bed just as Dwayne had done. While Dwayne had cloaked himself in his professional, clinical cloth of calm, passive acceptance, Brian kept on grinning, looking as though he wanted to break into wild laughter. As people went by in the hall, his head would jerk from side to side. He was a School Psychologist, with an emphasis on theories of learning. Not being a Clinical Psychologist, he was in a strange environment. How I appreciated his visit. It must have been a difficult thing for him to do.

Jack, never losing a chance, once again butted in on my visit. Brian became even more nervous, just smiling, and then, completely ignoring Jack. We both ignored Jack, with me finally asking him to leave. Brian went through all kinds of gyrations, cocking his head, screwing up his eyes, nodding after Jack as he left. I simply nodded, saying, "Yeah, Jack has some problems."

We talked mostly small talk. Brian was out of his depth. He had been the first person that I had met when I had returned to campus for my second try at that elusive doctorate. I had seen him from a couple of blocks away and had yelled at him, running toward him, finally getting his attention. He had been surprised to see me and had asked me what I was doing there. When I told him that I was going to give graduate school one more try, he became ebullient. He had said, "Okay. That's it. You don't deserve it but you've got your fellowship back, as of now." I replied, "Hell, I didn't deserve it the first time, but I accept."

He had immediately tried to enlist me in some of his projects, telling me that with some work, I could catch my class by that June. Even though I had been gone five quarters, he told me that I was bright enough to do my thesis while taking courses and that there was even a chance that I could graduate with the rest of my class. Hah. Little did he know that I was no longer the wunderkind that I was the first time I returned to graduate school. Later, he would show me a half finished research project that could serve as my master's thesis. I became dizzy and disoriented. The notes that he gave me were in my handwriting. Just as Dwayne had saved a file of my previous work (a requested critique of the School Psychology program from a graduate student's point of view), Brian had also saved a file of mine. This file was regarding a research project I had started with some other graduate students for one of his classes. When I had left school that first time, I returned to a manager's position in Chicago. All of my files for the projects I had been working on over a year earlier had been neatly boxed and saved. First Chicago, then Dwayne, and then Brian … I began thinking that it was my karma to go through life, forced to return to all of the places that I had been, forced to complete all of the things that I had started. Even today, I have such regret. How I wish that I could have fulfilled Brian and Dwayne's expectations of me. Actually, how I wish that I could have fulfilled my own expectations of me.

Sitting there, Brian was wearing a fur-lined coat that was almost as out of place in Florida as my parka was. That's what I remember the most about his visit: Brian sitting there, too nervous to take off his coat, constantly smiling. It was good to visit with him, to talk about the other students and life in general. It was nice of him to come.

After he left, I thought about him. He was kind of a card. Liam and I had always joked about him. Still, he has given me two of my fondest memories. We had had a seminar on attribution theory. There were only a handful of us in the class. We met at his house, sitting in a circle on the floor. He had put a couple of six packs of beer, a pitcher of lemonade and some pretzels in the center of the circle. "Okay, help yourself. The purpose of this seminar is to explore how we think." Having left big business as a senior analyst, forced to endure the low-life status of being a first year graduate student, I was filled with thanks. I had finally arrived. This is what I had always imagined advanced study in psychology to be. A group of us, treated as adults, were going to explore the processes of the human mind.

My second memory is also related to how we think. Between classes, a group of us had been walking around campus. Brian's little daughter had been talking to some flowers and a tree, saying everything that came into her head. One of the other students had mused about what kind of society we would have, if everyone did that, even as adults. Brian had replied, "Yeah. Some people call it thinking. We just don't do it aloud."

That afternoon, we had a special treat. There was an excursion to another part of the hospital. We were going to be able to go and see a movie. Well, sort of. Indicative of my new status and growing wellness, a nurse explained to me that my going with the group was optional. I quickly agreed to go. I would do anything to pass the time, anything to get off of the ward.

Mrs. S. and another nurse accompanied us. We were a motley crew. Dressed in the blue, ward outfits, not able to wear our street clothes, we all looked a little worse than normal, as we straggled through the halls. When we got to the showing room, we sat together, part of a larger group of staff and patients. People eyed us, quickly looking away. A young male and female were showing the films. I took them to be graduate students, probably getting advanced degrees in social work. They seemed nice enough, although they couldn't meet my eyes or those of the other ward patients. I guess that they had been warned that the crazies were coming.

The films were about Florida. They appeared to be "fun in the sun," promotional films. Once again, as with the physical therapy, I was struck by the irony of my situation. I looked over the people in the room. The ward patients sat quietly, slumped and tired looking. The other viewers appeared to be aware of us, but avoided us by concentrating on the film. Mrs. S. and the other nurse were like mother hens, first herding us into our seats and then watching over us. The graduate student running the projector had some initial trouble getting it started. He explained what the film was about, avoiding our eyes as a couple of us turned and watched him.

My attention wandered back and forth, from the film of beautiful young people splashing in a swimming pool, to those of us watching it. A day or two earlier, I would have probably sat there softly crying, filled with an intense desire to get outside and join the people in the film. Now, knowing that I was going home, I was struck by how different these young, healthy bodies appeared compared to us beaten down, slumped over patients. And here I was, one of the beaten down patients. Although I had cleaned up my act while on the ward, I was certainly as beaten down as any of the other patients.

The rest of my attention was centered on my body. I was nervous and tense, still reacting to my medication. Neither the pain nor the rubbery feeling was as intense as the last few days. It was more as though emery cloth were being rubbed on the inside of my bones. Not sharp or anywhere near as painful as the bone crunching of the last few days, it was still uncomfortable. I tensed myself against it, hoping only that it wouldn't get any worse and that I wouldn't do anything that would embarrass me in front of all these people. I was too close to going home to go ballistic and appear abnormal.

The movies were finished without incident. None of us flipped out or otherwise made a commotion. We straggled back to the ward. How different we appeared, first contrasted to the other patients and then, even more so, to the bright, healthy people in the film.

I saw Bertha for the last time later that afternoon. She looked good. She was wearing a new dress and freshly applied makeup and sported a tightly coiffed, new hairdo. I told her how good she looked. She became even happier and started flirting with me, touching my arm and shoulder. Her game playing was okay. I was well enough that I didn't flinch at her touch. She was as happy for me as I was for her. We talked for a little bit; then she rushed off to finish her packing.

It was time for supper. Just as I was going to get my tray, a nurse came up to me and told me that someone was there to see me. Since it wasn't visiting hours, they wouldn't let him in to see me. I could, however, say hello to him at the ward entrance. It was Ben. He was a fellow graduate student and a good friend. We had become close that first time around at graduate school. We had been the two old guys, my 28 to his 30, both of us redoing our lives to get that doctorate. After a rough start, almost not making it that first quarter (he received two "Cs," a third one and he would have been dropped from the program), he had done well. He would go on to become the first graduate student to receive a dual doctorate in School Psychology and in Clinical Psychology.

I had spent many hours tutoring him in statistics (he still received a C after all was said and done) and had argued with the team of professors who taught the Advanced Learning class (they had averaged his grades on the three segments of the course—two of which he had passed, treating them as a ratio scale which was a no-no, but they would not change his grade from a C) on his behalf. He barely scraped out a B on the second required course in statistics and was then home free as the clinical work was easy for him. There had been my promise and his perseverance. Thankfully, one of us made it.

It was good to see him. He was a deeply serious, sensitive human being. His dad's emotional problems and breakdown had been a major reason for him wanting to obtain a doctorate in the helping sciences. His wife was a treasure. I had thought that she was one of the nurse's at the emergency entrance when I was admitted. We talked quickly as I could only see him for a minute. We talked first through the partially open door and then, with an aide closing it, through a glass window. He wished me well and told me how surprised and sorry he had been when Dwayne had told him about what had happened to me.

Like the fool that I was, caught up in only my own problems, I told him that I now knew what his father had gone through. At the look of deep pain and sadness in his face, I immediately regretted my words. We talked for only a few minutes. I would never see him again.

I walked back to the television sitting room, feeling good about seeing him, but upset by my words and his reaction to them. I would have to stop my total self-absorption and begin to look beyond myself and remember the feelings of others.

My tray of food was waiting for me. It was filled to over flowing. As a child, I had been admonished to eat all of my food and to clean my plate. Almost always, even when the food was mediocre or an over-bearing hostess had forced too much on me, I would still try to finish whatever I have been given. More than just childhood training, I believe food to be precious, even sacred. It certainly shouldn't be wasted. Jack, throwing a tantrum, or just in one of his ornery moods, would occasionally waste a whole plate of food. I would invariably cringe.

I stared at the food. Surely, I didn't order all of this. I looked around to see if anyone was playing a trick on me. No, all of the other patients had their own food and were intently eating. Oh, well. I dug in. Making a valiant effort, there was just too much. I ate most of it. I even tried to give a dessert or two away, although no one else wanted anything.

After supper, I sat there, stuffed. Lillian came by, a sneaky grin on her face. She asked me how my supper had been. I answered, "Fine," still not catching on. She kept on hanging around, kept on hinting about the food. Finally, it dawned on me. "Well, there was an awful lot of it. I couldn't finish it." She burst out laughing. Bertha had done it. That morning, she had changed my menu, adding all kinds of things.

Oh boy. Wait until I see her. Now, I owed her double. First of all, she had told all those stories about me at the group therapy menu. Then, she had fooled around with my supper order. I had told her about my needing to finish my food and about how upset I would get when Jack would waste his. She had been too busy and distracted, too happy, for me to mention the group meeting when I had seen her before supper. Now, however, I would get even with her. Lillian told me that I might still be able to catch her. I went looking for her. I missed her, though. She had already left.

When visiting hours finally arrived, Liam and Linda came in with a rush, all excited and happy. They looked good. Both of them were wearing clean clothes. Liam had carefully brushed his long, floppy hair. Linda, although she used it sparingly, had fresh makeup on. They looked as though they were going out some place.

Although I couldn't meet their high energy level, I felt good, just a little shaky. I had already taken my medication and was beginning to feel it. For some reason, early afternoon and mid-evening were my worst times regarding adverse reactions to the medication. While I have vivid recollections of taking my medication in the early morning and right around visiting hours, I'm not sure if I also took it at midday. Although relatively mild, the evening reactions were immediate and noticeable. My early afternoon crunching (Tuesday, Wednesday, and to a lesser extent, Thursday, were all fearsome) was either a delayed reaction or else I was given medication three times a day, which seems more likely.

They had all kind of news. Yes, my mother, sister and brother-in-law were all coming. In fact, they would be there that night. Liam and Linda would have to leave early, in order to pick them up at the airport. Yes, I was going to be released the next morning. It was all arranged. My family would meet with Dr. D. on Saturday morning. I was definitely going home.

Oh boy. Excitement. And they were there to share it with me. Hugs and kisses. I was going home. Whew.

The three of us were all excited and bubbly. I kidded them about looking especially good for my family. They feigned surprise. "Hey, come on, we always look good." For the first time, the thought crossed my mind. I wondered at my mother's reaction to finding out that Linda and I were living together. Oh well. We were adults. Both my mother and my sister thought that Linda was the greatest. Hell, they must have already known about our living arrangements as Linda had been in constant phone contact with them.

Liam and Linda would probably take my family out to dinner. Everyone would probably stay at my apartment. It would all work out.

The rest of our visit was taken up with them asking about how I felt. No, the facial problems hadn't returned. I felt as good as I could under the circumstances.

The three of us kept on talking about anything that came to mind. We went over the impending visit, how I felt, and what Linda and Liam had been doing. It was a good time of shared happiness. It was as though they hated to leave. It was too good to just sit and talk and touch. Surprisingly, I was the one that became worried about them being too late for the plane. I got up several times to check the clock over the reception desk as none of us wore watches. They kept on telling me not to worry about it. The airport was only some 10 or 15 minutes away and planes were always late. I wasn't so sure.

Finally, I just let it go and settled down to enjoying their visit. All too soon, it was time for them to go. Time had switched on me. Instead of endless waiting for time to slowly pass, I now wanted every last possible second with them. Liam finally got caught up in not wanting to be late for the plane and said that he and Linda had to go. I walked them to the exit. We all hugged each other one last time. And then, they were gone. With their departure, I was immediately let down. I was too excited to just sit around. The other patients still had visitors. I wandered around my room, quickly getting my things together. I really didn't have that much. Although Linda had constantly brought me things, the cigarettes and candy had been devoured. Most of my clothes were used. It was simple enough to throw them in a bag. I carefully arranged my remaining clean clothes on one side of my closet. I arranged and accounted for all of my toilet articles. I even remembered to dig out the notes that I had hidden. Well, there you have it. Five minutes of waiting were taken up in doing something. I did it a second time, burning up another couple of minutes.

Wander here. Sit there. Talk a bit. Join the coffee clutch as visiting hours ended. Tell Lillian about how I would be leaving the next morning. I watched the other patients sit in their private worlds, spacing to who knows where, unable to share my joy. I felt some empathy with them and some sadness at my getting better so quickly while they remained wherever they were.

But then I would space into the thrill of release. I could feel my growing nervousness and some discomfort. Disregard it. I was going home. I was leaving. No real closure. Who cares? I was going home. The hell with the present and all of this foolishness, I was going home. Come on, time, do a number. Let it be twelve hours later. Let me be free.

Eventually, it was time for sleep. Ah, sweet dreams. On the morrow, I would be out of here. Thank you all, each and every one. May God bless us.

Thus ended my seventh and last day on the ward.

GETTING OUT

I was ready and waiting. My belongings were stacked neatly on my bed. I had gotten ready with care, shaving closely, brushing and combing my hair several times. I splashed cold water on my face more than once. There was nothing that I could do about my deep, sunken eyes. Wandering around, I continually took deep breaths, remembering to breathe through my nose, trying my best to relax. I was sweating so badly that after an hour of nervous pacing I had to change my shirt. Linda and my family finally arrived. Linda was acting as tour guide, leading the group. My sister followed her, holding my mother, helping her to walk. My brother-in-law, Tom, was in the background, bringing up the rear. Linda was the first to see me, exclaiming, "Oh, there he is. There he is."

Oh, how I remember that fearful look of concern and compassion in my mother's eyes. It's funny. Except for Linda and Liam, no one could really look me in the eye. Now, I had trouble looking my family in the eye. I broke eye contact with my mother. My attention centered on her feet. I had forgotten. She had just had foot surgery on both of them. Her feet were wrapped in bandages and she was wearing special, white, open shoes. She had trouble walking.

I was filled with deep shame. My mother, in her sixties, only able to hobble, forced to come and rescue her young, healthy son. She, who had spent so much of her life living for my sister and me, was probably in greater pain than I was.

I was immediately across the corridor, hugging my mom. I then hugged my sister and awkwardly shook hands with Tom. Linda stood by my side, holding my hand, as we all exchanged "hellos" and asked "How are you?" My mom was all concerned about me and kept asking me how I felt. There was nothing to say, but that I was okay. I was more concerned about her feet than my condition. She looked a little drawn and in pain.

My family began telling me about their airplane ride and how Liam and Linda had picked them up at the airport. They had all gone out to eat, at one of those inexpensive steak places. My mom, as was her wont, went on and on about how good the food had been. They had all stayed at our apartment, with my mom and Linda sleeping in our bed while Tom and Grace slept in the living room. Yes, the airplane ride had been okay, although there had been that one stretch of turbulence. Yes, they all fit in the apartment. It had been fine. They had slept well after the adventure of getting here. Yes, they had eaten that morning. Linda had fried them some eggs.

They went on and on about their trip. It was easier for them to talk about themselves than it was for me to talk about myself. We were still standing in the hall. Very quickly, Dr. D. was there. A nurse came to tell us that we were all to meet with him in the conference room. It was the one used for the group therapy sessions.

We trooped into the room. Everyone's attention immediately centered on Dr. D. My mother sat at rigid attention, totally concentrating on his every word. As he talked to us, explaining my condition, I listened with only half an ear. He explained that I was being given some anti-psychotic medication to take home with me and that I should take it as directed. I should get a local doctor and see him periodically. He talked to them, not me. It gave me a chance to look my family over without making eye contact with them. How glad I was that they were there. They all looked normal, the way that I remembered them.

I was relieved. On the way to the conference room, walking across the hall, the light from the room had spilled across the floor in a light, golden-like orange path, highlighting my poor mother's feet. I had flinched, but no, this wasn't the time or place for hallucination #356A.

When the meeting was over, my family was very solicitous of me. They insisted on carrying my things. We went down to the first floor. The women went to the administration offices to check me out. Tom and I went outside to wait for them.

OUTSIDE! Oh my! Thank you Lord. Thank you so very much. We stood there, looking off in the distance. It was very humid with a very light rain falling intermittently. It was warmish. It was northern Florida in February. I took deep breaths of the warm, humid air. It was incredibly fresh and beautiful. The ward had been clean and air conditioned. The air on the ward, however, had been nothing like this. Even now, I can still smell the way the air was when I first got outside. It was so very good, so very beautiful. With deep thanks I swore that I would never ever screw up again. No one would ever again have any cause for putting me in a cage. Tom and I stood around, making small talk. Small talk. I could even chat about minor things. The life and death struggles were over. My strongest memory about my discharge was simply standing there, talking with Tom in the fresh air.

After quite some time, Linda, my mom, and my sister joined us, all talking at once about the endless red tape. Tom drove. There was some debate as whether to make two trips as my Volkswagen beetle wasn't made for five adults. "No, no, we can make it in one trip." My mother and sister sat in the back holding my things while Linda sat on my lap in the front. Crowded, we slowly made it across town. Everything, including the streets, the houses, the cars, all of the foliage, appeared to be bright and new. I loved it.

At the apartment, there was limited chaos. Things were scattered here and there. They had already started packing. Everyone immediately got business-like and busy, packing here, moving things there. No one would let me help. I was just to get better. The plan was a simple one. Tom and Grace would drive my VW to Chicago. Linda and I would use their plane tickets and leave the next day with my mother. There was some question as to when Tom and Grace would leave, as he would have to work on Monday morning. It was about a 20-hour drive. It would depend on how soon the packing was finished and how they felt.

My sister was scrubbing down the kitchen. My mother was helping Linda pack. Tom was moving and carrying things. I insisted on going and telling the building managers that Linda and I would be moving out. Everyone said that I shouldn't worry about anything and that they would take care of it. Although weak, I couldn't just sit there. I insisted.

I went to the managers' apartment, proud that I was free and able to do things on my own. When I got to their apartment, there was a touch of Deja vu. As usual, the young, married pair was sprawled on the couch, watching television. It was my third or fourth time meeting with them. Each time, they had been in virtually the same position with the television going. I felt nervous and tense, not at my actions, but just in general. I had an urge to grate my teeth and found myself talking slightly out of the side of my mouth. Once again, in a very limited fashion, my medication was doing its thing.

I told them that I had suffered a nervous breakdown, that I had been forced to drop out of school, that Linda and I would be leaving the next day and that any paperwork would be taken care of by my family. They seemed nonplussed, even bored. The wife just asked me to remember to return the keys. On the way back to my apartment, I was struck by how an eternity of hell to me had only been a brief week out of their lives. They probably didn't even know that I had been gone.

Eventually, everything was taken care of. The VW was packed to overflowing. Tom and Grace would leave that evening, planning to drive all night. Before they left, we got a bucket of take-out chicken and several side orders. Liam and Bobby would come over and say goodbye.

Linda and I joked about the chicken. It was a nice memory. One evening we had eaten some eggs and were still hungry. We had ordered some chicken. We would always joke about it. "Which came first, the chicken or the egg? Why, the eggs, and then we ate the chicken."

Liam and I had no great words to say to each other. He and Bobby had come over, both looking a little stoned. I just hoped that my mom wouldn't notice. Bobby was quiet and sat to the side. Liam and I did a lot of well wishing. There wasn't really much to say. We made plans for him to drive us to the airport the next day. He had to work and would use his cab.

Sleep was uneventful, although I tossed and turned in nervous anticipation of the next day. Strange dreams tried to impinge on my consciousness. I was too up, however, to worry about them. They receded into the dim back corridors of my mind.

Going to the airport, getting on the plane, waving goodbye to Liam, a true friend, I was nervous and tense. I was beginning to come on to my medication and felt myself tensing against it. It had been a major question, discussed at length with Linda. Should I take my pills? Would something happen on the plane? We finally agreed that it would be better if I took them. It was okay, however. No flip outs. There was just a little extra tension, but no mind-blowing pain or hallucinations.

Back in Chicago, Linda and I would stay with my mother. She would use my room and I would sleep on the couch. Although I was still crippled with diminished faculties, we began making plans to get married.

I would go to a new doctor and receive a full physical. He came highly recommended. He was a medical doctor, who worked with some mental patients, but not a psychiatrist. I was in good shape, except for nervous tension. I explained my various symptoms and told him that I seemed to have a number of adverse reactions to my medication. He looked up my medicine in the *Physician Desk Reference*, a large thick book that included the typical side effects of the various prescription drugs. Yep, there they were, most of the things that I was complaining about were listed as possible side effects of the medication I was taking.

I seemed quite normal, although I still had severe problems with my fine motor dexterity. My hands were especially bad. I seemed so normal that he decided to put me on Librium, telling me to decrease and then stop taking the anti-psychotic medicine.

I began hallucinating once again. Without the anti-psychotic medicine, I was still nuts. I never told anyone about it, not even my mother or Linda. The tranquilizer and familiar surroundings helped me to put up with the sensory aberrations. The ward had taught me well. No matter what was happening, no matter if I were hallucinating my guts out, I would never let anyone know. I would never spend another week on a closed ward.

Linda and I got married in May. We had a glorious honeymoon, borrowing Tom and Grace's camper truck, traveling around the country for some six to eight weeks.

I would return to graduate school in Illinois that fall. I was afraid to return to Florida. Both Linda and I agreed that I could only be happy as a college teacher, doing research and writing. Taking the entrance exams, I had scored high. At the time, my scores were the best in the history of the department. I had always enjoyed taking standardized tests, sort of a test of will and capability. I prepared for them much like a gymnast or diver preparing for an athletic event. This time, however, when taking the graduate entrance exams, rather than being quick and facile, I had to dig my fingernails into the palms of my hands, bite my lips and curse the answers out of my memory banks. Taking a test was no longer the quick and easy task of my pre-ward days. I would receive a doctorate in Education, not Psychology. I did well enough, obtaining 10 A's and two B's in 12 courses. I completed a highly statistical dissertation on teaching effectiveness. My doctoral chairman said that my comprehensive exams were the best he had ever read in more than ten years of advising doctoral candidates.

It would have been a good story, one of triumph, with me overcoming impossible odds. The bright student breaks down, rebuilds himself, and then comes back as a success. Hah. Trained to teach high school teachers how to teach, I obtained my doctorate at one of the few times in history when this country didn't need high school teachers, let alone someone to teach them. Not only did I not get a college teaching position, I was not even able to obtain an interview.

It was the last straw. I would break up with Linda, leaving her with our meager possessions. I would go off in the distance, with no car, few possessions and near penniless.

Later, after finding work, I would try to reconcile with her. She would have none of it. She had found someone else, a loving, gentle high school teacher. Sort of the kind of guy that I thought I would always become.

It had been my hope to teach school (albeit college) and live in a college town with a white picket fence around the backyard, raising a couple of kids and having a good life. To this end, I had gotten Linda out of the city, away from her druggie roommate, and had begun sharing with her what I thought would be a better life for both of us. It never happened, at least not for me. Except for one class, I would never teach college. I would never remarry, never live the good life I had always imagined for myself.

While we had shared so much love and so many good things, I had also given Linda fear and pain, breaking into violence a couple of times. The person that she had loved so very much had been broken along the way. I would go on with my life, she with hers.

It was only a week on a ward, such a short time. I may have gotten out, but I have never really left. While time has healed the sharpness of it, my demons still lurk beneath the layers of my rational mind. May the dear Lord forgive me my weakness; I can only hope.

AFTER IMAGES

AFTER IMAGES

I was certainly not well when I was released from the ward. For the next six months I would basically rest and "get better." These are some random memories from my early time off of the ward. The rips in my consciousness would slowly abate. These after images have stayed with me. They are not necessarily in any order. Welcome to being schizoid.

Standing on my mother's porch in the crisp, Chicago winter, I bent over and scooped up some snow, methodically packing it into a hard, round ball. Straightening, I lobbed the missile at the metal clothes pole some 20 feet away. Ker bang. A hit. Curious, since I never have had an arm that could hit anything, I slowly fashioned another snowball and let it fly. Ker bang. Another hit. The arc was beautiful, the motion righteous. A vibrational plane had been eased out of the universe, across which an extension of myself (cleverly disguised as a ball of snow) unerringly traveled. Excited, I bent to the task, remembering to slow down and take a deep breath or two and then let fly another one. Ker bang. Oh my! Another hit. Easier than falling out of bed. Once again, the ease, the motion, the symmetry were there.

Reruns began filling my head. There was Robin Hood hitting an arrow within an arrow to beat the bad guys. Zen archery: "Ah, sweet student, the key is concentration. Become as one with the target. Allow the arrow to move from self to self." Drumbeats and trumpets filled my head.

I fell away from wherever I had been. The next snowball fell into a neighbor's yard. Successive misses proved to me that the hitch in my arm was still there, my eye was still bad and I really couldn't hit anything. If someone ever asks you why we settle for less than what we really are or can be, a simple reply of, "It's easier, somehow," will suffice.

Linda and I stood hugging each other. We were in the middle of a flat, empty, snow-covered field that was surrounded by frost-laden trees. It was a forest preserve, a few miles from my mother's house. Linda was facing south, I north with the moon (a pale silver in the light blue sky) directly east and the sun directly west. I was at the center of the only universe for which I had given everything that I had ever had. It seemed right, the terror of the ward momentarily forgotten. Tears filled my eyes as memories of the pain and anguish of the ward and awareness of my broken head and body did not allow the embrace to continue.

It was a follow-up visit to my local doctor. He had discontinued my anti-psychotic medicine due to my complaints about the physical problems it caused me. Now, I was only taking Librium, a light tranquilizer. Although everything was bright and I was edgy, I was maintaining.

As I approached the receptionist, I was startled. She was sitting behind glass with an open circle cut in the glass, enabling us to speak to each other. It appeared that she was sitting in the dark and the glass separating us was covered with frost. Yet, she did not appear to be cold. I held my tongue. This was obviously some kind of altered perception. She told me to take a seat and told me the doctor would be with me shortly. I sat quietly, reading a magazine when I heard what I took to be a female patient screaming. It was a scream of absolute terror that raised goose pimples on my arms. I nervously looked around but the few other people in the waiting room were all acting normal. I ignored the screams and sat quietly, breathing through my nose. I would never ever be confined to any ward again. Thankfully, when I saw the doctor, it was only him and me and there were no screaming patients. A lot of smiles and "I'm okay" and I was out of there. Except for occasional blips, I was getting better. No one would ever know that I was still having problems.

I was lying in bed, mom a room away and Linda two. I felt the labored, troubled sleep of my mother. My awareness reached for Linda. She was deeply asleep, many oceans away from wherever I was, untroubled, buried in herself. Shivering, I turned to the problem of trying to get some sleep.

I picked the car up a couple of blocks away. The radio was loud; it might as well have been pressed against my ear. Arggh!!! Ack! The sound filled my head and then I was the radio, or rather, the radio was a subset of me. Energy coursed through my wires and transistors. It passed quickly with me jerking back to the comforts of my bed.

Shivering worse, frightened, unable to sleep, I began lying on my back, arms at my side, assuming the "dead man" yoga position, dropping into passive, positive acceptance. It was then that I felt him coming off of the walls, out of the blankets. I tried to allow it to happen ("flowing is," "this too shall pass," "non-attachment is the secret to enlightenment"), but it only became worse.

My grandfather, in his 80's, suffering much, confined to a nursing home, had come to visit me. My skin turned, shriveling, my teeth left, my gums hardened and I became old, very old. Starting to resist, but remembering (oh dear, sweet Jesus, what did you mean by "do not resist evil") passive, positive acceptance, I allowed it to happen. I literally became a shrunken, old man, with the energy, youth and vitality squeezing out of me. My breathing fell to my grandfather's half of a lung as I lay trembling, now curled in a fetal position, scared shitless. I fell into a deep sleep.

Some weeks after I got off of the ward, Linda and I went to my bank located in downtown Chicago. It was connected to the Northwestern train station. We took the elevated (called the ell or subway as it went both above and below the ground) downtown. It was a shaky trip with me all hyper and nervous. Everything looked bright and different, although these were my familiar surroundings that were supposed to allow me to stop hallucinating. Basically, I had no responsibilities other than remembering not to freak out. Although the whole ride was testy, we made it to the bank without incident. It was there that the trouble began.

I was standing in line. Linda was off somewhere. The two gentlemen standing ahead of me in line were talking to each other in some foreign language (German?). Hard to explain, but I had the illusion that I was able to understand what they were saying while also knowing that I did not know what language they were speaking. It appeared that they began arguing about what day it was and then, oops, I was back on the ward. Time travelers? The exact day became quite important. I smelled a powerful, dangerous, drugging gas with both of them becoming less substantial. I became dizzy and altered; Linda came over and joined me. I turned to her, whimpering that we had to get out of there (a small portion of my mind was aware that after 10-15 minutes of waiting, I was almost next in line—I was getting better). She showed no surprise, not arguing with me, taking me by the arm and getting both of us out of there.

We stopped and sat down in the breezeway that connected the bank and some stores to the train station. There was room to sit along the sides of the breezeway. Having worked downtown, I had traveled this route many times. We sat there, with me all sweating and hyper and with Linda holding on to me, ready to hug me, to listen to me or do whatever her man needed.

An old woman, white haired and feeble, came walking slowly toward us hunched over her cane. Inadvertently, I began staring at her. Oh no. She began dissolving, coming apart at the seams. My world went tilt. She became, for all practical purposes, an amoeba. I began screaming, "oh no!" in my head. Only in my head, however, as nothing that ever happened to me again, no matter how outrageous, would ever give anyone an excuse for locking me up again, not even melting people, for if nothing else, I could hold my tongue. I began blinking furiously. The third or fourth blink was magic; I was able to see her as an old lady once again. Linda knew that something had happened, what with me going rigid and all. A look at my face even brought fear to her eyes. I buried my head in my hands and mumbled, "Let's get out of here." We did.

Drugs gave me visuals and audios (increased sensitivity and/or hallucinations); it took insanity to give me a full-blown olfactory. My nephew needed to take driving lessons to either get car insurance or to obtain it at reduced rates. Something like that. Driving along, I spotted a sign announcing free driving lessons for teen-agers. Curious, I stopped to investigate.

The office was closed and the door was locked. Peering inside, I could make out the dim lines of what appeared to be large embroidered traffic signs (stop, yield, and so forth). Amazed, I thought that this was a childish way to teach teen-agers and commented to myself, "This looks fishy." Oooops. My nostrils were filled with the pungent odor of fish; it was as though I were standing in an open fish market. Talk about easy. Shaken, I left.

One of the most courageous things that I would do in those early days off of the ward is to walk four blocks to the neighborhood drug store in order to buy cigarettes. At that time, my only duty in life was to drive Linda to work and to get better. Lying around the house, "getting better," trying to figure things out, attempting to minimize my paranoia and sensory aberrations, write (impossible), watch daytime television (difficult), read (hard to do for more than a few minutes), I would occasionally get myself together and take a walk for the daily paper or cigarettes.

Inevitably, I would do this when there was a tinge of suspense and danger connected with this simple act. When I was on the verge, so to speak. I had big mountains to weary over such as a couple of dogs whose barking would startle me, the possibility of kids getting out of school with their nervous energy and quick movements allowing me to almost lose it, and of course, there was always the problem of maybe having to have to talk to someone.

Additionally, "change" and "matches," both connected with buying cigarettes, were standbys in my altered state of awareness. For example, the elderly woman behind the counter would say, "Here's your <u>matches</u>", and flip me a <u>match</u>book. The covers were red, white and blue, with a picture of an enlisted man and the legend, "Save our Prisoners of War." Oh sure. Match. P.O.W. My match. My world would go tilt and I'd be back on the ward doing P.O.W. Or instead of flipping out over the matches, I would be doing some nightmare in my head, imagining myself becoming all kinds of terrible, wasted things and she would say, "Here's your CHANGE." I, of course, connected her words to what was going on in my head. Sure. Why not?

On one occasion, I stopped to browse through the paperbacks at the drugstore. I picked up one about a woman breaking a heroin habit. She talked of a gentle giant that protected her, that granted bliss, but who eventually turned into a bone crushing force satisfied only by more junk. Reading a few pages about her experiences, I did that move-over transition and began living her delusion, seeing and feeling her giant. The effect was similar to the oranges and reds of the knockout shot I had received in the emergency ward. Complete fear. I realized that I was experiencing what she was describing. Would I become a heroin addict? I didn't bother buying the book.

And then there was Linda. How it turned. In the weeks preceding my breakdown, she had been or at least had seemed to have been such a mystical being. She had been so "right on." Synchronous. If I were doing a bad head trip, her look, touch, and words were just what I needed to bring myself to a better present. If I were into something good, she would simply join me, sharing it with me. This harmony became totally discordant.

For example, on one occasion, she was at the front door, getting the paper, while we were talking about something. I had been momentarily rational when we were talking, but then I slipped away and began doing mind horror. I fell into the anti-war movie, *Johnny* or was it *Johnny goes to War*? It was about a conscious being that is completely paralyzed due to a war injury during World War I. He has no arms or legs and is just a head and a torso. Everyone thinks that he's an unknowing vegetable and acts accordingly, with him lying there for years. Having no lip movement, his mind screams over and over again, "Kill me. Kill me." And then I was there, from small talk with Linda to remembering the movie, to becoming Johnny. I became a lump of cortex, screaming in my head, "Kill me. Kill me."

I began surfacing from this experience, shaken and dizzy with a voice in my head still screaming, "Kill me." Only seconds had passed. Linda, who had simply walked across the room, while I did eons of mind time, turned and brought me back to the here and now by replying to a statement I had previously made to her. Her simple, "Yes, I think you're right," only brought more horror. In the pre-breakdown days, it would have been a, "Oh, don't be silly!" as if she knew what I had been thinking, or she would have seen my glazed eyes and quickly cleared them with a hug. These occasional rips in the fabric of my rational mind were not the worst of it. Subtler, but worse, was the dependency.

There I was, wrapped in blankets, smothered in weakness and passivity, taking a simple television program and weaving archetypical themes out of it, cascading through Greek mythology, Hinduism and more. Doing this, while my mother had a chance to have her baby with her once again, treating me as such. There she was, mothering me, babying me, with my mind rebelling (I'm a grown man!), while my state allowed it.

It was even worse with Linda. She could enter the room and I would need to touch her, need to hug her. Too often, rationality would drain out of me. I would melt, merging with her clothing, then her, then with a version of her that she will probably never know, becoming a mindless, clinging, vibrational parasite. I could feel a tangible energy flooding out of me as I filled her with my love and essence. She always grooved on it; while the dependent infant that I had become would repulse me.

I began seeing a different her. She had been my OTHER; some mystical being that was my mirror image, my female side, my complement, and the yin to my yang. Whatever. Now, I saw an everyday her, magnified by my childlike sensitivity. I would pick her up from work (at this time, she sold clothes at a suburban plaza near my mother's house), and she would sit in the car, legs crossed, bouncing a knee, chewing gum (goddesses don't chew gum, even I knew that), talking about what had happened at coffee break, about customers, ad infinitum.

In my delusion, I was still doing life and death battles, living on the edge, fighting portions of myself that still didn't work. In addition to the jagged, oddly spliced films that continually tried to bubble up from my subconscious, there was the more immediate problem of getting my hands to work. I was not that interested in what happened during her coffee break.

In those days, weeks and months following my release from the ward, I was certainly not well. In addition to the mental and physical disabilities, there was also the rage that occasionally broke to the surface.

For example, several weeks after my release from the hospital, I received a supplemental bill for my x-ray. There was no mention of the spot on my lung (obvious, if anyone had read the x-ray as I had had tuberculosis as a child and take an abnormal chest x-ray to this day, let alone so many years ago while on the ward).

As I stared at the bill, dim recollections of my god-awful x-ray trip while on the ward ripped through my consciousness. Staring at the bill, I was seized with an uncontrollable rage. I crumpled it into a ball, threw it across the room and began screaming, totally upset and frightening both Linda and my mother. I was finally able to control my anger and tell them why I was so very upset. Although they listened to me and tried to comfort me, the fear in their eyes had nothing to do with the x-ray bill.

My search for truth and understanding was forgotten as I worked on survival. One brief sojourn into trying to get to the bottom of what happened still haunts me, however.

I had driven Linda to work and had started home. It was mid-morning of a gray, overcast day. I felt very tense, more nervous than usual. I was slightly altered and felt very stoned. I also felt expectant, as though something very important was going to happen. I really didn't want to go home. As I drove along, I turned here, then there, and then, back another way. I found myself crisscrossing Chicago's north side and adjoining suburbs. I drove and drove, aimlessly turning this way and that.

I began thinking, "This is it. This is it." Although not as strong and certainly not with the determination and energy that occurred when I committed myself, I began feeling as if some confrontation, some climax or catharsis was about to take place. I continued to drive and then felt myself being drawn in a certain direction. Memories of the ward flooded my awareness. I continued on, however, feeling relatively safe in my car, driving through more or less familiar neighborhoods. Pre-ward, I had gotten stoned many times, wandering aimlessly into "happenings." It was something like that, with me operating on close to remote control. I began driving with a purpose, feeling that this, indeed, would be a moment of truth.

I ended up on Chicago's north side, somewhere around north Clark Street. It felt right, with me almost tugged toward some destination. I parked the car and realized that I was heading for some kind of shop or store. It was in a stand-alone building. The cloud cover had disappeared. In bright sun, I started across the street.

As I reached the center of the street, my foot on the dividing line, I looked up. There was an empty lot next to the building. To the right of the store at the back of the empty lot there was a large wooden fence, painted a dark green. Scrawled across the fence with what looked to be white paint was a large graffiti, "Linda and Vinnie?" I stopped, momentarily stunned.

My attention shifted to the shop. Just where was I going? I took another step. What was that in the window? There was some kind of a demon's head or witch mask. I could now read the writing on the door. Oh shoot. It was an occult shop. Better a Buddhist temple or an ice cream store.

I stopped, cursing under my breath. Enough was enough. I turned around and began walking back to my car. Back on the sidewalk, walking along with my head down, there was some writing etched in the cement of the walk. "Linda and Don." Linda had been going out with someone named Don when I had met her. He had been quickly forgotten as we were swept away in ecstasy.

I shook my head, continued on to my car and drove home. Enough was more than enough. My mind, of course, tried to make much ado of the whole incident. A message from God or was it the devil's laughter? Probably just another coincidence in a life filled with the improbable. Years later, curious, I would not be able to find the shop, the fence or the sidewalk. Just as well, although Linda, after leaving me and a difficult marriage, did marry someone named Don. You count. I'm tired.

Worst of all, was the fall from grace. I still believe. There *are* beings, who <u>do</u> identify with *spirit*, who can control brain waves and bodily illnesses, who can project essence through time and space, who do, with awareness, travel through the many levels of this onionskin universe of ours. There *are* people, who through the grace of God and the law of karma, do **know**. Okay, there must be. I no longer know, no longer travel in those circles, so to speak.

Perhaps vainglorious and stupid, I still feel that I had come so close to something very wonderful. I had lost control, shattering myself along the way. Broken, I had been forced to be reborn in the only real world that I have ever known, a material world of rationalism and dualism, ignorance and confusion. If only I would have known, I would have done everything in my power to avoid spending a week on a ward.

Ray was a good friend of mine who I had known for some dozen years before my week on the ward. Linda and I visited him and his wife on the west coast during our honeymoon. We spent several days with them. Ray, of all of the straight people that I knew, probably understood what I had been trying to do the best.

Ray: I don't know. You seem the same.

Me: Yes. Thank you. I feel the same.

Ray: I mean, you're just like the old you. You act like you always did. You still like to drink beer and shoot pool. You seem the same.

Me: Yes.

Ray: I mean, I think that you wanted to be different. But you seem the same.

Me: Yes, of course.

ABOUT THE AUTHOR

ABOUT THE AUTHOR

Vincent Blade Douglas is a former high school teacher (math, Russian, psychology) and system analyst. After obtaining his doctorate in Education, he worked as a federally funded evaluator of a demonstration project, a manager in a large health and welfare fund, and as an instructional designer. He spent 25 years as an independent contractor, providing training materials and services to over 50 different companies.

Before obtaining his doctorate, his head broke. This is his story.

Printed in the United States
By Bookmasters